LEARIE
CONSTANTINE

By the same author

From Chatham to Churchill
The Story of Health (with Anne Howat)
The Teaching of Empire and Commonwealth History
Dictionary of World History (ed.)
Documents in European History, 1789–1970
Stuart and Cromwellian Foreign Policy
Who Did What (ed.)

LEARIE
CONSTANTINE

Gerald Howat

London   George Allen & Unwin Ltd
Ruskin House   Museum Street

© George Allen & Unwin Ltd. 1975

ISBN 0 04 920043 7

Printed in Great Britain
in 11 point Monotype Baskerville type
by W & J Mackay Limited
Chatham

For David and Michael

ACKNOWLEDGEMENTS

Grateful acknowledgement is made to those who gave permission to quote from material in which copyright is held: to the Executors of the estate of the late Lord Constantine, and his daughter, the Hon. Mrs Gloria Valère, for use to be made of his writings and broadcasts; to the British Broadcasting Corporation for details of his association with the Corporation; to the publishers of Lord Constantine's books, and the proprietors, publishers and authors of books and newspapers from which quotations have been taken. A detailed list of such copyright-owners appears in the Note on Sources at the end of the book.

Acknowledgement is also made to the following agencies and individuals who have supplied photographs and given permission for their use: Miss Anne Bolt, the Central Press, Mrs Ruth Clegg, *The Cricketer* and Mr David Frith, Mrs Margaret Johnson, Mrs Karen Jonzen, Sport and General, the Trinidad Publishing Co. Ltd.

The author's thanks are due also to Mr A. F. Carpenter for his professional assistance in preparing old snapshots for reproduction.

PREFACE

I embarked upon this biography of Learie Constantine immediately after completing a book which had substantially to do with Oliver Cromwell. At first no comparison seemed sensible between two men separated by time and circumstance, especially as Cromwell did his best to stop 'Krickett' being played when he ordered the destruction of bats and balls in Ireland. Then I recalled Clarendon's judgement on Cromwell: 'He must have had a wonderful understanding in the natures and humours of men, who from a private and obscure birth without interest of estate, alliance or friendships, could raise himself to such a height.'

Learie Constantine, from the obscurity of slave ancestry and a small cocoa plantation, rose to become one of the great cricketers of his generation, a broadcaster, a cabinet minister, a diplomat, a knight-bachelor and the first Negro to take his seat in the House of Lords. Of Cromwell, it was said that his greatness at home was but a shadow of his greatness abroad. Constantine's homeland was Trinidad yet it was in the British Isles that he won greater recognition and where he believed he 'was accepted and honoured'.

The printed sources for this biography are principally newspapers, journals, *Wisden Cricketers' Almanack*, books on cricket and on the West Indies, the published volumes of the Legislative Council Debates of Trinidad and Tobago, and Lord Constantine's writings and broadcasts. I list these in some detail at the end of the book. Lord Constantine's own writings are to be found in several published volumes. All, except *Colour Bar*, are mainly about cricket. A very large number of broadcast-scripts is in the archives of the British Broadcasting Corporation. Some articles were contributed to various newspapers and journals.

I am indebted to the institutions which made their resources available to me and to an extensive list of individuals whom I interviewed or with whom I corresponded. My thanks are due to Mr R. D. Hewlett and his colleagues who made accessible material at the B.B.C. Reference and Registry Services in London and at the B.B.C. Written Archives Centre in Reading; to the staff at Rhodes House, Oxford, the Bodleian Library, Oxford, and at the British Museum Newspaper Section at Colindale, London; to Mr D. H. Simpson, Librarian of the Royal Commonwealth Society, London; to Mr Stephen Green, Librarian of the Marylebone Cricket Club, London; and to the Research Department of Amnesty International, London.

The Hon. Mrs Gloria Valère, daughter of Lord Constantine, and Mr Elias Constantine, his surviving brother, have been most helpful in answering my queries upon family events and in commenting upon passages of the book. Mr John Kirk, solicitor to the Estate of the late Lord Constantine, was most co-operative from the outset.

I was made particularly welcome in Nelson, Lancashire, where many players and friends associated with Lord and Lady Constantine's twenty years in that town met me. I received much courtesy from the Office of the High Commission for Trinidad and Tobago in Belgrave Square, London—in particular, from His Excellency the High Commissioner and from Mr Allen Charles, the Information Attaché. Other institutions to which I turned for assistance, which was willingly given, were Lord Constantine's former Chambers in the Temple; the West India Committee; the Office of the High Commission for Jamaica in Grosvenor Street, London; and Trinidad Texaco Incorporated (formerly Trinidad Leaseholds Ltd), Pointe-à-Pierre, Trinidad.

I must also record valuable conversations with, and help from, the following: Mr G. O. Allen, C.B.E.; Mr John Arlott, O.B.E.; the Hon. Mark Bonham Carter, chairman of the Community Relations Commission; Mr. R. St C. Charles of the Trinidad High Commission; Mr Alva Clarke, Head of the B.B.C. Caribbean Service; Dr C. B. Clarke; Mr Ivor Cummings, O.B.E., formerly of the Colonial Office; Dr and Mrs R. C. Dolly; Mr Cyril Duerden of Nelson Cricket Club; Mr

Colin Firth of Nelson Cricket Club; the Rt Hon. Sir Dingle Foot, P.C., Q.C.; Mr David Frith, Editor of *The Cricketer*; Mr Albert Gomes, formerly Minister of Commerce in Trinidad; Mr John Greenwood, chairman of Nelson Cricket Club; Mr Harold Hargreaves, formerly captain of Nelson Cricket Club; Mr L. Harvey of the Trinidad High Commission; The Rt Hon. Denis Howell, M.P., Minister of State (Sport) in the British Government; Mr J. A. C. Huggill, D.S.C., formerly chairman of the West India Committee; Mr C. L. R. James; Miss D. L. Jones of the Trinidad High Commission; Mrs Karen Jonzen; Mr James Kerrigan of Nelson Cricket Club; Sir Laurence Lindo, C.M.G.; Mr Winston Millington, formerly of Trinidad Leaseholds Ltd; Mr Sam Morris, Deputy Chief Officer of the Community Relations Commission; Lord Pitt of Hampstead; the Hon. Terence Prittie; Lt-Col. Max Robinson, D.S.O., O.B.E., Secretary of the West India Committee; Mrs Prunella Scarlett, Director of Public Affairs, the Royal Commonwealth Society; His Excellency Dr Patrick Solomon, formerly Deputy Prime Minister of Trinidad; Mr Harold Standage, Secretary of Nelson Cricket Club; Mr E. W. Swanton, O.B.E.; Miss Eleanor Weir-Breen; Mr Clarence Winslow of Nelson Cricket Club.

Among numerous correspondents, I am especially grateful to the following: Mr Rex Alston; Mr J. G. Andrews of Trinidad Texaco Incorporated, Pointe-à-Pierre, Trinidad; the Reverend Francis C. Berry of St Mary's College, Dublin; Mr Rowland Bowen, cricket historian; Mrs Ethel Bradley; Mr A. F. Brocklebank, I.S.O.; Mr Reynold Bullen; Mr P. D. C. R. Clark, formerly of Northern Counties Cricket Club, Scotland; Mrs Ruth H. Clegg, formerly of Nelson; Mr J. St F. Dare, formerly president of the British Guiana Cricket Board of Control; Mr E. G. Dashwood-Evans, of the Brazilian Consulate in Manchester; Mr Campbell Douglas, formerly of H. B. Rowan's XI, Scotland; Mr Gerald Duffy, of the Irish Cricket Union; Mr H. R. Foulkes; Mr G. C. Grant, formerly cricket captain of the West Indies; the Rt Hon. the Lord Hill of Luton, P.C., formerly chairman of the governors of the B.B.C.; Mr Frank Hulme; Mr. W. A. Hunt of New South Wales; Mrs R. G. Johnson, formerly of Nelson; Mr John Kay of the *Manchester Evening News*; Mr J. L. Keith, C.B.E., formerly Head of the Welfare Department at the Colonial Office; Mr Maurice Latey of the B.B.C.; Mr Larry Semmens; Mr Jack Sokell, secretary of the Wombwell Cricket Lovers' Society; Mr Eric Stafford; Mr J. B. Stollmeyer, formerly cricket captain of the West Indies; Mr Charles Sykes; Mr A. Thornton of the *Lancashire Evening Telegraph*; Mr A. H. Wagg, cricket statistician; Professor Glanmor Williams, formerly a governor of the B.B.C.; and the late the Rt Hon. Sir Hugh Wooding, T.C., P.C., O.B.E.

Apart from the newspaper resources of the Bodleian Library, Oxford, and the British Museum, I drew upon papers available in Edinburgh and Bristol. I acknowledge with thanks the research done there on my behalf by Mrs Agatha Henderson-Howat and Miss Kate Woodall, respectively. My secretary, Mrs Angela Griffiths, has my thanks for typing the manuscript, and my son, David Howat, for compiling the index.

The pleasure of writing about Learie Constantine has been enhanced by meeting, and corresponding with, so many interesting people for whom the common denominator has been an association with my subject. If at times this biography seems to be too fulsome, it has proved difficult to be otherwise. There seemed fewer warts on Constantine than on Cromwell.

I do not believe I could have attempted this book had I myself not known Learie Constantine and his wife; had I not seen him play cricket; had I not lived for some years in Trinidad; and had I not shared his view that the Commonwealth can still be an agency for world co-operation and peace.

G.M.D.H.

Radley College
Oxfordshire

CONTENTS

ILLUSTRATIONS

I

A CRICKETING
CHILDHOOD
1902-1917

Grandpa Ali Pascall was about a hundred years old when he
died. His grandchildren took a last look at him in the open
coffin, then they were lifted over it three times by their parents
and told to go outside the house until the burial had taken
place. Eight-year-old Learie asked why. 'Because it was an
African custom of the tribe grandpa came from', he was told.
The child remembered the event vividly, for the funeral rites
were lengthy, accompanied by wakes and vigils. A few days
earlier the old Negro had sat in the sunshine on the steps of
his bungalow leaning his back against the door and watching
his grandchildren play. At the end of a long life he was content. Although he had never learnt to read or write, his
daughter Anaise had done so. He had started life owning
nothing—not even himself—but he had become the care-
taker of a few acres of cocoa estate.

Ali Pascall's parents had lived in the Niger Delta. They
had crossed the Atlantic Ocean in a slave-ship and found
themselves working for some Spanish-speaking master on the
north-east coast of South America. Ali became a child-slave.
One day he and another child-slave, a Negro girl called
Malvina, stole a canoe and sailed away to the land of Trinidad which they could see across the water. In their excitement,
they overturned the canoe in the last moments before landing
and lost their few possessions. They waded ashore and tramped

their way till they came to a little village called Maraval.

So the story was told by Anaise, their daughter, to her own children. Learie Constantine remembered how reluctantly his mother would tell it: '. . . slavery was something my mother and my grandparents didn't like to talk about'. But the customs of their peoples were not forgotten. The Negro in Trinidad, though freed, had remained in a low social and economic stratum with no opportunity to take part in the creation of a Trinidadian society, so he clung to the remnants of tradition from an African past; the cultural elements of his ancestry remained important to succeeding generations. The funeral ceremonies at the death of Grandpa Pascall indicated that his people were of the Yoruba tribe.

Anaise Pascall, daughter of slaves, married in 1900 Lebrun Constantine, a grandson of slaves. Lebrun's grandparents had been among the last slaves to cross the Atlantic to bondage in the West Indies, where they had been sold to masters in Trinidad. Slavery there had no long-established roots, as it had in Barbados and Jamaica, yet it was a fact of existence for some forty years. Lebrun's grandparents rejoiced in that moment of political and individual liberation which finally came for all in slavery in the British Empire on 1 August 1834. The next generation was born into freedom. Lebrun, unlike his wife, was therefore the child of a freeman and a freewoman. The tales of slavery which their children picked up belonged to Anaise's parentage and not to Lebrun's. Lebrun Constantine was born at Diego Martin, not far from Maraval, on 25 May 1874. Although his own parents were born in freedom, life yet remained a stern economic and social struggle comparable, in some ways, with the lot of many in the new industrial society of Europe.

The surname 'Constantine' which the family bore probably derived from that of the slave-owners of Learie Constantine's great-grandparents on his father's side. In the list of claims lodged with the Commissioners of Claims in London,* there are three bearers of the name Constantine among the 2,356

* *Accounts of Slave Compensation*, prepared in the Office of Commissioners of Claims, House of Commons, London, 1838.

claimants. Jean Baptiste Constantin* lodged a claim for £54 2s 8d for one slave, Rose Constantine one for £477 16s 10d for ten slaves, and Catherine Constantine one for £145 0s 10d for four slaves. In all, compensation claims were lodged for the loss of 17,539 slaves in Trinidad who became free men, women and children. It is reasonable to assume that the name 'Constantine' was adopted by some, at any rate, of the fifteen slaves freed from owners bearing that name. Lebrun Constantine's French first name may further suggest that Jean Baptiste Constantin was the original owner of his slave grandfather.

Trinidad was a mixed community of Europeans, Africans, East Indians and Chinese, with a tiny survival of indigenous Amerindian peoples. Since the end of slavery much of the labour on the sugar estates had been done by the East Indians, who came as indentured servants and continued to do so until 1917. Many Africans who had worked on the slave sugar estates had become labourers on cocoa estates, and on such an estate at Diego Martin grew up Lebrun. Fashioning his own bat from a coconut branch and his ball from lime or orange, cricket became his passionate pursuit. While the Negro lad taught himself his craft in the remote north-western peninsula of a tropical island, an Anglo-Saxon of his own age, born in the same island, learnt the game at Rugby School in England under the tutelage of professional coaches. Pelham Warner, son of Charles Warner, Attorney-General of Trinidad, had his early upbringing in the island and his early education at Harrison College, Barbados, before going to England where he was to gain considerable eminence as both a cricketer and an administrator of the game. His earliest cricket had been played in the gallery of his home at Port of Spain, a few miles from Diego Martin. Lebrun Constantine and Pelham Warner, from their different antecedents, were both to adorn the game and make their contribution to the distinctive characteristics of West Indian and English cricket.

Among his friends on the cocoa estate of Diego Martin,

* Spelt without an 'e'. This Constantin was a Trinidad slave-owner of French descent.

Lebrun raised a cricket side which played against teams from other villages such as Petit Valley and Four Roads. They were not very far apart, all lying in a valley surrounded by mountainous countryside which looked westwards towards the narrow waterway separating the north-west of Trinidad from the mainland of Venezuela. A few miles to the south lay Port of Spain, capital of the island. There the twenty-year-old Lebrun took his own cricket team in 1894 to win a local competition.

Cricket had spread rapidly from England to Europe and the British Empire at the end of the eighteenth century. It was being played by Dutch merchants in 1793; by troops in Brussels before the battle of Waterloo; by English lace-makers in Boulogne; by Danes and Portuguese. If trade followed the flag, so cricket pursued the Empire. Colonists in New South Wales, East India Company servants in India, soldiers at the Cape were all playing the game long before Napoleon's defeat in 1815.

In the West Indies—an eighteenth-century battleground of competing European and economic interests—cricket had found some hold in islands which came under British influence. Barbados, eldest of Crown colonies, had by 1806 a flourishing club called St Anne's. In 1842 there had been a Trinidad Cricket Club for some years, in an island whose British associations went back no further than 1797. In 1865 West Indian inter-colonial cricket began when Barbados played British Guiana. West Indian cricket, in the second half of the nineteenth century, centred in those three colonial territories of Trinidad, Barbados and British Guiana. Distances in the Caribbean were immense, so Jamaica was unable to participate in colonial cricket until 1929.

By the 1890s West Indian cricket deserved the attention of a team from the country where the game had originated. Some English amateurs led by R. Slade Lucas visited the West Indies in 1895. Among those selected to play for Trinidad against the Englishmen was Lebrun Constantine. In a low-scoring match, Trinidad beat the visitors by eight wickets. *Wisden's Cricketers' Almanack* described Trinidad's form as being 'well up to the standard of good club cricket in England'. R. Slade Lucas's XI was largely composed of Oxford and Cambridge players with a few first-class county men such as Lucas himself.

Soon afterwards, Lebrun became an overseer on the estate with responsibility for supervising the work of a group of labourers. Meanwhile, his cricketing ability led to his selection to tour England in 1900 with the first-ever West Indian side. It was led by R. S. A. Warner, brother of Pelham.

The tour opened in June at the Crystal Palace against London County of which W. G. Grace—by now over fifty years of age, and still the Grand Old Man of English Cricket —was captain and secretary. London County scored 538, Grace making 71, and the tourists lost by an innings and 198 runs. On the second day of the match, Tuesday 12 June 1900, Lebrun Constantine lost his wicket to Grace, in a general collapse against W.G.'s bowling. Twenty-eight years later to the day, 12 June 1928, this uncertain start to West Indian cricket in England was to be avenged by Lebrun's son in a display at Lord's which established the status of West Indian cricket.

Later in the month Lebrun made the first century by a West Indian in England in the match at Lord's against the M.C.C. The West Indians faced an innings defeat when Constantine and W. J. Burton, from British Guiana, put on 162 for the ninth wicket in an hour, Constantine scoring 113 before falling to W. G. Grace. Pelham Warner, now an England cricketer, called Constantine's innings 'a dashing and faultless display'—but his side still lost by five wickets (see p. 24).

In the rest of the tour, Constantine scored freely against Gloucestershire, Nottinghamshire and Derbyshire and finished the tour second in the batting averages, having scored 610 runs with an average of 30.50.

From England, Lebrun returned to marry Anaise Pascall. At Diego Martin, on 21 September 1902, their first child was born. He was christened Learie Nicholas.* The 'Learie' was

---

* Constantine had several nicknames during his lifetime—Cons, Connie, Electric Heels being the most common. I have called him 'Learie' when there is a risk of confusion with his father, and thereafter generally used his surname.

M.C.C.

W. G. Grace c Ollivierre b Woods......	11	b Burton......		3
A. E. Stoddart c Ollivierre b Woods.....	30	c Cox b Woods......		18
J. Gilman b Burton......	33	lbw, b Woods......		6
Lord Harris c Burton b Woods......	35	c Sproston b Woods......		3
E. C. Mordaunt b Burton......	31	not out......		51
A. Page b Burton......	0	run out......		22
A. F. Somerset b Ollivierre......	118	not out......		0
A. B. Reynolds b Woods......	37			
M. M. Barker b Goodman......	26			
E. R. de Little b Goodman......	0			
A. Montague not out......	32			
Extras	26	Extras		4
	379	(5 wkts)		107

	O	M	R	W		O	M	R	W
Burton.......	37	6	118	3	....	17	5	39	1
Woods.......	41	8	109	4	....	19.1	8	47	3
Ollivierre.....	13.5	2	55	1	....	2	0	17	0
Cox..........	3	0	13	0					
Goodman.....	11	0	49	2					
Sproston......	1	0	4	0					

WEST INDIANS

C. A. Ollivierre lbw, b Grace......	21	b Stoddart......		32
G. C. Learmond b de Little......	52	b Stoddart......		6
S. W. Sproston b Grace......	14	c and b Grace......		33
P. I. Cox b Grace......	17	b Stoddart......		6
P. A. Goodman c and b Grace......	0	b Stoddart......		6
W. Bowring b Grace......	0	b Stoddart......		7
A. Warner c Gilman b de Little......	22	b Stoddart......		3
L. S. D'Ade run out......	4	b Stoddart......		2
L. S. Constantine not out......	24	st Reynolds b Grace.....		113
W. J. Burton b Stoddart......	18	not out......		64
S. Woods st Reynolds b Harris......	0	b Montague......		0
Extras	18	Extras		23
	190			295

	O	M	R	W		O	M	R	W
Stoddart......	10	2	32	1	....	32	6	92	7
Mordaunt.....	5	1	30	0	....				
Grace........	18	3	56	5	....	21	5	87	2
De Little......	18	3	46	2	....	8	2	39	0
Harris........	2.3	0	8	1	....	7	0	39	0
Montague.....					....	4.1	3	15	1

chosen because an Irishman of that name had befriended Lebrun on his cricket tour. The child's godfather was his father's employer, Sidney Smith. So Learie was called after one white man and had another for his godfather. In the innocence of infancy, no racial prejudice clouded his environment. 'I lived a carefree life, and I cannot recall that I thought about such things at all', he once remarked in a broadcast. What he did not realise was that Mr Smith was an unusual employer who would allow no subservience on Lebrun's part, expecting only the respect and loyalty due to any business relationship.

One day in March 1906 when Learie was three and a half, he had to bid his father a hasty and unexpected farewell. The ship taking the 1906 West Indian tourists to England lay in Port of Spain harbour. Lebrun, unable to afford to leave work or family, wandered down town to watch its departure. Michael Maillard, a merchant in Frederick Street, bade him good luck for the tour and was told that Lebrun did not see how he could go to England. Within minutes Maillard had sent Lebrun home to Maraval by carriage to collect his things. Meanwhile, a trunk of clothes and kit was purchased. By the time they reached the jetty, the ship had sailed for England. Undaunted, Maillard chartered a fast launch, and Lebrun Constantine boarded the steamer before it had sailed out of the Bocas straits into the open sea. Suddenly, the Constantine household was bereft of its head for six months— sad at Lebrun's absence, glad for his success. By his efforts and his financial support, Maillard helped to make it possible for a Constantine, father or son, to be on every West Indian tour to England between 1900 and 1939 (see p. 48).

The tour itself did not fulfil expectations. The West Indians, although granted first-class status, won only three of their thirteen major matches. A string of defeats at the start of the tour forfeited public support, and only a victory by 268 runs against Yorkshire redeemed their reputation. Lebrun Constantine, a little less successful than in 1900, came third in the averages, his best performance being 89 against W. G. Grace's XI at the Crystal Palace and a fifty in each innings against an England XI at Blackpool.

Soon after his return from this second visit to England, Lebrun moved his family to Cascade, near Maraval, four miles from Port of Spain. Lebrun was given full charge of a cocoa estate, and Learie later recalled in one of his broadcasts:

'As children we never really wanted for anything because we had the run of two estates; this one and my grandfather's, which my uncles, aunts and mother worked. There was always something to eat. We could go hunting for meat, we kept pigs, chickens and goats, and there were fruit and vegetables. My father believed if a child ate well and slept well there couldn't really be much wrong. We were lucky. It wasn't every coloured family that was so fortunate. I remember one worker on the estate with a wife and five children. Sometimes my father caught the children stealing from the estate but all he ever did was scold them and let them go. This made a deep impression on me as a child, because my father was very strict with us about taking anything that didn't belong to us.'

For the four Constantine children, stealing was seen as a major crime. 'I was five-and-a-half when I learnt my first lesson about stealing. I found a fresh egg lying in a drain, and picked it up and took it home to my mother. "Did it belong to you?" she asked. And she took a switch and switched me right back to the place where I found it and made me put it back again.' When Learie asked his father why the other children were not punished, he was told that to stop them stealing would be to starve them. He was learning his first lessons in the economics of society. Years later, when he was ready to secure the best possible cricket contract from some club or for some tour, he did so in order to give security to his own family.

Childhood games included playing in the nutmeg trees whose willowy branches did not easily break. Everyone would climb a tree except for one child deliberately left on the ground. His task was to catch somebody falling from the trees as the other children swung from one branch to another. Even washing-up was made fun. Dishes were used for catching-practice: 'Our kitchen was set a little away from the rest of the house. When we had finished a meal my brother would stand on the kitchen steps and I would stand in the dining-room, and I would throw him all the plates, crockery and cutlery.' A more serious pursuit was learning how to aim a gun—though it was a long time before ammunition was allowed. One day some illicit shooting of wild animals such as lapp and agouti was discovered by their father, and duly punished.

It was a happy home, if a patriarchal one. The children respected the authority of their father. 'Parental approval in that household mattered both when they were small and as they grew up', recalled a childhood friend of those distant days. The family was 'considerably more prosperous than many a Port of Spain one where the father might be in local government service and enjoy a higher salary'. Learie himself thought they were happy days. 'A happy childhood is one of the greatest defences a man can have against the world', he said when he was a man over fifty.

So days were passed under the hot Trinidad sun. Picture a stockily-built Negro lad clad in khaki shorts and shirt made, according to Learie 'from a kind of flour bag which used to come from America and which washed well and was very tough and didn't tear easily. When the rain fell, we would take our shirts off and roll our shorts up, and play in the water'. Set him and his friends against a backcloth of mountains wild and unreclaimed in their forested beauty, with cacoa trees engulfing the small estate, samaan trees casting their rich colouring, and keskides setting up a ceaseless chatter. There were the scarlet flowers of the immortelle and a fragrance all about. 'All you had to fear were snakes.'

Learie's first recollection of a world beyond, where prejudice reigned and bitterness might become manifest, came when he was five. While he and his brothers were throwing oranges to one another, a frenzied cry came from their mother. 'Get into the house or he'll ride over you!' A white estate-owner from nearby had aroused her fears—a man known to be indifferent to the Negro peoples. 'He'll ride over you.' Learie Constantine was to make it his business to see that no white man rode over him.

Advancement for a Negro might come through education or through sport. Cricket—but not education—had given Learie's father a certain status in the Trinidad community. Lebrun Constantine was anxious that his children should learn what school might offer. He was also ready to make cricketers of them—boys and girl alike.

Life for Learie and the other children between 1908 and 1917 crystallised into these two pursuits of education and cricket. Cricket meant more: there were ready-made coaches in his father and in two uncles—St Croix Constantine and Victor Pascall. Pascall, like his father, was a colony player. Behind the estate house there was a ready-made strip of matting, twelve yards long, laid out. 'We played every day in the dry season and waited for the pitch to dry in the wet one.' Lebrun's coaching policy was varied in its approach. Learie and his brothers were allowed to bat as they wished provided they felt comfortable in their stance and hit the ball hard. They were shown how to hold the ball to make it turn, and taught the value of bowling a length. But it was in fielding that Lebrun took the strongest line. He would give them endless catching practice, often hitting the ball over his shoulders to the waiting fielders behind. No catch should ever be dropped: if it were, the offender had not paid attention. 'Pay attention' was the simple but effective dictum and philosophy. These cricket practices were a family affair: Learie's mother Anaise kept wicket and his sister also played. Of those occasions, Learie has written:

'Family cricket went forward with redoubled zest. We were kept at it in every spare moment of daylight: my father knew the dictum that genius is one-tenth inspiration and nine-tenths perspiration, and those of us who showed no inspiration had to perspire the more to make up for it. He did not coach us, being convinced that more good cricket is coached out than coached in—a theory which I have had reason to respect since—but he made us practise, practise, practise, knowing that you learn a thing best by doing it. He would bowl at us just as he bowled at inter-colonial batsmen or veterans from England; the pace was just as wicked, the ball broke off the pitch just as disconcertingly; if we got out, we went to our place in the field without a second chance, and the work there was even hotter than at the wicket, so we stuck in as long as human ingenuity could do it. My sister Leonora was able to hit a ball so that many a first-class cricketer, seeing her, would have felt like giving up the game. My mother and I and my two younger brothers and she were all treated alike; sex and age made no difference; and if one made a blunder, one had to pay for it in full.'

It is doubtful if Learie really appreciated his schooldays. He attended St Ann's Government School in Port of Spain until he was twelve. His friend of later years, C. L. R. James, whose father was the headmaster, recalled 'a thickset, rather slow boy' avoiding the rough-and-tumble of the playground. He was already aware of what James has described as his 'royal ancestry', for everyone knew he was Lebrun's son and Pascall's nephew. From there Learie went on to St Ann's Roman Catholic School where he stayed from 1914 to 1917, 'reaching the seventh standard'. He said himself that his father was not prepared to pay fees for him to go on to St Mary's College, but had Learie shown any real enthusiasm for the idea of continuing his education, Lebrun would surely have found the money; benefactors like the Smiths and their cousins the Maillards (who had financed Lebrun's cricket tour in 1906) might have helped. The Learie Constantine who in 1943 declared his anxiety to have been educated when he was a child took an adult view of the situation. Another contemporary of those days at the second St Ann's school recollects that there was 'no real desire to learn'. He lacked, one may judge, the burning ambition to attain secondary education. Still less did he aspire to an island scholarship. These few accolades were for brilliant boys among whom were to be numbered some of his friends and colleagues of later years.

Life's real attractions lay beyond the boundaries of the classroom. Cricket was there to be played in the precious hours before the light fell at six o'clock or so. When he was over sixty years of age, Learie still remembered those hours of cricket, when 'the joy, the tension, the exhilaration, and the happiness, brought into our lives served as a cushion, I am sure, for the sterner life which was ahead for all of us'. And not only hours of cricket: Learie, as a schoolfriend remembers, was an extremely competent footballer, especially good at dribbling—in those days more important in the game than the modern technique of precision passing. He was also a sprinter. All this made him a popular schoolboy who paid tribute to his headmaster, Andrew de Four, for what he was taught on the cricket field rather than in the classroom.

Under the influence of de Four, he learnt at Queen's Park Savannah in Port of Spain the discipline of match play. De Four was a hard taskmaster. For being bowled for a duck two matches running—on the second occasion, first ball—Learie was banned from the School XI by de Four for four weeks. The ban even extended to watching others play. His mother was told to report his absence from home on match days to the headmaster: Queen's Park Savannah is a vast playing area capable of sustaining thirty cricket matches simultaneously, and a boy could easily have watched from afar, either his own school game or anyone else's.

Learie owed much to de Four, who encouraged him to use the bat 'for hitting the ball'. He captained St Ann's XI in 1916 and 1917 during which time only one match was lost—to Tranquillity, a team of older schoolboys, formidable in white trousers and white boots while Learie and his friends had to be content with khaki shorts and black boots. School matches took place on Fridays. On Saturdays, Learie watched senior cricket on the Savannah. There was an occasion when his father's club, Victoria, played a local 'Derby' against Stingo. Two of the Stingo XI, George John and Joe Small, were players of international ability. Such was the rivalry between the two clubs that Stingo, on winning the toss, put Victoria in to bat in the hope of achieving an innings victory. Learie has recorded his delight at the way in which his own heroes dealt with Stingo's attack. Rarely in later life did he experience the 'fullness of satisfaction' which that match gave. Learie Constantine was always to be loyal to the team of the moment with an intensity which made him play cricket with all the fervour he could arouse. It did not always win him friends among the opposition who sometimes felt that there was conceit in his spoken warning to a new arrival that he would soon get his wicket or run him out.

These were the years of the First World War. In the period before the outbreak of war Learie, as a child, would have heard German ships practising gunnery in the Gulf of Paria. In August 1914 they sailed away, taking with them their bands who had often played in Port of Spain. They left behind a floating wharf, while their submarines lurked off the Bocas and caused lighting restrictions to be imposed in the colony. Lebrun's cocoa estate enjoyed a modest prosperity from the cocoa boom which the war brought. Sugar-estate owners benefited from the ending of the supply of German bounty-fed beet sugar to Britain. All over the island increased cultivation took place to offset the reduction of food imports.

Learie left school in 1917 when he was fifteen. He had been too young to join the 1,500 men who sailed from Trinidad to serve in the West Indies Regiment, but he must have seen the recruiting meetings in Port of Spain and possibly been amongst those who lined the streets to welcome the return of the survivors in 1919.

After the war, the factors which created unemployment in the great industrial belts of the world had little special relevance to Trinidad. The limitations for young Constantine were social ones conditioned by his colour and his lack of education. His father might dream of the professions—medicine, dentistry, law—for these were ways in which an African in Trinidad might achieve personal independence and some status. It was to law that Learie was assigned, and as an office boy that he began his working life in the solicitor's firm of Jonathan Ryan in Queen Street, Port of Spain. Ten years of work as a clerk might allow him to sit solicitor's examinations himself.

As a first step, he attended the Contaste School of Commerce to learn typing. He became extremely efficient at this, both in the speed at which he typed and in his ability to strip down and service his own machine. The dexterity in fingerwork which gave him such mastery over a cricket ball was applied to the typewriter. For the moment, cricket was just a pipe-dream.

2

AMATEUR CRICKETER
1917-1928

Constantine stayed in Ryan's office from 1917 until 1922; Ryan was a good employer who gave him every encouragement. Constantine advanced through the various stages of district court clerk, supreme court clerk and, finally, chief clerk. His job involved preparing summonses, taking statements and being in attendance at court. There was a great deal of typing to do, and a lot of moving around from office to courts. He used these trips—short as the distances were—for exercise. 'He would run rather than walk' remembered a colleague, for he was determined to keep himself in tip-top condition. Running exercised his limbs, typing his fingers. There were always oranges to throw around to practise catching. He was a lad of boundless energy—never still.

The office hours were not strenuous. He did not have to be there until 8.30 a.m.—late by Trinidad standards, where work often began at 7.00. By four in the afternoon he was free to go. He was paid three shillings a day which he gave to his mother, and she handed him back sixpence for a meal in town. Constantine worked hard enough but he was not temperamentally suited—at that stage in his life—to spend his leisure time in studying. The compulsion to play cricket as often as he could was irresistible.

But first, for a mixture of reasons, his father barred him from playing organised cricket in 1917, 1918 and 1919. On the one hand, he suspected that cricket would always win pride of place over office work, and he was determined that

Learie should establish himself in his career. On the other, he realised that his son's talents would quickly take him into major cricket where he might come up against top-class cricketers before he was ready for it. In the West Indies the ordinary club side—then as now—could contain one or two men who were in the current West Indies side, or at least played for Trinidad. In English cricket, the first-class cricketer is largely separated from all other cricketers, thus creating a gulf in both technique and temperament.

Lebrun Constantine was captain of Victoria, later re-organised as Shannon, and the club's old name is itself a reminder of the tradition in which Lebrun had grown up. Queen Victoria, mistress of an empire, and after whom countless clubs, institutions and an Australian state were named, reflected in her person the stern parental attitude of the late nineteenth century. Lebrun was a child of that Victorian outlook with its external image of unbending parenthood concealing rather than revealing a kindly interior. Only years after the event did Learie himself realise why his father had stood down from the Trinidad cricket trials in 1921. 'How little I knew! He had deliberately stood down from the trials so as to give me a chance, though he was keen to play.'

After three years in the wilderness, apart from ceaseless practice on the matting wicket at home, Learie appeared for the Victoria-Shannon 2nd XI—once he had raised the money for his white flannels. In his third match, he scored 50 out of 72 in an hour. It was a performance good enough to win him selection for the 1st XI.

That Learie should play for Shannon was inevitable not only because it was his father's club. The major clubs around Port of Spain in the 1920s were a reflection of social and economic circumstances. Thus, Queen's Park Oval was the club for prosperous white men. Shannon suited Negroes and Indians in the lower ranks of white-collar workers. Poorer men joined Stingo. If this seems exaggerated in its emphasis, one need but recall that English club cricket in the same period imposed similar distinctions created by accent, school and occupation. Only the question of colour was absent.

The first real test of Learie's abilities came in 1921 when he faced George John in the match against Stingo. John was extremely fast and capable of making the ball rise sharply. Constantine was aware, as he walked to the wicket, that John was bent on getting his wicket. 'People had begun to talk of me as a second George John', he wrote later. He realised that John was determined to show who was the better man. They had met once earlier, before Constantine had begun to be talked about. On that occasion John had bowled him third ball. Years later, in a broadcast at the time of John's death in 1944, Constantine recalled that John remarked: 'You ought to be at school instead of coming here worrying big cricketers.'

This time the duel went Constantine's way. He attacked from the start, scoring 67 within the hour before his wicket was sent tumbling several yards by John. No malice was shown on either side, and Constantine's obituary tribute to John was generous.

But by 1921 there were other things on his mind than cricket. He had met a girl from Port of Spain called Norma Agatha Cox, a chemist's daughter whose father had died when she was seven. At first he had 'made no impression at all'. Norma was not interested in cricket and certainly had not envisaged marrying a cricketer. But by the middle of 1921 they were meeting regularly—or as often as cricket and work permitted. There were partings—a short one during the British Guiana inter-colonial tournament in 1922, and a six-month one when Constantine toured England in 1923. Norma accepted these. But she resented the little amount of time he could find for her when he was working in Port of Spain. 'Learie could spare only about five minutes a day for me. He was living in the country and I was in the city. His last train went about seven o'clock, and after work he would go to the nets to practise. I was a very poor second to the cricket.'

At that time Norma was far more conscious of their relationship than was Learie. She was not introduced to his cricketing friends. Gradually, however, Norma accepted the discipline demanded of a cricketer who played for Shannon. Constantine always felt that it was his experience in Shannon cricket which moulded him as a cricketer. When sides came from England, Shannon men in the Trinidad side performed well against them. When Test matches began for the West Indies in 1928, Shannon men were there. The coconut wickets in Queen's Park Savannah, where Shannon played, demanded skill from those who batted on them, especially when old age and much use rendered them threadbare. A high standard of fielding was axiomatic. A personal discipline that demanded total dedication to the claims of the team was cardinal. These were qualities which Constantine felt, in later years, were not always to be found in West Indian representative sides.

Largely as a result of the confidence in which he was held by A. E. Harragin, the Trinidad captain, Constantine won selection in the list of twelve named for Trinidad in September 1921 against British Guiana at Port of Spain Oval. Fearful of arriving early and of suffering agonies of nervousness in the pavilion, he turned up at the ground at 11.45 a.m. only to find that play had begun at 11.30 and that he would have been put in the final XI. There was little consolation in telling the captain that the newspaper had billed the start as midday. From the pavilion the dejected young cricketer watched Trinidad beat British Guiana. The second match of the inter-colonial tournament was between Trinidad and Barbados in which Constantine made his début in first-class cricket, scoring 0 in his first innings and 24 in his second. He fielded well and took two wickets for 44. Rain delayed the progress of the match which had to be abandoned in order that the Barbados players might catch their boat home. Constantine learned another hard lesson. He tossed the ball up after taking a catch . . . and dropped it! 'I had to face Major Harragin at the end of the over and hear his brief and accurate summing-up of what I had done', Constantine noted. It did not cure him of the habit of tossing a catch up in the air, but it taught him to hold it when the ball came down again.

TRINIDAD

A. Cipriani	c C. F. Browne b Emptage...	33	not out.............. 29
C. A. Wiles	c Hoad b Griffith..........	30	not out.............. 88
W. H. St Hill	c Ince b Griffith........	6	c Gilkes b Challenor..... 48
J. A. Small	b Griffith................	12	c & b Challenor........ 10
A. E. Harragin	b Gilkes..............	17	
F. de Gannes	not out................	30	c Mason b Gilkes........ 11
J. C. Rogers	c Ince b Griffith..........	0	c Tarilton b Mason...... 37
L. N. Constantine	c Challenor b Griffith.	0	b Griffith.............. 24
V. S. Pascall	b Griffith................	1	
G. A. Dewhurst	c Mason b Griffith......	7	
A. V. Waddell	b C. F. Browne.........	19	
	Extras	19	Extras 19
		174	**(5 wkts) 266**

	O	M	R	W		O	M	R	W
Challenor.....	4	3	2	0	....	17	4	46	2
Griffith.......	20	7	38	7	....	26	6	53	1
Gilkes........	16	1	42	1	....	14	0	37	1
Emptage......	12	0	28	1	....	13	2	24	0
Mason........	10	3	30	0	....	23	7	43	1
Hoad.........	2	0	8	0	....	2	0	8	0
C. F. Browne..	3.1	0	7	1	....	16	5	26	0

BARBADOS.

G. Challenor	st Dewhurst b de Gannes.......	16
P. H. Tarilton	c Constantine b Pascall.......	8
B. H. Emptage	b Constantine..............	2
H. W. Ince	b Pascall.....................	5
C. A. Browne	c Harragin b Pascall..........	48
E. L. G. Hoad	b de Gannes................	0
C. F. Browne	c Cipriani b Constantine.......	1
J. M. Kidney	b Waddell..................	17
B. I. Gilkes	c Dewhurst b Waddell..........	0
K. Mason	not out........................	9
H. C. Griffith	b Waddell..................	34
	Extras	15
		155

	O	M	R	W	O	M	R	W
Pascall.......	27	13	33	3				
Constantine...	21	4	44	2				
Waddell......	14.2	5	20	3				
Cipriani......	7	2	12	0				
Small........	2	0	7	0				
de Gannes....	7	1	17	2				
St Hill.......	3	1	7	0				

A year later, in September 1922, Constantine went with the Trinidad side to British Guiana. It was the first time he had left his homeland. He sailed southwards to a more distant part of that vast South American mainland which he had seen all his life, remote and unapproachable, from Trinidad across the Gulf of Paria. The brief tour was one of great happiness for the Constantine family. Lebrun, almost fifty, returned to the Trinidad party. Victor Pascall, Learie's uncle, was also a member. In the first match, against British Guiana at Georgetown, Learie Constantine opened the batting, scoring 14 in each innings. He had two short spells with the ball, taking one for 5 and two for 7. Trinidad's victory—by 29 runs—qualified them to play against Barbados in the final. Lebrun Constantine was selected for Trinidad, and the match provides one of the few examples in first-class cricket of father and son playing together. It was the only time the Constantines were to do so. The father could look back to playing cricket against W. G. Grace. The son would end his first-class career playing in a side with Keith Miller after the Second World War.

The game at Georgetown against Barbados produced tremendous scoring. On the first day Barbados could feel reasonably content in having got the first eight Trinidad wickets for 200 runs. Then came Victor Pascall, batting at number nine, the third member of the Constantine family in the side, whose 92 runs encouraged each of the last two men to make fifties themselves. Barbados replied to Trinidad's 359 with an opening partnership of 174 between George Challenor and P. H. Tarilton. Trinidad's score was overtaken with the loss of three wickets. Runs came relentlessly until the total reached 673. Trinidad, in reply, could make only 141, and lost by an innings and 173 runs. Few sides, whose last three batsmen in the first innings totalled 219 runs between them, can have lost so severely. For Learie Constantine, the emotional importance of the match was playing with his father, and the practical importance, fielding at cover. The outfield was far superior to that of Trinidad's Oval, and Constantine could field in the assurance that the ball would

TRINIDAD

W. H. St Hill	run out			0	c & b Pilgrim			36
A. Cipriani	c Kidney b Hoad			11	b Hoad			7
J. A. Small	c & b Hoad			36	b Hoad			5
C. A. Wiles	lbw b Hoad			13	lbw b Hoad			16
N. Betancourt	lbw b Griffith			12	b Griffith			11
F. de Gannes	lbw b Griffith			29	b Griffith			30
L. N. Constantine	lbw b Pilgrim			17	lbw b Griffith			13
L. S. Constantine	b Hoad			6	c Austin b Hoad			1
V. S. Pascall	c Browne b Griffith			92	b Griffith			0
G. A. Dewhurst	st Austin b Tarilton			58	not out			2
C. Fraser	not out			69	run out			8
			Extras	16			Extras	12
				359				**141**

	O	M	R	W	O	M	R	W
Challenor	9	1	40	0	8	0	40	0
Griffith	29	3	101	3	13	2	37	4
Pilgrim	16	2	57	1	7	0	14	1
Hoad	33	1	131	4	13	1	38	4
Ince	2	0	10	0				
Hutson	2	0	4	0				
Tarilton	0.3	0	0	1				

BARBADOS

G. Challenor	lbw b L. N. Constantine	96
P. H. Tarilton	b Small	100
E. A. Collymore	b Pascall	30
J. M. Kidney	b Betancourt	73
C. A. Browne	b Small	3
H. W. Ince	c & b Fraser	151
H. B. G. Austin	lbw b Pascall	53
E. L. G. Hoad	st Dewhurst b Fraser	24
H. C. Griffith	c St Hill b L. S. Constantine	60
L. Hutson	c Fraser b Pascall	45
O. A. Pilgrim	not out	0
	Extras	38
		673

	O	M	R	W
Betancourt	14	1	65	1
Small	35	5	111	2
L. N. Constantine	45	0	97	1
Pascall	54.1	11	146	3
Cipriani	10	0	49	0
Fraser	24	1	76	2
L. S. Constantine	22	1	74	1
St Hill	3	0	17	0

come to him fast and true. 'When the game began, I was a novice,' he recorded, 'when it was over, I was a cover-point.'

Learie Constantine, on the strength of three first-class matches and the confidence in him as a fielder of H. G. B. Austin, the West Indian captain, was chosen to go to England in 1923. Clearly, cricket was winning over law. Yet before his selection for the 1923 tour, Constantine had left the firm of Ryan to join that of Llewellyn Roberts. It was a larger practice and gave him some experience of conveyancing work. For a man now considering marriage, it offered better prospects and pay. Unfortunately, it meant longer hours. Roberts had a habit of keeping the staff till 6.30 in the evening, after which it was too dark to play cricket. Constantine left the firm when he knew he was going to England. Somewhat rashly, he decided that 'the future could look after itself'. The S.S. *Intaba* bound from Port of Spain to Bristol in April 1923 carried a carefree young man making his first visit to England, a country with which so much of his life was later to be identified. In the years to come he would know the land well, and would be the recipient there of honours and distinctions and of snubs and insults.

What did this twenty-one-year-old West Indian Negro, ignorant of all that lay in the future, make of England in the 1920s? He found a country still licking its wounds from the First World War; idealistic hopes of eternal peace offered by the League of Nations fending off the first whispers of discontent from Munich beer-cellars; clear-cut social divisions and English reserve. Constantine and his colleagues in the West Indies side took life as they found it. Money was tight, and the thirty-shilling allowance per week, over and above hotel and travelling expenses, did not go far. Constantine recalled an occasion when the team attended an official lunch and were each given ten shillings with which to tip the waiter—a sum equal to a third of their week's allowance. One of the team thought that seven shillings and sixpence was quite enough for any waiter, and pocketed the difference. Constantine thought little of the waiter who reported the player, and in any case considered the tip excessive. It was

cheaper to go for walks and play practical jokes on each other
than to go sightseeing. If the English were reserved, Constantine realised, it was not an attitude adopted towards West
Indians specifically. The English were simply people who did
not speak even to other Englishmen 'unless firmly introduced with no hope of escape'. The orderliness of the English
countryside intrigued him, 'with its prim, green fields and
well-arranged trees'. The English Sunday, for a young West
Indian far from home, was dull and lonely. He was good at
writing letters regularly both to Norma and to a friend from
Port of Spain, Winston Millington. They were most descrip-
tions of the week's matches, for Constantine's thoughts were
centred on the business on hand.

He wrote that West Indian cricket had to re-establish itself
since the tours of 1900 and 1906 were forgotten in England.
The Australians had visited England three times since the
last West Indian side. He and his fellow-players were the
first representatives of their islands for seventeen years. New
friends had to be made and a reputation established afresh.
Bleak and bitter weather for the first six weeks of the tour gave
the visitors little chance. Constantine noted:

'Day after day we were positively shivering, playing for hours
in the damp and drizzle with scarcely a ray of sunlight. It was
difficult to appreciate what that really meant for us. I shall
never forget that so-called summer! The rigours of it robbed
us of our captain, froze up poor George John's bowling, upset
Victor Pascall, and chilled the rest of us into pessimism. Being
naturally exuberant, we fought against it; but it lay in wait
for us and trickled down our necks, damped the clammy
sweaters we tried to hide in, and made our wrinkling flesh
creep. I recall miserable journeys in freezing trains from one
damp hotel to another; dressing-rooms with their own
private chills laid on, and afternoons in the field when it was
impossible to pay attention because one kept thinking about
overcoats.'

Despite these conditions, by the end of June the side had
won five out of twelve matches, though without exciting the

public imagination. At Oxford, where they defeated the University by eight wickets, they showed their ability to hit hard. The University scored 390 for six wickets declared. After losing three wickets very cheaply, the tourists were in trouble. Constantine had to listen to some mild taunts in the Christ Church pavilion at the expense of his team. Rash promises of what would follow were made to critical undergraduate spectators. But each promise was fulfilled: Small scored a quick 29, J. K. Holt's 52 came in under an hour, Constantine scored 77 in sixty-five minutes:

'The wicket was perfect, far different from the matting wicket on which I had played nearly all my cricket. I could come to meet the short ball and devote all my attention to hitting it as hard as I could. I could drive anything the smallest degree over-pitched, and late in the innings I was gliding from the off-stump to fine leg.'

The contrast may be pictured between Constantine sitting ill-at-ease and unsure of himself, an uneducated Negro of twenty-one struggling to make something of his life, and the suavity and self-confidence of Oxford undergraduates of the 1920s—young men of his own age but white, from upper-middle-class backgrounds, assured, and smilingly contemptuous of the colonials. Constantine reacted in the only way for the moment open to him—by making runs.

Late in the summer, the match against Surrey at the Oval gave the West Indians their first sense of triumph. Challenor, one of the greatest batsmen in the early history of West Indian cricket, scored 155 not out and 66 not out, and the tourists beat a side lying fourth in the County Championship by ten wickets. The *Morning Post* described Challenor's batting as 'good enough for any Test side'.

This victory secured for the West Indies an invitation to play in the Scarborough Festival against H. D. G. Leveson-Gower's XI. It proved an historic encounter. Trailing throughout the match, the West Indies left an XI of England calibre a mere 31 runs to win. 'Thirty-one runs did not give anyone much of a chance', wrote Constantine to a friend, 'but the West Indies took the field prepared to make the England eleven fight for every run they made. This was our last day's cricket in England.' The wickets of Jack Hobbs, G. T. S. Stevens, Ernest Tyldesley, Wilfred Rhodes, A. P. F. Chapman and F. T. Mann fell, before J. W. H. T. Douglas and P. G. H. Fender scrambled home. 'We felt,' Constantine recorded, 'we had put the West Indies far on the road to parity with England, Australia and South Africa. Much was still to be done, but we had laid a true foundation.' The team had won six and lost seven of twenty first-class matches.

Constantine had gone to England primarily for his fielding. He was, said *Wisden* 'an amazingly good cover-point'. He had held 18 catches, scored 425 runs and taken 37 wickets. P. F. Warner, by now retired from the first-class scene, described him as 'the finest fielder in the world'.

When Constantine returned home in September 1923, he determined to put cricket before work. It was 'not entirely a foolish decision. I thought that one day I could become an English professional.' Already, the first trickle of overseas players had started coming to England, but it was far-sighted, not to say vain, of the young Constantine to see himself among them. He was now unemployed, and secured temporary work at £7 a month holding acting appointments in the civil service in the Registrar's office of the Supreme Court and in the Education Department. The work was of a routine nature—typing and filing. There was no security in acting appointments, and soon he was unemployed again. The period 1924 to 1925 was not a happy one. Constantine was out of work part of the time and dependent on his family. His father supported him but the son hated to ask for the money necessary to play cricket, however modestly. His cricket cost him little more than fares and equipment. 'He didn't drink and after a match he would go to Pacheco's Billiard Saloon in Frederick Street where he would play pin-pool or snooker', one of his cricketing friends recollected. Norma had long ago decided, in her own words, that 'she loved him anyway and would get herself interested in cricket'. But she saw little of him and he was lucky not to lose her.

From a cricketing point of view, his best game in this period was for Shannon against Queen's Park at the Oval in 1924. Shannon were set to get over 250 in an hour and a half. Constantine's 167 not out brought victory but not the favour of the Queen's Park authorities, between whom and Lebrun Constantine some long-standing ill-feeling had persisted—its precise origins now forgotten.

Although Constantine appeared for Trinidad in 1924 and 1925 he did not do especially well with bat or ball. His best performances were eight for 38 against Barbados at Bridgetown in 1924 and 36 runs against them at Port of Spain in 1925. J. St F. Dare, who played against him in the British Guiana matches, recalled 'a sparkling and often unorthodox opponent. His ebullience on the field was inoffensive. One just realised he was on the attack all the time, wholeheartedly but fairly.' Among his team-mates he was 'accepted as a pleasant and lively companion and, with an English tour behind him, already held in high esteem'. In the 1925 match between Trinidad and British Guiana, Dare lifted a ball safely over Constantine at cover ('as I thought') only to be caught out as Constantine 'gave the impression of climbing an invisible ladder to get the ball'.

Early in 1926 an M.C.C. side led by the Hon. F. S. G. Calthorpe came out to the West Indies—the first since before the war. Though largely a team of amateurs, it included the England and Gloucestershire professional, W. R. Hammond, then at his peak. Constantine was not selected in the party of Trinidad players to go to Barbados and so missed participating in the first Representative match in the West Indies (not a Test match) between the West Indies and the M.C.C. Rain saved the West Indies from defeat after the M.C.C. declared at 597 for eight wickets (Hammond 238 not out). The West Indies replied with 147 and 21 for six wickets. When the West Indian party arrived in Trinidad, Austin, the captain, insisted that Constantine be in the Trinidad colony side and subsequently in the Representative XI. Constantine always believed that it was Austin—a white Barbadian—who kept him in the game, and that the Queen's Park authorities would have limited his prospects. The Representative match was won by the M.C.C. by five wickets. Constantine's contributions were 7 and 18, and two wickets for 53. The bowling figures did not do him justice. In the M.C.C.'s second innings, when 240 runs were needed for victory, he had bowled a sustained spell of accurate, fast bowling, which had restricted the English batsmen and delayed the moment of defeat. In the next match, in British Guiana, Constantine had the satisfaction of seeing the M.C.C. follow on against the West Indies score of 462. The M.C.C. led by only 45 in the second innings when rain stopped play. Constantine, in that innings, took four for 54, and headed the bowling averages for the 'rubber' with seven wickets for 129.

Meanwhile, his fortunes had been restored by an offer of employment from Trinidad Leaseholds Ltd. Oil was a fairly new dimension in Trinidad's economy. It had been known to exist since the middle of the nineteenth century, and a company to exploit it had first been founded in 1886. But Trinidad oil could scarcely compete with the oil boom in America and little was achieved until after 1900. In the years before the First World War hundreds of millions of gallons were exported and several large companies were formed in the south-west of the island. Trinidad Leaseholds Ltd had been founded in 1914. The idea of employing Constantine had been suggested to the Trinidad Leaseholds' staff by the old Trinidad player, Joe Small, who was a stores clerk with the firm. Constantine joined as a machine-shop clerk and then became a quantity-stock account ledger clerk at £8 a month, working in the south at Fyzabad. There he shared rooms in the barracks at various times with Bruce Hunte and Winston Millington. Millington was his friend from clerking days in Port of Spain. With both men he maintained contacts for the rest of his life, and Hunte was a bearer at his funeral. A 'boarder' (caterer) provided a hot meal at midday brought round in a carrier. Otherwise, men were expected to cook for themselves. While at Fyzabad Constantine played on Saturdays for Trinidad Leaseholds in the Rahamut Cup competition, the major trophy offered for senior clubs in south Trinidad. Matches were two innings apiece, spread over three Saturdays. On Sundays he made the forty-mile journey to the north to play for Stanmore in the Oxavin Cup. He continued to keep himself immensely fit, exercising with a trapezium and rings and taking part in athletics competitions. As a sprinter he won several events at Trinidad Leaseholds, and played football on the right wing for Forest Reserve.

His appearances for Shannon were very infrequent at this time, but two performances may be noted. Reynold Dolly recalled a match at Siparia:

'The redoubtable Lebrun Constantine took the then invincible Shannon team to Siparia by train for the feast of La Divina Pastora and to play the local team. The home team made 205 runs and by a strategic prolongation of the lunch interval left Shannon only 80 minutes to make the runs before the last train left for Port of Spain. Learie implored his father to let him open the innings, and with five minutes to spare Shannon beat Siparia by seven wickets, Learie's contribution being 185 not out in 75 minutes.'

A cricket match against the Sporting Club came to an untimely end when Constantine dismissed them, almost single-handed, for 7. Shannon made the necessary runs in an over, and the Shannon team were free to keep an engagement to attend a wedding at two o'clock that afternoon. Constantine also represented Shannon with three other cricketers in the 4 × 100 yards relay race at an Empire Day track meeting at the Queen's Park Oval. The four cricketers —all colony players as well as Shannon players—won the event.

The only cloud on Constantine's horizon in 1927 was his immediate superior at Fyzabad, who was not interested in cricket and accused him of wasting time. It was an unfair accusation. Constantine often worked well into the night to bring his ledgers up to date. Constantine threatened to resign when a crucial Rahamut Cup match was due the same afternoon. A phone call saved the day and he was transferred in 1927, to Pointe-à-Pierre, where he was employed in the Stores and had a net set up behind them. Constantine was grateful for the security which Trinidad Leaseholds Ltd offered, for he was now able to get married to Norma, an event which took place on 25 July 1927. It proved to be a marriage of great mutual devotion for over forty years. In April 1928 their only child, Gloria, was born.

A few months after joining Trinidad Leaseholds, Constantine played at Bridgetown against Barbados. The match extended from 24 January to 2 February 1927 and produced 1,677 runs. Constantine has described it as the greatest game he ever played in, although his own personal contribution was small. Barbados, almost 400 runs behind on the first innings, managed to win by 125 runs. Their second-innings score of 726 for seven wickets declared included a double century by Challenor, 174 not out by E. L. G. Hoad and 123 by Tarilton. Constantine took three wickets in the match at a cost of 210 runs, and made 11 and 13. In his book *Cricket and I* he paid a long tribute to his fellow-players, and to the three Barbados centurions in particular.

At the end of the year, in December 1927 and January 1928, Constantine played in three trial matches in Barbados which ranked as first-class. In one of them he made a quick 63 runs, and in another took five wickets for 32. He also used these matches to bowl faster than ever before. He was selected to go to England with the 1928 West Indies party, perhaps a little luckily. No large scores had come his way in inter-colonial cricket and he had taken fewer wickets than expected over the years. But his fielding saved stacks of runs, his catching got wickets, and a cautionary word was uttered by Austin, before he left for England, about batting with a little more restraint.

Trinidad Leaseholds put him on half pay and he set off, 'not this time as a slightly nervous youngster, but as a young man of experience, veteran of a previous tour'. Norma and her infant daughter were left behind in Trinidad to await the outcome of the tour.

Constantine was aware that the future might hold more for him than the summer of 1928 in England. As events turned out, he did return to play cricket in Trinidad again, but never to be a part of the domestic scene as he was for so much of the 1920s. Henceforth he would come back *peregrinus* —a stranger in the land.

1. The West Indians in England in 1906. *Left to right, standing*: R. C. Ollivierre, C. S. Morrison, L. S. Constantine, G. Challenor, J. E. Parker, J. Burton, O. H. Layne, C. P. Cumberbatch. *Sitting*: A. E. Harrigin, H. B. G. Austin, P. Goodman, G. C. Learmond. *In front*: C. K. Bancroft, S. G. Smith.

2. Queen's Park Savannah, Port of Spain where Constantine played cricket as a schoolboy and for Victoria-Shannon. As many as thirty games could take place simultaneously.

3. Gloria Constantine aged three in 1931. Her entire childhood was spent in England.

4. Norma Constantine during the early years in Nelson.

5. An outing to the Lake District with friends in 1935.

3

CRICKET
ROUND THE WORLD
1928-1930

From April 1928 until September 1931 Constantine played
cricket almost continuously. Up until that time, he had made
thirty-six appearances in first-class cricket. Between 1928 and
1931 he made a further forty-seven. Only thirty-four remained in his career. As a first-class cricketer, these were his
best years. They were also the years in which he began to
establish himself as a professional cricketer in the Lancashire
League. His cricket, at all levels, may be summarised as
follows, first-class matches being marked with asterisks:

April–September 1928	West Indies' tour in England*
January and February 1929	Trinidad at Port of Spain*
February–March 1929	Guest player in Jamaica*
April–September 1929	Nelson in the Lancashire League
September 1929	L. N. Constantine's XI on tour in Scotland
November 1929	Guest player in the United States
December 1929–April 1930	M.C.C. tour in the West Indies*
April–September 1930	Nelson in the Lancashire League

November 1930–March 1931 West Indies' tour in
                                        Australia*
April–September 1931   Nelson in the Lancashire
                                        League

These busy years began when Constantine, for the second
time, set sail for England in April 1928. The tour itself was
not a great success in terms of results. For the first time, the
West Indies met England in official Test matches, losing each
one by an innings, while defeats at the hands of both Ireland
and Wales scarcely suggested that they could match, even
those countries which had little claim to first-class status.
Wisden pessimistically commented that 'whatever the future
may have in store, the time is certainly not yet when the West
Indies can hope to challenge England with a reasonable hope
of success'. But even if it proved disappointing, the tour was
not an unmitigated disaster. The team won five first-class
matches and held their opponents to a draw in a further
thirteen. Of those players making their second visit, Constantine alone enhanced his reputation, but in one all-
important respect he failed. In the Test matches, he took
only five wickets at a cost of 52 runs apiece, and scored only
89 runs in six innings.

He began the tour in exciting fashion. Against Derbyshire
40 runs were needed to win with two wickets left. Constantine, instructed to 'save the game', won it instead by hitting
five fours and a three, and then two more fours. With his
partner's contribution, it was enough to give the West
Indies a win in their opening game.

In the next game, against Essex, in bitterly cold weather
at Leyton, he scored 130 out of 190 in ninety minutes. Essex
had made 369, and the tourists had replied with 183 for six
when Constantine joined F. R. Martin. Three sixes and
fourteen fours came in a devastating innings which gave the
West Indies a first-innings lead. Immediately afterwards, the
tourists met Surrey at the Oval. Constantine took 50 off their
bowlers and followed this up with 60 not out in the second
innings. A match that might have been lost was saved.

Quite apart from Constantine's natural instinct to hit the ball hard, there was another aspect to which he himself attached much importance. The West Indian tour was privately financed by businessmen. Early defeats would lose the public's support and interest, and would threaten economic disaster not only to the promoters but to the prospect of future tours being sponsored. A photograph of the game against Derbyshire shows a single row of spectators scattered on a bench watching the game in bleak conditions. If the weather would not help the cause of the tourists, Constantine himself must do so (see p. 65).

More runs came for him against Oxford University, but rain restricted play in the first appearance of the West Indies at Lord's—against the M.C.C.—to 31 overs in three days. Against Cambridge University Constantine took five wickets in each innings, and thereafter rested torn fibres in a muscle. He was scarcely fit for the match against Middlesex in mid-June, by which time the weather had turned in the West Indies' favour, and they were once again at Lord's.

'I went up not too confidently for medical examination before our match with Middlesex. The doctor shook his head and said I must not touch a ball for a week or ten days, or I might do myself permanent harm. I went out from that examination with an unpleasant decision to face. I knew that our tour had failed so far to cover its costs. If we failed against Middlesex, interest in the Tests would be knocked to bits just at a time when our bright displays were raising everyone's hopes. Mr Mallett, our team manager, to whom I put my problem, was in as big a hole as I was. "You are our draw card," he said. "If you drop out, we shan't do much business. But you must decide yourself. I don't want you to harm yourself." Well, it was my year, and I said I would play. The doctor was summoned and told he must somehow get me fit. I remember that June morning so well—the glorious heat of the sun, the tense air of expectancy, and the feeling in my bones that muscle or no muscle I would show them some cricket at Lord's. The doctor's face grew as long as his arm.

"It is my place to warn you that it is most unwise for you to play. Probably you will break down on the field, and the consequences may be serious. You must make up your mind what you intend to do." "I'll play," I said. "You're mad!" he said; but he gave me a great grin.'

At once Constantine went on to bowl, getting an early wicket before having to rest. He had opened the attack with G. N. Francis. They and H. C. Griffith made up the triumvirate of fast bowlers on whom the West Indians primarily depended during the tour. Despite bowling on wickets unsuitable for their pace, all three had performed reasonably well so far. But against Middlesex, Francis and Constantine could do little—Griffith was not playing. Middlesex's total of 352 for four wickets declared included a hundred by 'Patsy' Hendren, often a scourge of West Indies' bowling. The West Indies could muster only 79 for five and faced the follow-on and an innings defeat when Constantine came in. In an innings of great power, distinguished by his driving and pulling, Constantine scored 86 in an hour. The follow-on was saved and immediately he attacked the Middlesex batsmen with such a spell of fast bowling that he hit the stumps five times and took seven for 57 in 14.3 overs. As he returned to the pavilion, the Middlesex members stood up to him. He was touched and embarrassed: 'I had a sudden vivid fancy of myself dusty amongst dusty files in a lawyer's office in Trinidad waiting for the newspapers with the cables of the Middlesex match.' He had made a victory possible for the West Indians who were set 259 to get to win. But at 121 for five, their chance of success seemed to be diminishing until Constantine—by now the hero of the large Lord's crowd—joined M. P. Fernandes. He gave a hard chance to extra-cover off his first ball. This was the only concession to the Middlesex attack. Within an hour came a century which included two sixes and twelve fours. The West Indies won by three wickets, and Constantine's personal contribution had been 189 runs and eight wickets—to say nothing of his brilliant fielding. One of his strokes was so powerful that it struck the pavilion rail and ricocheted among the seats, damaging wood and paint. A fielder who had tried to stop that ball played no more cricket that summer (see p. 54).

Again the members in the pavilion, and the entire Lord's crowd, stood to him as he came off the field. Among those in the pavilion watching was Lord Dunglass—eventually (as Sir Alec Douglas-Home) to become British prime minister and a president of the M.C.C. Lord Home, nearly fifty years later, still remembered that innings: 'the best shot I ever saw him make was off a none-too-short ball which he sent over cover point to the feet of Father Time on the top of the north stand at Lord's. It was prodigious.'

Constantine, on that afternoon of 12 June 1928, had taken up the challenge first presented by his father on that same ground twenty-eight years earlier. West Indian cricket was established as a major force from that point onwards. The significance of that victory for both the West Indies and Constantine was profound. The match had been watched by the Australian cricketer C. G. Macartney. His influence led to the first invitation the West Indies received to visit Australia two years later. For Constantine himself came an invitation to turn professional and to join Nelson in the Lancashire League. His cricket, if successful in the three-day game, clearly had a great future in the shorter one-day contests demanding quick runs and a rapid fall of wickets. Macartney advised him on the terms of his contract, and his immediate future was decided. The long-term implications of that decision could not be foreseen.

The rest of the tour was something of an anti-climax. All three Test matches were lost—by a margin of an innings in each case. Constantine himself did badly apart from taking 4 for 62 in the Lord's Test in an England total of 401. Only twice did the West Indies' total exceed 200 in their six innings. In the second Test, at Old Trafford, Constantine came in for some criticism for bowling bumpers at Jack Hobbs, Hammond and D. R. Jardine. Bowling for England was Harold Larwood around whom the controversy about 'body-line' bowling would presently erupt.

MIDDLESEX

N. Haig b Small	119	b Constantine	5
H. W. Lee c Martin b Constantine	7	b Constantine	15
J. W. Hearne c Nunes b Roach	75	lbw b Small	28
E. Hendren not out	100	c Francis b Constantine	52
E. T. Killick b Francis	6	c Francis b Constantine	4
G. O. Allen run out	4	c & b Francis	7
F. T. Mann b Francis	32	b Small	4
I. A. R. Peebles not out	0	b Constantine	0
T. J. Durston ⎫		not out	9
W. F. Price ⎬ did not bat		b Constantine	3
J. A. Powell ⎭		b Constantine	1
Extras	9	Extras	8
(6 wkts decl.)	352		136

	O	M	R	W		O	M	R	W
Francis	35.5	4	107	2	....	10	3	30	1
Constantine	20	1	77	1	....	14.3	1	57	7
Browne	11	2	21	0	....				
Small	29	5	72	1	....	11	3	36	2
Martin	13	0	30	0	....	3	0	5	0
Roach	7	0	36	1	....				

WEST INDIES

G. Challenor c Hendren b Durston	23	b Haig	33
C. A. Roach c Lee b Durston	0	run out	10
M. P. Fernandes c Hearne b Allen	29	c Allen b Haig	54
W. H. St Hill c Hendren b Peebles	5	b Durston	5
E. L. Bartlett st Price b Powell	13	lbw b Hearne	26
F. R. Martin not out	26	not out	1
L. N. Constantine b Peebles	86	c Haig b Lee	103
J. A. Small c Hendren b Haig	7	c & b Peebles	5
R. K. Nunes b Durston	17		
C. R. Browne c Allen b Durston	0	not out	4
G. N. Francis lbw b Haig	1		
Extras	23	Extras	18
	230	(7 wkts)	259

	O	M	R	W		O	M	R	W
Durston	21	10	16	4	....	15	3	32	1
Haig	24.4	7	32	2	....	22	5	80	2
Hearne	11	4	25	0	....	15	3	51	1
Peebles	18	2	51	2	....	11	2	45	1
Allen	8	2	43	1	....				
Powell	7	1	40	1	....	1	0	6	0
Lee					....	4.4	0	27	1

For Constantine himself, the match against Northampton-shire was another personal triumph. He took thirteen wickets, including a hat-trick in the second innings, and scored a century in ninety minutes, of which 78 runs came in boundaries. The West Indies, in scoring 434 for 9 wickets, beat the county by an innings and 126 runs.

He played a major part in most of the remaining matches. In both the Festival games, at Folkestone and Scarborough, he got runs and wickets. A 62 in three-quarters of an hour against an England XI at Folkestone was followed, at Scarborough, by a fifty and seven for 68 in the match against H. D. G. Leveson-Gower's XI. He ended the tour second in the batting averages, having scored 1,381 runs for an average of 34.52, and he was top in the bowling, with 107 wickets for 22.95. He had bowled more overs than anyone else, and taken the most catches. He had enjoyed his summer much more than five years earlier; he had got to know the English people better, and was ready to come and live amongst them in Lancashire in 1929. But the tour had taken its toll. As with Don Bradman in the 1930s, much was expected of him in every match. The critics applauded when he succeeded, and accused him of playing to the gallery when he failed. He often needed twelve hours' sleep before the next day's cricket. He considered that the captain, R. K. Nunes, grossly over-bowled him, and their relations on the tour were not good. With the exception of Austin in 1923, Constantine was critical of the white captains under whom he played in England and in the West Indies, and believed there were better leaders among the coloured cricketers. At the end of the tour, the voyage home was a chance to rest and to take stock before his final season as an amateur—the inter-colonial tournament of 1929.

Constantine played in both colony games. Against British Guiana in January 1929 he bowled extremely fast to take four for 32 and five for 64 besides making a half-century. Trinidad's victory of 223 runs was a substantial one. In the second game of the inter-colonial tournament he broke the record for Trinidad in these matches by scoring 133 against

Barbados. It beat the previous highest score of 116 held by his father since 1910. It was the highest score of his career in first-class cricket, and he matched it by taking seven wickets in the game for 71 runs. He was never again to play for Trinidad in a colony match. His record between 1921 and 1929 read:

Batting: Innings, 19; Times not-out, 0; Runs, 472; Highest Score, 133; Average 24.84.
Bowling: Runs, 688; Wickets, 37; Average 18.59.

The colony matches received wide coverage in the Trinidad press and competed for attention with reports on King George V's serious illness. The *Trinidad Guardian* commented that in Constantine, Francis and Griffith, the West Indies had 'a bowling combination superior to anything of that class in the Empire'. After the second match there followed a one-day game between a Combined XI of Barbados and British Guiana, and the Trinidad side. The Combined XI made 151, and Constantine contributed 32 to Trinidad's 154 for three. A quarter of the proceeds of the match were given to Constantine as a benefit to help him in his expenses in going to England. It was a gesture from the Queen's Park authorities which pleased the Constantine family and did something towards easing the strained relations which had existed between them. A dinner at the French Restaurant in Port of Spain concluded both the entertainment of the visitors and the farewells to Learie Constantine.

Constantine then went to Jamaica in February 1929 to play against a touring side from England sponsored by Julien Cahn and captained by Lord Tennyson. In the final match of the short tour, the West Indian Representative XI defeated Cahn's XI by 144 runs, Constantine taking four for 66 and holding six catches. Then it was time to return briefly to Trinidad and thence make his way to Lancashire to begin his professional life with Nelson, a career which is the subject of chapter 5.

At the end of 1929, Constantine was free to return to the West Indies in preparation for the forthcoming visit of the

TRINIDAD

C. A. Roach	c Skeete b Birkett	86
C. A. Wiles	lbw b Walcott	46
W. H. St Hill	lbw b Rogers	5
G. Liddelow	c Walcott b Griffith	23
L. N. Constantine	c Clarke b Walcott	133
J. A. Small	c Griffith b Rogers	6
E. A. C. Hunte	lbw b Rogers	1
N. Betancourt	lbw b Griffith	13
B. J. Sealy	run out	37
E. St Hill	not out	20
C. St Hill	c Griffith b Walcott	2
	Extras	8
		380

	O	M	R	W	O	M	R	W
Griffith	22	3	91	2				
Rogers	23	3	110	3				
Skeete	14	0	92	0				
Birkett	10	4	39	1				
Walcott	6.1	1	30	3				
Ward	3	0	10	0				

BARBADOS

L. A. Walcott	b Constantine	0	lbw b E. St Hill		9
C. de L. Inniss	c Constantine b Sealy	22	c E. St Hill b Constantine		4
L. S. Birkett	c Sealy b Constantine	30	b Small		28
J. M. Kidney	c Hunte b Constantine	9	c Wiles b Small		0
J. E. D. Sealey	run out	9	c Hunte b Constantine		7
M. W. Clarke	c Hunte b Small	1	b Constantine		0
E. L. Ward	c Constantine b Sealy	0	c sub b Sealy		16
H. C. Griffith	c Constantine b Sealy	3	c sub b E. St Hill		13
C. Waithe	c Roach b Sealy	3	c Betancourt b Constantine		5
H. E. Skeete	b E. St Hill	24	b E. St Hill		18
H. M. Rogers	not out	2	not out		0
	Extras	5		Extras	9
		108			109

	O	M	R	W	O	M	R	W
Constantine	11	2	41	3	9.4	3	30	4
E. St Hill	10	1	30	1	10	3	28	3
Small	8	3	18	1	7	2	31	2
B. J. Sealy	8	1	14	4	2	0	11	1

M.C.C. In the few weeks intervening, he fitted in a short visit to the United States in November 1929 where he played as a guest of West Indian cricketers in New York. His visit was given great publicity:

'Come and see L. N. Constantine, the fastest bowler in the world. Incomparable as a fieldsman. A harder hitter than G. L. Jessop.'

This assumed that American spectators had heard of Jessop! Babe Ruth, the US baseball player, might have been a better comparison. Constantine made only five runs, but he took seven wickets for 9, feeling satisfied with his performance until a messenger came on to the field from the pavilion. 'You've got to do something, boy,' he whispered. 'A demon bowler ought to knock the men about. The people are getting sort of restless.' Constantine put something extra into his next ball and, to his horror, knocked out the batsman. The Press report next day was full of praise! One catch he took in the match brought crowds on to the ground pressing dollar notes into his hands. The visit was enjoyable with one reservation. On the day after the match Constantine was asked to change his seat in a Roman Catholic Church. Few 'colour' incidents in his life made such a deep impression upon him as that. It came at a particularly disturbing time just after he had spent his first summer in Lancashire and had begun to be accepted there by white people.

With the visit to the United States he had played cricket in almost every calendar month of 1929. This was how he had wanted it to be. He was the complete professional; he had played in Trinidad, Jamaica, England, Scotland and the United States. Here was his livelihood. He spent December 1929 in the Trinidad nets preparing for the Test series against England.

The M.C.C. sent two sides overseas in 1929–30. One went to New Zealand and Australia, playing mainly in New Zealand; the other to the West Indies. It was a reflection of English first-class cricket of the time that both were strong touring parties and both contained amateur cricketers able to find time to go. The tourists to the West Indies were led, for the second time, by Calthorpe and included R. E. S. Wyatt, a future England captain, Rhodes, and George Gunn, two veterans of over fifty. Rhodes had first played for England in 1899, Gunn in 1907. Both ended their Test careers with honour on this tour. Hendren, L. E. G. Ames and W. Voce gave strength to batting, wicket-keeping and bowling.

The tour opened with two high-scoring draws against Barbados. Then came the first Test match.* England scored 467 in reply to a West Indies' total of 369 to which Constantine had contributed 13. George Headley's 176 was the main feature of the West Indies second innings of 384. The match was drawn with England 120 short of victory with seven wickets left. Constantine had bowled thirty-nine overs in the first innings and taken three for 121. He had also held three fine catches, one coming full face off the bat when he was fielding short in the gully. He had had a hand in the dismissal of six batsmen and the *Barbados Advocate* gave him its main banner headline in reporting the third day's play:

'There was only one player whose performance overshadowed all others. That player was Learie Constantine. He out-witted Sandham, bowled Ames, took a good catch to dismiss Hendren, and then mystified his spectators by taking two magnificent catches whereby O'Connor and Astill were returned to the pavilion. He is a wonder. This term admirably sums up his greatness.'

After the match, Austin, the former West Indies captain, made presentations. Constantine got a bat for the best all-round performance in the West Indies side. Austin paid tribute to Constantine, father and son:

'There is no more charming and keen cricketer than Mr Constantine senior, and as you see, ladies and gentlemen, the son has inherited the father's manners and keenness for

* The West Indies Press regarded the matches between the M.C.C. and a full West Indies side as Test matches. *Wisden* in 1931 treated them as 'Representative' matches. They were subsequently given official Test match status.

the game. We enjoy watching you, Mr Constantine, as much
as you enjoy your cricket.'

In the evening a dinner was given to both teams by the
Barbados Cricket Committee, attended by the Governor, the
Colonial Secretary, the Bishop of Barbados, and a large
number of players and officials associated with Barbados
cricket. The speeches were long. They paid customary tribute
to the identity between cricket and the Empire. The only
critical note came from the England captain who considered
that there was no chance of a result while Constantine
bowled 'with four short legs and two deep'. He suggested that
if Constantine had had three men in the slips and a gully and
had bowled at the wickets he might have won the match for
the West Indies. It was a guarded reference to 'body-line'
bowling. Within a couple of years, the policy of fast bowling
to a packed leg-side field, as exploited by Larwood in
Australia, was to cause a crisis of international dimensions in
Anglo-Australian relations, and the 'body-line' controversy
dominated the cricket scene in the early 1930s. Meanwhile,
Calthorpe's comments brought a long letter to the Editor in
the *Barbados Advocate* of 18 January 1930, in which the
correspondent, Dr L. C. Hutson, pointed out that Larwood
in England the previous summer and Voce in the current
match had bowled with equal speed to similar field-settings
and had gone uncriticised.

Constantine's own views were that an occasional ball
pitched short down the leg side was legitimate. But he was
approached by the English manager, R. H. Mallett, before
the Trinidad Test and asked not to bowl short down the leg-
side. To avoid ill-feeling he agreed, despite the fact that Voce,
who took eleven wickets in the match, bowled at a great pace
with some balls that Constantine felt were intimidating.

Constantine appeared three times against the M.C.C. at
Port of Spain—twice for Trinidad and once for the West
Indies. Trinidad won the first colony game and M.C.C. the
second. Apart from one innings of 333 by Trinidad, they
were extremely low-scoring games by Caribbean standards.

In the second game Voce's fast bowling, rising sharply, secured twelve Trinidad wickets.

Constantine did little with the bat and was able to bowl only in the first game because of cramp. But nothing affected his fielding. He took nine catches in the two matches and, by his own admission, 'had never fielded so well before'. In the second Test at Port of Spain, Constantine and his fellow opening bowler Griffith, were largely responsible for England being dismissed for 208. Constantine then contributed 58 in fifty minutes to the West Indies total of 254. When England batted again, Hendren and Ames put on 237 for the fourth wicket. Constantine dropped Hendren early from a chance which 'I would have taken nine times out of ten'. His four wickets were scarcely any compensation for England's total of 425. West Indies lost the match by 167 runs.

Three weeks later, at Georgetown in February 1930, Constantine played a notable part in the first victory of the West Indies in a Test match. The West Indies scored 471, led by C. A. Roach (209) and Headley (114). In reply, England lost three wickets for 33, and were all out for 145. Constantine took four for 35. When West Indies batted again, Headley became the first West Indian to score a century in each innings of a Test match. England were set 617 to win. They nearly succeeded in saving the game, being all out for 327 with only fifteen minutes left. Constantine, in forty overs, took five for 87.

Constantine's dismissal of Hendren in the first innings was a subject of mirth to the numerous schoolboys watching the match. Hendren had been coaching them, and offering the advice that there was no reason why a strong batsman should allow himself to be bowled on a good wicket. To good-humoured delight, Constantine clean-bowled him with a fast one which kept low when he was attempting a hook.

For Constantine that was the end of the tour. His omission from the final Test in Jamaica was nothing to do with form but illustrated the problem of raising West Indies sides. Twenty-nine men were picked for the four Test matches and four separate captains led the team. The composition of West

Indian XIs throughout the years have reflected strongly the place where a match is being played. Several factors contributed to this: communications, until the establishment of frequent air-travel, were difficult, so that players were faced with long sea journeys; local feeling was so strong that popular and known heroes were preferred by the home crowds; unless his claims to be selected were outstanding, expense militated against a man playing away from his own territory when another man's abilities were similar. Selectors tended to be appointed for a particular Test match, sometimes from within the administration of the host territory.

So the M.C.C. sailed to Jamaica where they played four matches including the final Test, in which they amassed the mammoth total of 849 (Sandham 325). By mid-April, when the M.C.C. tour ended, Constantine and his family were on the boat for England and a second season with Nelson.

4
DOWN UNDER
1930-1931

As early as 1926, during the visit to England of the Australians, the possibility of a West Indies' tour of Australia had been discussed between Australian players and the West Indies batsman Challenor, who was in England at the time. Nothing came of the idea, largely because the Australian Board of Control refused to ratify it. It was an unfortunate decision: the West Indians were probably a stronger side at that time than they proved to be four years later when a tour eventually took place.

One Australian who had been foremost in suggesting a tour had been the former Test player, Macartney. Macartney was a fine player, whose batting had been the basis of Australia's resounding successes in Test cricket after the First World War, and a sound judge of the game. Macartney believed the West Indians would learn much from a tour of Australia, while accepting the fact that they would be unlikely to defeat the full Australian XI. He rated their abilities far above those of New Zealand, who, like the West Indies, were recent arrivals on the Test match scene. After seeing the 1928 West Indians in England Macartney was able to persuade the Australian Board of Control to invite the West Indians to come to Australia in the season 1930-1.

Constantine returned to Trinidad from his second season with Nelson in time to join the party, composed of Trinidad, Barbados and British Guiana players. They met up with the Jamaican contingent at Panama where an exhibition match was played before they sailed on to cross the Pacific to New Zealand. They played a solitary game at Wellington before beginning the Australian tour at Sydney. On paper, the West Indian tourists were a reasonably strong party, containing their usual three fast bowlers in Constantine, Griffith and Francis and strong batting in George Headley and C. A. Roach. But they suffered from the besetting weakness of nearly all West Indian teams, then and later. The players did not know each other well, coming from their scattered islands or, as in the case of both Constantine and the captain, G. C. Grant, direct from England. Grant was a Trinidadian who had gained a 'blue' at Cambridge and had not yet returned to his homeland. He had seen none of the players perform recently.

Despite almost a month at sea, Constantine found his form at once against Wellington, taking six wickets for 24 in a total of 195. Rain deprived the West Indians of likely victory. Eight days later, the West Indians played their first-ever game on Australian soil against a New South Wales side which included the new star in the firmament—Don Bradman, fresh from triumphs in England and the amassing of 334 in the third Test match at Leeds. In reply to the West Indians' first innings total of 188, New South Wales scored 206, Bradman making 73. Constantine clean-bowled A. G. Fairfax, A. F. Kippax and S. J. McCabe and had A. A. Jackson leg-before-wicket in a spell of eleven overs. They had made 46 runs between them and, with Bradman, were all to appear in the Test side later in the season. Had the West Indians—and Constantine himself—maintained that form, the Test matches might have been more equally poised. When the West Indians batted a second time, Constantine got 59 in thirty-five minutes. The former Australian captain M. A. Noble, writing in the Sydney *Sun*, said that Australians had to go back to 'times before 1914 to recall such a sensational innings'. The match was eventually lost by four wickets but an impression had been made. The visitors could hope to command substantial 'gates' for their matches and in both innings they had contained Australia's leading batsmen.

6. Learie Constantine bowling.

7. The early part of the 1928 West Indies' tour of England was hampered by bleak weather which affected gate receipts. A few spectators see Constantine catching G. M. Lee in the match against Derbyshire. The wicketkeeper is R. K. Nunes, the West Indies' captain.

Against Victoria at Melbourne the West Indians came up against H. Ironmonger, who was later to top the bowling averages in the Test matches. Ironmonger took thirteen wickets in the match for 118 runs, and only a fine century by Headley redeemed the West Indians' batting. He and Constantine came together when the score was 36 for six and put on 76 together. Headley's century was described as a 'fine, free and unblemished' display. Constantine bowled extremely fast, though with little movement off the pitch, taking five wickets for 64 in Victoria's score of 594, of which W. H. Ponsford, another of the Australian Test side, made 187. Victoria won by an innings and 284 runs.

During the match Constantine met an old Negro Barbadian, Sam Morris, who had come to Victoria half a century earlier during the later stages of the Australian 'gold rush'. He had not made his fortune but won fame instead as the first West Indian to play in a Test match. The facts were unusual. The Victorian selectors had picked the Test team to play against England at Melbourne in January 1885. The chosen XI refused to play because of a pay dispute, and a 'reserve' side appeared for which Morris was selected. He took two wickets for 34 and opened the batting. It was Constantine's most interesting memory of the match.

Defeat by South Australia brought the West Indians to their first Test match against Australia at Adelaide with a record of three defeats and no successes. Australia made only one change from the side which had defeated England by an innings four months earlier.

The game was played in scorching weather which had its own appeal for West Indian players. On the first two days the West Indians held their own, scoring 296 and taking three Australian wickets for 64. Thereafter the Australians scored a first-innings lead of 80 and went on to win by ten wickets. Constantine had, as ever, fielded attractively, but had little success with bat or ball. The Australians were particularly struck by the speed and accuracy of his returns.

Constantine learnt during this game the thoroughness of the Australian approach to Test matches. W. M. Woodfull, the Australian captain, could consult a chart showing the direction of all scoring shots by individual players on the opposing side during most of their first-class careers. It was a far cry from the West Indian captain meeting his players virtually for the first time when the tour began.

The West Indians spent Christmas in Tasmania. Constantine scored a century in fifty-two minutes at Launceston, a match which gave the West Indians their first victory. For Constantine, as for many of the others, it was the first Christmas he had spent away from Trinidad. But home now was Nelson, and to Nelson had gone his Christmas letters and greetings to Norma and two-and-a-half-year-old Gloria.

New Year's Day 1931 found the West Indians facing Australia in the second Test at Sydney. While they dismissed many of the leading Australians cheaply, Ponsford's 183 ensured a large total. To Australia's 369 the West Indians could only reply with 107 and 90. Once again Constantine failed as a batsman and had little luck as a bowler. But the West Indians' fielding, and his own in particular, were described as the 'best seen at Sydney for many years'.

Against Queensland at Brisbane Constantine had an outstanding game, scoring 172 runs, dismissing seven batsmen and taking three catches. On the first day he made 75 in under an hour in the West Indians' total of 309. Queensland were dismissed for 167, Constantine taking four for 33 in twelve overs. When West Indies batted again, Constantine's 97 came in an hour and a half.

'When I reached 97 I decided to get the three runs by singles. I pushed the first ball to cover and called my partner for an easy single. "No," he screamed, and I had to get back. Whereupon I decided to hit a six. I waited for my ball, timed it to a nicety, and let myself go like that tiger leaping. It was meant to be a stroke past the bowler's hand, but it hit that hand, and as it seemed to me, bounced sideways like a ricocheting bullet, struck my partner's bat as loudly as a pistol-shot, deflected into the hands of mid-on, trickled out of his palms and was grabbed up by somebody running in behind him before it could drop to the turf. I went indoors a sadly injured man.'

The West Indies' second-innings total of 265 left Queensland to score over 400 for victory. Constantine's three for 23 contributed to their dismissal for 188. It was the West Indies' first victory on the Australian mainland.

Constantine had been fascinated to play against the aboriginal bowler, E. Gilbert, who bowled fast, unusually gathering pace as the over progressed. Gilbert had once been suspected of throwing and had practised with his bowling-arm in a splint to ensure a straight arm. Constantine became the first player ever to hit him for a six.

Once again, the West Indies fared badly at Test level. The third Test at Brisbane followed immediately upon the Queensland game. Australia batted first and Constantine got Bradman's wicket for the first time—but not when he would have wished. Before Bradman got going, Constantine set a field with three slips and a gully. Bradman, Constantine felt, was a little vulnerable to pace bowling outside the off-stump. After bowling several straight balls with no movement in them, Constantine sent down an extremely fast ball which moved away late from the off-stump. Bradman edged it—as intended by Constantine—to first slip. The catch went down. 'Don gave me one look as much as to say that he saw it all, and then settled down grimly', wrote Constantine. Not till the next morning did Constantine get that wicket when Australia were 423 and Bradman had reached 223. As Ponsford (109) and Kippax (84) were also dropped off Constantine's bowling, it was an innings of 'might have beens'. Australia's total of 558 left the West Indies demoralised. Only Headley with a century redeemed their own performances of 193 and 148. Constantine had held his catches and wrote that he would have liked to have been able to field in the slips to his own bowling—but he contributed nothing as batsman, and much of his bowling had been erratic in length and direction.

An 'up-country' match at Newcastle against a New South

Wales Country XI gave Constantine the chance to bat as if playing for Nelson in a Saturday afternoon game. Off sixty-seven balls in ninety-three minutes, he scored 147. The tourists won by an innings. Constantine enjoyed himself but deplored the fact that the West Indies could not produce 'the form of which they were capable' in the major matches. Through a clash of fixtures, they played Victoria's 2nd XI—the 1st XI being involved in a Sheffield Shield match at Brisbane against Queensland. The West Indies failed to force a win, being 129 runs short with five wickets in hand at the close of play. Constantine had a good game in the return match against South Australia. After scoring 63 in little more than an hour, he bowled so fast and so effectively that South Australia had four wickets down for less than 20. In the process, he strained himself so badly that he was unable to bowl more than four overs in the second innings. A match that looked as if it was going the West Indies' way was won by the last South Australian pair putting on 22 to win.

The fourth Test at Melbourne was a disaster. Defeat by an innings and 122 runs in two days destroyed all hopes of the tour being a financial success. Only Headley, with 33, made a score of any status at all in either innings. Constantine got rid of Ponsford and Jackson cheaply and proved the least expensive of the fast bowlers, but Bradman's 152 and Iron-monger's eleven wickets effectively destroyed West Indies' hopes.

And so to Sydney where the West Indies were due to play New South Wales and then the fifth Test. Those Australians who had pinned their hopes on the West Indies doing reason-ably well in Australia were convinced that they had not done themselves justice. They had had the sun on their backs—more than in their two recent tours of England—but they had not had the fast wickets to which they were accustomed. M. A. Noble, one of the elder statesmen of New South Wales cricket who had supported the West Indies so much in his articles in the Press, urged the Sydney authorities to prepare the fastest wicket possible for the final two games. The wicket, wrote Constantine, was 'a real Barbados' one, and the West

Indies responded in kind. Runs against New South Wales came from Roach, Headley, J. E. D. Sealey and Constantine. Wickets came from Constantine and Griffith. Constantine took six for 45, hitting the stumps on all six occasions and getting rid of Bradman for 10 and McCabe for 26. Constantine has described how he got some of those six wickets:

Davidson: 'I let him have a very fast off-break. He shaped at it just as he had done to the out-swingers, and his wicket fell in a heap to my first ball.'

Bradman: 'I bowl him a "Davidson's ruin" but rather slower, so as to bring Don out to make his pet stroke—steering the ball away through the slips. He does so before realising that there is a devil in it; and his off-stump goes for a walk.'

McCabe: 'A sudden express breaking from the off-side, but delivered with the identical action of the other balls before it. McCabe goes to play it, snicks it with the edge of the bat, and plays on.'

Hunt: 'A fast one between middle and leg is smothered. An even faster one breaking on to the leg stump causes him to move out a little too far, and the wicket goes down in a heap.'

Encouraged by a first-innings lead of 149, the West Indies scored freely when they batted again. Constantine's 93 in 100 minutes was the highest score.* With Sealey—at that time the youngest player ever to have appeared in a Test match—Constantine added 150 for the fifth wicket. New South Wales were set 552 to win. Constantine, with a recurrence of strain, was substantially rested, and his fellow-bowlers had a hard task restraining New South Wales from getting all those runs. But victory by 86 runs came to the tourists. The Australian Press was full of enthusiasm. At last, the West Indians had shown what they were worth. They had, said one journalist, 'taken the bit between their teeth'.

* Unusually, it was an innings without a six in it. Constantine had bet the old Australian player, A. A. Mailey, that he could play a long innings without hitting a six. He did so, and Mailey paid up. Constantine, writing twenty years later, described this as his best innings in first-class cricket.

The West Indians were ready for the last Test, and a chance to avert a run of five successive defeats. G. C. Grant, who had himself batted solidly throughout the tour, and learnt much as a captain, won the toss and chose to bat on a wicket that had had rain. Thanks to F. R. Martin and Headley, the West Indies were 222 before their second wicket fell, and 298 for two at the end of the day. Rain fell in the night and delayed the start, Grant declaring after an hour's batting leaving the Australians to bat in the late afternoon with a hot sun drying out a wet wicket. Before bad light stopped play, Grant's decision had been justified. Five Australian wickets fell for 89, including those of Woodfull, Ponsford and Bradman. Sunday intervened, and on the Monday Australia averted the follow-on by reaching 224.

The West Indies, with a lead of 126 and the threat of more rain, scored quickly on the Monday afternoon and evening, reaching 124 for five. The light got increasingly worse but it was West Indian policy to make runs while the rain kept off. It rained all Tuesday, and Wednesday brought a hot sun and the inevitable 'sticky' wicket. The West Indians declared at their Monday night score leaving the Australians 251 to win. Francis and Constantine opened the bowling against Woodfull and Ponsford. With victory in their grasp—given the conditions under which Australia were batting—West Indian nerves went to pieces. Two catches were dropped in the opening overs. Then, at 49, Woodfull skied a ball from Griffith to Constantine. Constantine was once asked in a broadcast programme in 1955 to select a passage from his own writings on cricket which he regarded as important in the history of West Indian Test cricket. He chose to read his description of this catch:

'Woodfull threw his bat at one from Griffith and the ball shot up to the skies straight over the wicket. "Learie!" screamed the team at me standing in the gully. There was Barrow, the wicket-keeper with his gloves, as near to the ball as I was, but they called for me and I stepped forward from the gully. And as I moved to follow the catch more closely, I put my eyes straight on the solitary little scrap of sun and lost sight of the ball completely. For a desperate moment I could not find it. "Woodfull!" beat through my mind, "My God, Woodfull!" Never before have I ever been frightened at a catch and I hope I never shall be again. I went stone cold and my heart began to throb, but I grabbed at my cap, pulled it down over my eyes to shade the sun, and caught sight of the lost wanderer again. I opened my fingers wide high up in front of me and took the ball above my chin, so that if I had missed I should have had another chance below; but I held it safely at the first attempt and stood trembling.'

Certainly the dismissal of Woodfull gave the West Indians their first break-through. Ponsford was caught by Constantine moments later, and Bradman went for o. Before lunch Kippax went to an off-break from Constantine, and Australia had lost four wickets for 53. After lunch, McCabe and Fairfax stood between the West Indians and victory, taking the total up to 155 before McCabe was caught. Fairfax was to stay to the end, but gradually lost his partners. When Ironmonger was run out, the West Indies had won their first Test match against Australia, their first away from home, and the second in their history.

That Wednesday, 4 March 1931, was a red-letter day in West Indian cricket. Not for twenty years were the Australians to get their revenge, when J. D. Goddard took the West Indies to Australia in 1951–2. Bradman never again played against the West Indies, nor met Constantine on the cricket field. Years later, in a fanciful and imaginary match in his book *Cricket Carnival*, Constantine selected himself and Bradman for an XI of Contemporaries to play an XI of Old Timers. Unlike recent computerised Test matches which have been based on the 'memory-bank' of the computer fed with cricket statistics, Constantine created his own score-sheet and produced an honourable tie. He let Bradman make 159 in the match, and gave himself five wickets and two catches.

Of Constantine on that tour of 1930–1, Bradman wrote in his *Farewell to Cricket*:

'Constantine became a great favourite with the crowds in Australia. Without hesitation I rank him the greatest fields-man ever seen. The phenomenal agility and anticipation of Constantine made him a perpetual danger in any position. One can understand why his name became first on the list of all Lancashire League cricketers.'

Constantine returned the compliment in his *Cricket and I*:

'Bradman the prodigy is a batsman who scores phenomenally. He is a beautiful timer of the ball and at all times he seems merely to be hitting good length balls where he pleases and when he pleases. As long as he is there, it is runs, runs, runs all the time.'

Both men were thus 'phenomenal' to each other. Both had learnt their cricket using the resources of their environment— Constantine the coconut bat, Bradman a ball hit against a water-tank. Both became cricket knights. Both were men of public importance in their own right after their playing days were over.

That victory against Australia did an immense amount of good to West Indian cricket. The West Indians were cheered by the Sydney crowd, and those who had encouraged the tour to take place felt, in the end, vindicated. It was rated 'a happy and enjoyable event'. For Constantine personally, there was the great pleasure of being asked for his portrait to have it placed in Sydney Cricket Pavilion. At the time, he doubted if few things in the game would ever give him greater pleasure. Sensitive as he was to matters of race and colour, he had wondered how he and his colleagues would be received in 'white' Australia. There were no worries on that score. The hospitality and reception of both Australians and Lancashire 'exiles' left Constantine with a fondness for Australia which he always retained. If, indeed, he was gradually adding to his political education, there could have been no greater contrast than this large, sparsely populated white dominion in the old Empire and his own densely packed Trinidad of varied races. Yet both had become parts of that

Empire within a few years of each other; Australia's penal settlements in 1788 followed upon the Botany Bay landing; Trinidad had become *de facto* British after Colonel Thomas Picton had assumed command of the island from the Spanish in 1797, in the Napoleonic wars. Australia had reached, in the very year of this cricket tour—1931—a high degree of independence within the Empire under the Statute of Westminster. Could this have been entirely lost on the future chairman of Trinidad's People's National Movement Party?

But Constantine had gone to Australia as a young man of twenty-eight to play cricket, not to study the politics of Empire. As a cricketer he had performed with distinction in first-class matches. He had topped the bowling, taking forty-seven wickets at a cost of 20.23 runs, and come fourth in the batting with 708 runs for an average of 30.78. Only in the Test matches had success eluded him except in the field. It was the only time Australian crowds saw Constantine as a cricketer. Of his performances on that tour, the Australian critic, A. G. Moyes, wrote:

'Now and again he looked hostile. His fielding was always a sight for the gods. Sometimes he hit well but our recollection is not one of achievement so much as of genius badly directed. Nevertheless, we can be glad of the genius. We recall his manner of playing cricket.'

It was time to return home—to Lancashire, Nelson and the family. On his own admission, Constantine had been worried about them in his absence, partly for financial reasons. Although the £300 which the West Indies Board of Control had paid him for the tour was far in excess of what he had received for his 1923 and 1928 English tours, by now not only was he a married man with responsibilities but he was also setting his sights higher. He had already earned £500 in the summer of 1930 before setting off on the Australian tour, and was now receiving far more from cricket than he could have dreamt of as a clerk in an oil firm.

5

NELSON
1929-1939

The 'digs'—two rooms in Howard Street—faced Whitefield
Elementary School in a low-lying part of the town. Children
from the school ran out into the playground to catch a
glimpse of the black couple who had arrived the night before.
Learie Constantine and Norma, leaving Gloria behind with
Learie's parents, had been met at Liverpool Docks by T. E.
Morgan, Chairman of Nelson, and Harold Hargreaves, the
captain. They had been driven over on a cold April evening
in 1929 and introduced to their landlady. 'She made it quite
plain that nobody else would take us', Constantine said some
years later. The accuracy of the remark may be doubted
since only one or two people had been approached but it was
true that the people of Nelson were on the whole wary and
their new arrivals were on the defensive. The cricket committee had made a decision involving far more than cricket.
They had assumed responsibility for a West Indian Negro
family settling into the tightly-knit community of a Lancashire cotton town, the majority of whose inhabitants worked
in the mills.

Constantine himself was able to settle down quickly enough
because his work lay in Nelson. Things were less easy for
Norma. Everyone recognised her, of course, as the black
cricketer's wife, but they still stared as she went shopping.
The family continued to be a novelty to the children at
Whitefield School. Not content with gazing from across the
playground, they would 'jump up at the window to peep at

us'. Then there came the anonymous letters—not many of them, but still able to hurt. At the end of the summer, Constantine at any rate had had enough, although his wife had borne the brunt. 'We are going home and we are not coming back'. he said. 'No, we're going to stay. Let's make it! Let's stick it out!' Norma, always the dominant partner, persuaded him of the wisdom of staying, of the financial status they enjoyed, of the alternatives in Trinidad. None of this bitterness lasted. Gradually, the Constantines realised that rudeness was a cloak for ignorance. Most of Nelson had never seen a coloured person. 'Soon people asked us out in an atmosphere of curiosity.' Constantine rightly analysed curiosity as the major factor in white attitudes. 'They were laughing at us, not because we had black faces, but because we were different from what they expected.'

The Constantines returned to Trinidad in September 1929 —Learie to play in the Test series against England—and came back the following April. This time two-year-old Gloria came with her parents. They moved a hundred yards away from Howard Street to rented rooms in Buccleugh Road. By the end of the second summer Constantine had earned in two years—with collections as well as salary— nearly £1,200. They had already saved a great deal, and they decided they would rent a house at number 3, Meredith Street. The Constantines had come to stay.

Meredith Street, set high in the town, contained a row of terraced houses built in portland stone. Each had four rooms and a small yard at the back. They overlooked Thomas Street Bowling Green. Beyond, chimney stacks pierced the sky and distant Pendle Hill pointed the way to Yorkshire. The houses had been built at a time of expansion in the cotton industry at the turn of the century. By moving to Meredith Street, the Constantines had established themselves in 'a good quality district'. By the standards of the place and the day, they lived in a middle-class environment. Number 3 Meredith Street remained their home until 1949, long after Constantine ceased to play cricket for Nelson. The move gave permanence to their life in Nelson. By now 'we had

settled down, made friends and had our own house'. Both
sides had made an effort in adjustment, but it was immensely
harder for the Constantines. They were watched, central
figures on the stage all the time, ambassadors for Trinidad
and the coloured races. Sometimes Constantine revolted
against being under constant observation and went off for a
day or two to lose himself in the anonymity of some large
city, Liverpool or Manchester.

In their fourth summer—1932—the household took in a
lodger. C. L. R. James cannot have been the easiest of guests
in a four-roomed house with no garden and a lively four-
year-old child. He was a Trinidadian with ambitions to
write and with some abilities as a cricketer. He kept late
hours, read intensely and was deeply interested in politics.
He and Constantine had struck a bargain in Trinidad:
James would help Constantine write a book; Constantine
would give James a home, if necessary, while he took stock for
the future. James's presence affected Constantine's life in
Lancashire. He persuaded him that they must present the
image of the West Indies to those around them. It was not
enough to play cricket and be seen; the West Indies must be
talked about. 'By the winter [of 1932] we were in full cry all
over the place', James has recorded. They talked to rotary
clubs, church organisations and sports clubs. While James
sought to teach the people of Lancashire about the West
Indies, Constantine confined his talks to cricket. He would
describe tours he had been on, or discuss the techniques of the
game. James, on the other hand, learnt much from Constantine about the attitude of Englishmen to questions of
colour. The motives of the two men differed, for Constantine
was not yet ready for politics. Harold Hargreaves, the Nelson captain at the time, sometimes took the chair for these
meetings. On one occasion, at the Carr Road Wesleyan
Institute, Constantine was late, and Hargreaves recalled how
he filled in the time that autumn evening in 1932.

'Most of the houses at that time had large fireplaces with side
ovens all of black cast iron, and Friday was the popular day

to clean and polish them with blacklead. I told the audience Constantine would be late because Mrs Constantine would be busy blackleading him ready for the weekend. Constantine then arrived to be greeted with laughter. On being told what I'd said, he grinned all over, and turned the situation to his advantage.'

Constantine could take a good-natured 'colour' joke against himself. He could tell one too, as in the story of who came off worst walking along the street in opposite directions during the war-time 'black-out'—he or a white man. Later, James left to become a journalist, to go to the United States and to play a role in Trinidad post-war politics, but not before he had been a witness to a bad spell when weeks went by and Constantine failed with the bat. He still got wickets and he fielded well, but runs would not come. 'It was a horrible business,' James reflected. 'On Saturday he would leave home full of confidence, by Saturday night it was the same old story.' Eventually all came right and a good innings was played.

James had been an astute observer of Constantine at a time of crisis. He had seen the rough edge of a professional's career. Perhaps the very proximity of James to Constantine had brought that crisis, for there was a tenseness in their relationship—the mirror-image frightened. The cricketer of talent hesitant to plead the politics of Trinidad to north-country audiences; the political theorist for West Indian self-government almost accepting £3 10s a week to be some club's professional. But a bargain had been kept, and *Cricket and I* appeared in 1933. Despite errors of fact, it gave a picture of Constantine's cricketing experience, and James had had the home-base he needed at a critical stage in his own literary development. He was grateful to the Constantines and the friendship remained between him and Learie for the rest of Learie's life.

At this time Constantine had no intention of becoming seriously involved in questions of colour. Virtually his only concession in this direction was to join the League of Coloured

Peoples. This organisation was the first of its kind to be multi-racial in membership. Bodies such as the African Association, founded in 1897, and the African Progress Union, founded in 1921, had had a specifically Negro membership. The League of Coloured Peoples came into existence at the London Central Y.M.C.A. in 1931, to 'make representations to government authorities, hospital managements, medical faculties, commercial concerns, factory proprietors, hotels and boarding house keepers on behalf of coloured people in Britain. Its founder was Dr Harold Moody, a medical prac-titioner and a man of devout Christian principles. With the broad aims of the League Constantine was in agreement, and he accepted its evidence of racial injustice in British cities such as Liverpool. His friend James had joined the League and later gave Moody some credit for its achievements be-cause he 'would be able to speak now and then to a member of parliament or get a letter to the papers'. But James was mildly sceptical of the League because he doubted if it really made an impact. Constantine belonged because James did, and because he accepted that 'our people are badly mis-understood in this country'. 'I am trying to keep my end up in the North', he wrote enigmatically to Moody.

Constantine was still uninterested in the wider concept of Pan-Africanism which was fundamental to Moody's in-tentions. His concern was with the exiled Negro who had gone to the West Indies in slavery. Only later, partly because of his responsibilities for West Africans during the war, did Con-stantine take a broader view of Negro hopes and frustration. Secondly, he was not prepared to give time to the League's affairs. Cricket made great demands upon him in the 1930s and it was his livelihood. Thirdly, he felt out of touch with the League. He was unable to make the sort of contacts which Moody—and, up to a point, James—could make. Doors which opened for Moody in the 1930s did not do so for Con-stantine till the 1940s. Most of the League's business was conducted in London or through its journal, *The Keys*, which appeared quarterly from 1933 to 1939. Constantine seldom visited London in the 1930s, nor did he write articles. His sole book in those years, *Cricket and I,* was almost entirely about cricket. The League was of more importance once war broke out; then Constantine became professionally involved in the sphere of race relations and his association with the League became closer. He was eventually its president.

The main reason why Constantine avoided colour issues and the cause of colonialism lay in his simple decision to live an uncomplicated life in Nelson. This was what was expected of him—he was there to play cricket. He must have recognised the possibility of his contract not being renewed if he had allowed himself to become a 'political' figure. Neither his financial aspirations nor his personal feelings at the time would have made him want to run this risk. Nevertheless, he had no illusions about the implications of being a coloured man. He was, for instance, fond of a neighbour's child,

'a little white boy whose parents were old friends of mine. Soon the little fellow started school. On his very first day he ran home streaming with tears and crying out at me in broken-hearted reproach, "Uncle Learie, you never told me you were coloured!" They had given him a bad time, those other little boys and girls, when they discovered that he had a friend with a different coloured skin.'

The story has a happy ending; the two remained friends over the years. Both the boy and Constantine entered the legal profession. Less directly, Constantine was made aware that he would be unacceptable to Lancashire County Cricket Club as a professional, partly on account of his colour, when the Australian E. A. McDonald retired.

Over the years, a way of life in Nelson developed. Norma Constantine devoted her time to her family and her home. Gloria would be taken for walks to Walverden Park. Sometimes they would all go in their Austin Seven to Marsden Park where the flowers in the heated conservatory reminded them of Trinidad's tropical colouring. Shopping was mainly done at near-by corner stores at the ends of terraced streets. Going down into the town meant a walk of the best part of a mile, and a climb back. There were friends who shopped for Norma on cold days. Among the friends of those days were the Cookes, whose daughter was called Gloria after the Constantines' own daughter. Many years later, during his time as High Commissioner in London, Learie came to Nelson with his wife to give Gloria Cooke away at her wedding, as her father was ill. Then there were the Johnsons who gave a temporary home to the Constantines in the first few weeks of the 1930 season before the rooms in Buccleugh Road were available. Norma had also stayed with Margaret Johnson while Rowland, Margaret's husband, and Learie were away on the cricket tour of Scotland the year before. There were picnic expeditions with the Johnsons to the Lake District and a holiday in London when the two families went together. Norma and Margaret would exchange recipes while their daughters, Ruth and Gloria, exchanged measles. Later, the two girls would go to film shows together and play tennis. In the winter months the Constantines went with their friends to Skipton to listen to the local orchestra and sometimes, more grandly, to Liverpool to hear the Philharmonic Orchestra play. Constantine had an appreciation for music and as a boy had had a good treble voice, but he did not keep up his singing nor did he play any instrument. Among other friendships made by the Constantines were those with some of the officials who worked in Nelson Town Hall and their wives. The Constantines used to go to the annual dinner of the 'Spuds'—an informal social club formed by some of these men—and take part in the summer outings of the 'Spuds' to the Lake District and other resorts (see p. 49).

The friendships which the Constantines made outside cricket were largely with middle-class families. From the Constantines' point of view this is understandable: their income put them on a par with such people, and Constantine had the sort of ambitions for himself and for his daughter which, in the context of the 1930s, were 'middle-class'. Nevertheless, there must be some surprise that the Constantines were accepted in these circles. The explanation may be found in the status Learie enjoyed as a player, in the acceptability of him and his wife as people, and in the goodwill of their Anglo-Saxon neighbours.

Despite these friendships, Norma remained a difficult person to get to know. She was much quieter than her husband. 'We made her welcome and she was charming,' recalled another friend, 'but she was self-effacing. She didn't join anything.' But people recognised the strength of character which lay behind her shyness. 'She was a dominant person in her own home. She encouraged her husband to stay. She looked to the future, and made him work for some examinations.'

As a step towards academic success, Constantine joined the local library where, as he once said, he 'found books and more books, the friends of kings and commoners alike, the symbol of culture and achievement'. He began studying for the Cambridge Local Examinations by correspondence courses and in 1939 was taken into the family solicitor's office of a fellow Nelson cricketer, Alec Birtwell. Had it not been for the war, he would have become articled to the firm.

For Gloria, Nelson was home from infancy until she went to university after the war. She attended Miss Washington's Academy, a preparatory school, until 1935, then went to the convent at nearby Colne, the Convent of our Lady of Lourdes, from which she went on in 1939 to Nelson Grammar School, where she became a prefect and a house captain. In many ways she was protected from the slights that might have come her way. By the time she was three years of age her parents were happily and securely settled in Nelson. Indeed, she enjoyed a certain kudos as her father's daughter, but she was not insensitive to the significance of her colour. A family holiday in Brighton in 1938 was spoilt by rejection at an hotel—'we're in the wrong place, Daddy, they don't take coloured people'. But such instances were rare enough in Lancashire—had they been otherwise it is doubtful if her parents would have stayed.

So through the 1930s the Constantines were financially secure. They saved for the future, and were generous to West Indians whom they learnt were in distress. They had their share of begging-letters, and Norma was ready to send something if she felt there was genuine need. All this was something apart from their life in Nelson—they had too much common sense to touch the pride of their hosts by giving or lending money in Nelson. Instead, Constantine visited hospitals and talked about cricket. They were not indifferent to the effect of the Depression. They saw mills close down. Unemployment increased and poverty was apparent. The Constantines were horrified at the number of neglected children they saw, but realised that 'the inadequacy of the single wage made it necessary for a man and his wife to work in the mill'. 'I never knew till then the extent of poverty', Learie said in a war-time broadcast.

There was nothing Constantine could do about it all. His business was to play cricket, and for that reason—and that reason alone—he was part of the life of Nelson in the 1930s. He was a professional in the heyday of the Lancashire League.

League cricket in its broadest terms means the playing of cricket within a competition. Thus a group of clubs in an area might play 'friendly' matches against each other on Saturdays and participate in a competitive league on Sundays. Unlike a knock-out cup competition, a league involves its members throughout the season in a given number of matches. Points are obtained and at the end of the season a victor emerges. In a world of sport dominated by television and press coverage, few people can be unaware of the significance of leagues in football. Indeed, scarcely any football is played outside some competition. Nowhere is league cricket in the British Isles more popular than in the Midlands and North and, in particular, Lancashire. The Lancashire League centres around some fourteen clubs based on manufacturing towns or large villages in the Blackburn and Burnley area and was founded in 1890. Basically, it has remained a competition for amateurs whose abilities, enthusiasm and sacrifices have produced standards of play and play surfaces which would not disgrace the first-class professional game. Much has depended upon the co-operation of local businessmen and the encouragement of the Press. The Lancashire League allows its clubs to employ professionals and this has brought them players of top-class calibre. Such men often (but not always) have had a distinguished Test-match record behind them. They are expected to show their talents on the field, to coach the amateurs in the club—especially youngsters—and to assist in preparing wickets for play. In the early days of professionalism, before the First World War, the Lancashire League clubs could secure the man they wanted for about £5 a week. This represented about £100 a year since there was no payment in the 'close' season. Among the early professionals had been Sydney Barnes, whom A. C. MacLaren took to Australia with him straight from League cricket. Just before the First World War, the Lancashire League clubs began to look beyond England. Accrington secured C. B. Llewellyn, a South African Test player, and Nelson, E. A. McDonald, the Australian bowler who had played havoc with England in the 1921 Test series. Then, in September 1928, came their offer of a contract to Constantine.

John Kay, in his *Cricket in the Leagues*, has described Constantine as 'the ideal league cricketer' whose 'fast bowling was always a magnet for the crowd, his big hitting an added attraction, and his superlative fielding a third factor'. Constantine was first approached by Nelson after his performance against Middlesex in June 1928. Although his employers in Trinidad had been good to him in terms of cricket, there was a vast difference between an assurance of a clerkship in an oil firm linked to weekend cricket and a professional contract. Nelson's financial offer was the same as they had previously made to McDonald. Constantine's mentor, the Australian, Macartney, advised him to ask for more. Nelson accepted his request and terms were signed. It was a momentous decision for Constantine, one which changed the whole of his life. In its own way, it was also a momentous decision for Nelson. They had brought into their community a coloured man who was to be of influence far beyond the boundaries of the cricket field.

The style of cricket played in the League bore some relation to the games which Constantine had played for Shannon on the Savannah, and for Trinidad Leaseholds in the Rahamut Competition. Batsmen, Constantine found, were there to hit the ball—his father's advice—and bowlers were charged with taking wickets. A League match lasted five hours and runs had to be got quickly. A man who made 30 had done well: a team that scored 200 was likely to win. Players were no respecters of persons: a first-class player coming into the League from county cricket could be knocked around by a batsman anxious to keep the score moving. Constantine soon learnt what was the essential role of a professional such as he. Fundamentally, he was expected to score 50 or 60 runs and to take several wickets. Beyond that, his task was to contribute to the side's overall welfare. If the professional on the other side was taking wickets, it was his opposite number's job to restore confidence by scoring runs and protecting his partners from the bowling. If that professional was scoring himself rather rapidly, then he had to be contained. The other ten men in a League side were all worth their place, but it was the professional's role to act as the sheet-anchor of the team, and to encourage men to play above their level. All this—before packed and excited crowds —made strong demands on a man, but Constantine had exactly the right temperament for it. He was there to provide spectators with furious bowling, dynamic batting and lightning fielding. Yet all this happened unselfishly. If his wicket fell cheaply to an unknown youngster, he would be the first to provide a word of encouragement. If someone 'collared' his bowling, he was usually ready to applaud—and to try harder next time. There was a quality of sportsmanship which the Lancashire crowds at once recognised. In the words of John Kay—who played with him often, 'he dominated yet did not obliterate. He encouraged the amateurs and praised them as fellow cricketers.'

The cricket ground at Seedhill where Nelson plays its home matches lies on the edge of the town. Several parallel streets of terraced houses are situated behind the large green pavilion with its changing rooms, committee room and rows of seats. In Constantine's days, hanging baskets of flowers decorated the pavilion and a permanent cloud of smoke hung over the ground. From the centre of the field players can see a large part of Nelson on one side—chimney stacks predominating and an occasional church spire. Turning in another direction the players would see the slopes of Pendle Hill—the same view Constantine had from Meredith Street. A Nelson home match in the 1930s would involve the use of four turnstiles and extra ticket-sellers using the front windows of nearby houses. Nelson's secretary in 1974, Harold Standage, looked back wistfully to the Constantine era:

'He was a man of many talents on the cricket field and should he fail with either bat or ball, which of course he did from time to time, he was sure to electrify spectators in the field. Matches commenced at 2 p.m. on Saturdays. The cotton mills closed at 11 a.m. The cricket ground possessed large seated enclosures and a twin line of seats all round the ground. To ensure obtaining a seat, if the weather was reasonable, one had to be on the ground by 12.30. Later arrivals had to be content to stand for five hours. No grass ever grew on the terraces.'

Seedhill might hope, on a fine day, for 8–10,000 spectators. The match against Bacup in 1930 drew 14,000. Even midweek games, which started at 3 p.m., drew large crowds after the mills closed at 5.20. Week-night nets, with as many as thirty men practising, would attract 300 spectators. From the start of his career with Nelson in 1929, Constantine's presence ensured a 'gate' four times as large as normal. Six thousand extra spectators meant £150 to the club.

Constantine's first season for Nelson—the summer of 1929 —set the style for later years. He made nearly 1,000 runs for an average of 34 and took 88 wickets in 361 overs for an average of 12. At the end of that first season, Constantine went with Nelson to Scotland, a tour which one player asserted 'was instrumental in welding the team and their professional into the highly efficient unit which dominated the cricket scene in North-East Lancashire for years to come'. It was a tribute to the new professional in his first season that his colleagues in Nelson asked him to be captain for the tour. The trip began with a visit to the battlefield of Culloden, scene of Prince Charles's defeat in 1746, where a lament was played by a pipe-major on the graves of fallen Highlanders. Pipers were, indeed, attached to the team for the entire tour, and played at hotels and grounds. At a civic reception in Inverness, Constantine told the Provost and the Town Council that 'no game helped the solidification of the Empire as much as cricket'. It was a point of view he was to retain all his life.

The first match was against Northern Counties in the Northern Meeting Park, a club which had had a reputation for bringing distinguished sides and players to Inverness since a visit by W. G. Grace. Constantine's own innings was the third highest of his career, his 175 not out including four sixes and twenty-nine fours. It was, said *The Scotsman*, 'a display of hurricane hitting, putting the ball clean out of the ground on three occasions'. One disappeared into the nearby garden of the Provost of Inverness Cathedral. Many years later, in 1964, Constantine returned to Inverness. He was invited to tea with the Provost (by then retired) who had remembered the incident. When Constantine died, the local Press recalled his appearance in 1929 as a 'red-letter day in the cricket annals of the Highlands'. Constantine's team won by 271 runs.

Against Morayshire at Elgin, Constantine took seven for 15 as his side dismissed the Scottish county side for 45 and defeated them by 79 runs. The tour concluded with the defeat of Ayr—a club one day to produce an England captain in Michael Denness—and of the West of Scotland at Partick, Glasgow. Against Ayr, Constantine took six for 46, and against the West of Scotland five for 29. It was a pleasant conclusion to a hard-working season in League cricket. It was also Constantine's first introduction to a country of which he became very fond, where he played a lot of cricket in the 1940s and where he helped to establish a Regional Sports Council in the 1960s.

Constantine played cricket almost continuously between

December 1928 and September 1931, a period of almost three years. He was never to play so much in future years. He was probably at the height of his powers at this time—extremely fit, taking constant exercise, still under thirty years of age. The amount of cricket he played leads to some consideration of what he was now earning from the game.

Nelson could hope to take as much as £200 at a gate on a really fine day. Overall, the home matches on a Saturday in the season might produce a revenue of over £1,500. Nelson could afford to pay their professional well. In addition to that, there were generous collections round the ground when anyone—professional or amateur—made a 50 in a match. Constantine himself could hope to augment his annual income by over £100 in this way in the course of a season. His first three-year contract brought him £500 a year; his second (1932–4) rose to £650 a year. Between 1935 and 1937 he was earning £750 a year, far in excess of the maximum wage for a professional footballer; he was almost certainly the best-paid sporting entertainer in the British Isles. By comparison the cotton workers, who played with him or watched him, earned between thirty-five and forty-four shillings a week—approximately £100 a year. Coal miners in nearby Yorkshire pits might earn £150 a year. Many of those who played or watched cricket in the 1930s drew unemployment benefit of 15s 3d a week. Constantine's income put him in the top half-million salary earners in the country.

Apart from the mill owners, he was one of the best paid men in Nelson—doing the job he wanted for money he could scarcely have dreamed of in Trinidad. Norma's advice, 'Let's stick it out!', had been wise. His value to both Nelson and the League as a whole was such that rumours that another League was bidding for his services led to the various clubs in the Lancashire League contributing to a pool of money to keep him at Nelson. His presence in away matches ensured at least £100 for the home club's gate. In 1934 he was offered £1,100 to go elsewhere; he refused the offer but was flattered that the figure was greater than one being mentioned in similar negotiations to get Bradman. The chairman of the

Lancashire League that year commented that Constantine in five years had ensured that the other thirteen clubs had taken £10,000 at the gate in games in which Constantine had played away from Nelson.

Yet there was some public criticism outside the Leagues of the money spent on Nelson's professional. Nelson's employment of Constantine might be defended on figures alone: Nelson's gate-receipts since he came to them had been three-quarters of those of the other thirteen clubs put together. Constantine's own view of his financial worth may be gauged from an incident in his second season with Nelson. The club was chasing championship points, and in a match against Haslingden at Nelson on 16 August 1930, the visitors batted first, making a score of 169. Nelson's opening bats were progressing steadily and Constantine sat with his captain, Hargreaves, padded up to bat at number three. Hargreaves impressed on him that he wanted him to bat steadily until he got his eye in, then open up later. The first wicket fell at 28 and in went Constantine. The first ball brought two runs followed by 4, 2, 4. He went on to score at almost the same rate, reaching 90 not out when the match was won by seven wickets. Another member of the team remembers what happened next:

'Hargreaves waited, sat upon his locker in the dressing room for an explanation of his disobeying orders to play himself in before going for the runs. With his disarming smile Constantine said: "Now, Harold, if I played my cricket like some professionals play theirs, I should be paid the same as them. As I play my cricket to entertain the paying public, I draw two to three times as much as them and we get gate receipts in proportion."'

Despite this incident, Constantine's relations with Nelson captains were, on the whole, good. Hargreaves, who had first become a member of Nelson in 1904, was captain in Constantine's first year.* A player of twenty-five years' stand-

* As late in his own career as 1937, Hargreaves took all ten wickets for 48 against Lancaster (in a non-league match) with Constantine bowling at the other end.

ing in 1929, he 'had no trouble with Constantine'. But another former captain found him 'ready to make difficulties. He would sulk in the field if things went wrong and he was not getting wickets.' The remedy for this was to put him on the boundary where his attempt to talk 'Lancashire' with the spectators restored his good humour.

Although Nelson is in Lancashire, its closeness to Yorkshire has always meant that some of the club's supporters have come from the 'white rose' county. This was especially true in Constantine's day. On one occasion the Nelson team went to Long Preston, a Yorkshire village, to play a charity match. A spectator's recollections were:

'Such was the drawing power of the Nelson team with Constantine in it that every seat from Sunday schools, churches, pubs and private houses was carried to the ground to allow spectators to see the match in comfort. This cricket match was the highlight of the district and is still remembered and spoken of by the older local people.'

Another charity match in aid of the North Staffordshire Royal Infirmary found a huge crowd gathered—and the rain pouring down. In an effort to salvage something of the day, Constantine entertained the crowd for half an hour by a display of fielding which included an invitation to the other cricketers to throw the ball at him at point-blank range. 'He invariably caught it', recalls a spectator at that game.

Very early in his time at Nelson, Constantine went to stay with Yorkshire friends in Stockton-on-Tees and agreed to play in an evening game for Stockton against a Stockton District XI. Two thousand people saw him make seven in three balls before being out. Already he was 'news' and the Press coverage of the match devoted a paragraph to his brief innings. He was also interviewed by a reporter from the *Northern Echo* and asked his views on the 'Roses' matches— the bi-annual encounters between Yorkshire and Lancashire. He replied:

'Cricket as played in a Lancashire v. Yorkshire game, where they take six or seven hours for 200 runs is a wash-out. There is no virtue in orthodox cricket. You get an orthodox batsman, playing an orthodox bowler to an orthodox field, and nothing enlivening results. You must take a chance. The perfect wickets have something to do with it too. A bowler in England is afraid of being hit. If a batsman is hitting about the field and the bowler is too keen to get rid of him, while the fielders are expectant of the ball that will be hit their way, everyone enjoys it, both players and spectators. Why pat a half-volley because a man is on the boundary? Hit it over his head; hit it hard, at any rate, for even the best fieldsmen think twice before putting their hands to a hard shot. Put nine men on the boundary, and I would still hit the ball hard. In England they take so long to get their eye in. They pat every ball back. I also get my eye in, but I don't forget to hit the loose balls. The key to the whole matter is the batsman. It rests with the batsman whether the game shall be lively or dull. In our tour of 1928 we played a match where we were all out before lunch on the first day for under 200 runs. This meant that the match must finish, which I say is much better than the "no boundaries before lunch" game.'

The 'no boundaries before lunch' comment was a jibe at a tradition in 'Roses' matches. The local paper gave a double-spread column, an illustration and three banner headlines to his remarks and the national Press took up the interview. Constantine had touched a sensitive nerve in the hearts of Yorkshire and Lancashire supporters. There was an outcry of hostility. Who was he to criticise the game in England?

Constantine was unhappy that his remarks were blown up. He was still, in 1929, unused to Press publicity. Then—as on several occasions later in his life, on cricket and on other matters—he spoke out fearlessly but with some impetuosity. His Nelson supporters did not mind; Lancashire, as a whole, did, and the affair was remembered in 1932 by those who opposed the idea that he should join Lancashire County Cricket Club. So far as Stockton was concerned, nobody minded either and he continued to play for them annually in matches that aided their funds considerably. In these early months in Lancashire, recalled Larry Semmens, the reporter who interviewed him at Stockton, Constantine was a man who 'responded quickly to the kindness of others and who had a complete and aggressive faith in his own cricket talent'.

Constantine was remarkably injury-free until 1933 when he suffered from cartilage trouble for most of the season. It subdued his batting and reduced the speed of his bowling. He even confessed to missing a few catches which he would normally have jumped to. On a day when his leg was causing him particular pain, he confined himself to hitting twenty fours and two sixes. No doubt he had to run his partner's singles! It was the year of his benefit, towards which the other clubs in the Lancashire League made a contribution of £250. He chose his benefit year to produce his best bowling performance for Nelson in a match against Accrington. After Nelson had been dismissed for 116, he sent back Accrington for 12. In thirty-seven balls he took ten wickets for ten runs. The bowler at the other end—A. Pollard—bowled six overs, five of which were maidens, one run being scored from the other. With one extra, Accrington had been dismissed for 12 runs in thirty-nine minutes.

ACCRINGTON

W. Finney c Dowden b Constantine	3
R. Loughlin b Constantine	0
A. Smith b Constantine	0
T. Walmsley not out	2
J. Pollard b Constantine	0
G. Higgins b Constantine	0
W. McDonough b Constantine	4
R. Tyldesley b Constantine	0
F. Sproul b Constantine	0
D. Whittaker b Constantine	0
W. H. Hartley c Smith b Constantine	2
Extras	1
Total	12

Eight thousand people paid sixpence each that May Saturday afternoon in 1933 to watch.

Constantine's highest innings for Nelson—and the highest in his career—is remembered by his captain that year, Hargreaves:

'Nelson played East Lancashire at Blackburn on August Bank Holiday 1937. Nelson batted first on a plumb batting wicket, full of runs, on a glorious day. The East Lancashire professional was the New Zealander, W. E. Merritt. Constantine was number four in the batting order. Wickets fell steadily, all to Merritt, except that of Constantine, and I came in at number nine; the position then was 141 for eight. I was met by Constantine and tactics were discussed: I decided I would count the deliveries and advise Constantine of the last ball of the over when he would be expected to get a single. This worked admirably and fours and sixes flashed from Constantine's bat and, at one time, there were three balls in use, two out of the field and one in play. I was eventually out at 262. This gave Merritt nine wickets, and when Constantine realised the last over was being bowled prior to a declaration he danced down the wicket in a fairly obvious attempt to let Merritt finish with the ten wickets, but this was not to be as, for one reason or another, the bails were not removed and a declaration was made at the end of the over with the score of 284 for nine. The wicket was truly plumb for Nelson could not remove East Lancashire, who compiled 187 runs for the loss of five wickets and the match was drawn, 471 runs being scored in five hours' cricket.'

One of Constantine's memories from his Lancashire League career was of playing against the great Sydney Barnes, first of the famous professionals recruited to the League. Barnes was older than Constantine's father. He had played in twenty-seven Tests, in the days when the only opponents were Australia and South Africa, and taken 189 wickets. He had first played for England in 1901. Constantine, in his second year with Nelson, found himself sent in to save the situation against Barnes's club, Rawtenstall. Nelson were 68

NELSON

C. Hawkwood b Merritt.................... 28
C. Winslow c Ayres b Merritt.............. 2
J. Kerrigan lbw b Merritt................. 8
L. N. Constantine not out................. 192
W. E. Windle st Bibby b Merritt........... 1
C. Duerden c Chadwick (J. H.) b Merritt.... 5
E. Bradshaw b Merritt..................... 11
K. MacKenzie lbw b Merritt............... 5
F. Dowden lbw b Merritt.................. 0
H. Hargreaves c Lavery b Merritt.......... 10
A. Riley not out......................... 4
Extras 18

(9 wkts decl.) 284

	O	M	R	W
Ayres........	22	1	72	0
Merritt......	24	2	136	9
Chadwick, J. H.......	2	0	27	0
Chadwick, J...	3	1	21	0
Walsh.......	2	0	10	0

EAST LANCASHIRE

J. Chadwick c Constantine b Riley.......... 0
C. R. Davies not out...................... 103
W. E. Merritt c Hargreaves b Hawkwood..... 4
A. F. Green run out...................... 38
G. B. Eccles b Bradshaw.................. 8
G. T. Lavery c Constantine b Mackenzie..... 25
G. Holden not out....................... 7
Extras 2

(5 wkts) 187

	O	M	R	W
Riley.............	8	1	17	1
Hawkwood........	9	1	24	1
Hargreaves........	16	2	50	0
Constantine........	7	1	22	0
MacKenzie........	8	0	41	1
Bradshaw..........	5	0	28	1
Winslow..........	2	1	3	0

for three when Constantine went in to bat. Wickets fell
steadily until the total was 118 for nine, of which Constantine
had got 45. 'I shall never forget the length, spin and guile
Barnes produced to stop me getting the bowling', wrote
Constantine of that day's play. 'He set two men in the gully,
very close in, and two silly mid-ons, and neither I nor anyone
else could shift them. His bowling was as good as that, and
they never looked to be in danger.' It was a duel which
Constantine just won—though Barnes caught-and-bowled
him in the end when his score had reached 98 and the total
175. Constantine regarded it as one of the best innings he ever
played.

In 1937 Constantine decided to stop playing for Nelson.
His own explanation was two-fold: he wanted a change, and
he wanted more time to study. He had stayed with Nelson far
longer than it was customary for any player in the League to
be one club's professional. The rumour that another club
that year offered him more than Nelson seems without
foundation. Constantine's negotiations with Rochdale in the
Central Lancashire League led to an offer for 1938 similar
to his salary for 1937. The time had come to leave Nelson
cricket. Constantine's career with Nelson had contributed to
the club winning the League championship seven times, and
being runners-up on the other two occasions. The Worsley
Knock-out Cup was won twice. His best bowling performances
had been ten for 10 against Accrington and eight for 7
against Bacup. He had made several centuries. In 1934 he
scored half-centuries in six out of seven successive innings
while taking thirty-five wickets at a cost of 251 runs. The only
triumph he failed to achieve was the cricketer's 'double' of
1,000 runs and 100 wickets in a season—hard enough in the
county game. Playing two or three times a week in single-
innings matches it was almost impossible, and the nearest he
got was in 1933 when he made 1,000 runs and took 96 wickets
no one else has ever got nearer. He had always taken his
wickets for an average of less than 12 each, and with one
exception he had always had a batting average of over 30.
In nine seasons he had scored 6,363 runs and taken 776 wickets.

Such were the statistics. What was the significance of Constantine's cricket career in the Lancashire League? He had enabled the League to enjoy a financial stability it never achieved before or after. Clubs could afford professionals of the calibre of E. A. Martindale, brought in on Constantine's recommendation, and entertain the possibility of having Bradman. While other clubs were in no doubt about his value to the League, individual players in those clubs had to face his bowling—and the realities of his value. Ellis Dickinson, who kept wicket for Colne, the local 'derby' rivals, recalled having to withstand Constantine's bowling for forty-five minutes: 'the ball flew at my head, whizzed past my ear, and fizzed all over the place. He got furious when time ran out for Nelson.'

To the town of Nelson he was, wrote John Kay of the *Manchester Evening News*, 'the perfect citizen'. To Nelson's chairman, T. E. Morgan, he was a player 'who never gave the club a moment's trouble during the whole of his association with us'. To the people of the town he gave entertainment, whether to those enjoying respite from work in the mills or to those on the dole eking out the hours of enforced idleness. To the children of Nelson, he was approachable—the man who 'would play cricket with them on the recreation ground in an evening' and 'pile them into his Green Austin 7 after a match'. Jimmy Kerrigan, a player of the 1930s and, in 1974, groundsman at Nelson, remembered the thrill a car-ride from Seedhill up to the Manchester Road gave to youngsters who scarcely ever went in a car. Harold Hargreaves, mill-worker, operatic conductor, composer and cricketer, whose association with Nelson Cricket Club went back seventy years, talked, in his house in Dale Street by the Leeds-Liverpool canal, to the author. 'Connie was the greatest cricketer we ever had in Nelson. He was a good man and a simple one.' There lies part of the clue to Constantine's acceptance in Nelson. He conformed to the conventions of the community he had come among.

His relations with fellow-players such as Hargreaves invite further comment. Fundamentally, he was acceptable to them because he was good at his job. No one disputed the large salary he was paid because he justified it. The comparative affluence which gave him a car and a house in Meredith Street was seen without rancour because it denoted his achievements on the cricket field. Sending his child to a private school at the behest of the club committee was appropriate. He was a professional, entitled by his success to the attributes of a professional man.

This attitude on the part of Nelson players towards Constantine must be seen in the context of the Depression. Cricket flourished because of unemployment—where else than at the cricket field might the unemployed pass five cheerful hours for sixpence? Thousands did so every Saturday, and the players they watched were all heroes. Constantine's performance might have the quality of stardom, but all basked in reflected glory. Jimmy Kerrigan recalled that he and 'the others were personalities in the town, whether we had a job or were out of work'. The Depression was linked both to the appeal of cricket and to its standard. Many players were out of work, so were able to spend hours practising, and the Nelson ground might be packed with cricketers on an ordinary day. Among them would often be their professional—'not lying in bed as some professionals might do in the mornings but out coaching'. Cyril Duerden remembered that Constantine gave a lot of attention to coaching children. 'I went, for example, twice a week to his house for coaching in the back room winter and summer alike.'

The quality of tact contributed to Constantine's popularity. His own boyhood on a cocoa estate in Trinidad had been spent in happier circumstances than that of many a Nelson cricketer. He chose not to talk of this. When he was twelve, his life had been school and cricket at Maraval with enough to eat from the garden, and the sun on his back. Harold Hargreaves at that age was in the mill by six o'clock. Neither did Constantine question his colleagues about the toil of the cotton-mills or the desolation of unemployment. Although he listened to men talking politics, read for the first time the works of thinkers such as the Webbs and G. B. Shaw, and was interested in 'the condition of England', he said little. The common meeting-ground was cricket and there, to a great extent, Constantine was ready to let matters stand. Nor, as we have seen, did Constantine let his mild acquaintance with the League of Coloured Peoples touch his life in Nelson before the Second World War. The other players were totally unaware of its existence, and Constantine did nothing to enlighten them. They knew that James wanted to involve Constantine in politics. They were pretty sure Constantine did not want to become involved. Whether or not Constantine owed it to anyone to become involved is another matter.

Constantine was acceptable to many in Nelson Cricket Club because he was a man of sound principles and high moral standing. The Nelson of the 1930s reflected the Nonconformist ethic of sober living and thrift. Constantine did not smoke or drink, nor did he gamble. Drink made the children of poor men poorer, as did gambling. 'My father didn't drink much,' commented a Nelson player of those days, 'but the money would have been better spent on our backs.' Cards were not allowed to appear when the rain came down during a match.

Constantine spent modestly. In relation to what he earned, a few thought him mean. On the other hand, as someone remarked with reference to a former Nelson professional as well as to Constantine: 'I'd rather have a man that looked after his money than one who owed pounds to the fish shop and paper shop.' But the underlying differences in colour and in wealth that lay between Constantine and the Nelson players occasionally produced discord, as the following related incident shows.

Constantine, at the non-striker's end, failed to hear the call for a single by a batsman on 49. The man was run out and so deprived of a collection which might have brought him upwards of £30. In his disappointment he called Constantine 'a black b——r'. Constantine did not mind the noun, but bitterly resented the adjective. Yet both men had suffered. Constantine was sensitive to the barbed remark directed at his colour; the player had lost the equivalent of three months' earnings in the mill. Relations between the two men were cool for a couple of years.

As the 1937 season came to an end, there were tremendous demonstrations of affection. Constantine was bidden farewell at every turn when he went down a street. A band played 'Abide with me' at a match. The Mayor of Nelson made a personal appeal to Constantine to stay. But he had made up his mind—and it was not as if he were even leaving the town.

Constantine's cricket career with Nelson had ended, but he continued to live in Meredith Street for another twelve years. As he had shared the Depression with the people of Nelson, so he shared the war. 'My heart is with them now that we know each other', he said in a broadcast. Yet the years after 1937 are an anti-climax. Cricket with Rochdale in 1938 was less enjoyable and Constantine was less content in the Central Lancashire League. Later in the year, he made the decision—at some financial loss—to help the 1939 West Indian tourists and not to play for Rochdale. During the war he was in Nelson only at weekends, though he occasionally played for the club as an amateur in 1943 and 1944. It is a curiosity of his association with the town that he played cricket at Seedhill for less than half the years he lived in Nelson as a whole. Yet the image of him as a celebrity remained and did so still to the author visiting Nelson in 1974.

What Nelson did for Constantine is a larger issue. His life there made all that followed possible.

'If I had not come; if I had remained in my island, I could not have been the person I am today. I am a better person for coming; I am better materially, I am better socially. I have grown more tolerant. I have grown less selfish. I am a better citizen for the time I have spent in Nelson.'

In that apologia in 1954, on the eve of returning to the West Indies, Constantine assessed the years he had spent in Lancashire. His Nelson contemporaries had visualised some sort of distinction for him in the future. 'We knew he was studying in the winter', one remarked. 'We read about what he was doing in Liverpool during the war while he lived in Nelson', echoed another. 'There was the M.B.E.', commented a third. But cabinet office in Trinidad, a knighthood, a peerage, and the Freedom of the Borough of Nelson were scarcely even distant prospects.

6

FIRST-CLASS CRICKET
1933–1939

By becoming a League cricketer in 1929, Constantine limited his first-class appearances. It was something to which the statistician attached more importance than he did himself. In Trinidad, the distinction was blurred: Constantine often spoke of 'first-class' cricket when he meant the 1st XI matches played by the major clubs in Trinidad tournaments. What statisticians regard as first-class he would call 'inter-colonial' games. And statisticians themselves do not always agree on the nature of what is a 'first-class' match. For example, Constantine played some cricket in India in 1934 about whose status there is dispute.

Between 1933 and 1939 he played thirty-three first-class matches apart from his visit to India. He returned only briefly to the first-class scene when the West Indians visited England in 1933. He was a Nelson professional with obligations—and highly-paid ones—which he had to honour. He never disputed this himself, though his critics accused him of preferring Nelson's rich rewards to the modest remuneration the West Indies offered. He had no options: Nelson came first.

Unlike conditions on their 1928 visit, the 1933 West Indians enjoyed a fine English summer, indeed the warmest since 1921. Yet they failed, as a side, to live up to expectations. They leant heavily on the batting of Headley and the bowling of Martindale. Headley scored more than twice as many runs as any other player; Martindale took far and away the most wickets. The tourists won five and lost nine of their thirty first-class matches. They drew one Test match and lost the other two. Not till the end of May did Constantine appear for them when he scored a fifty in twenty-seven minutes at Lord's against the M.C.C. and captured the important wickets of J. W. Hearne, Hendren, Chapman and Jardine. The West Indians beat a strong M.C.C. side by 152 runs. Unfortunately, the West Indies fast bowlers found themselves accused of body-line bowling. It was a lively wicket and the ball jumped. Constantine usually bowled to a fine-leg, short-leg and mid-on on the leg side. He considered he was 'not especially intimidating'. 'Batsmen who got hit did so', he wrote, 'because they ran blindly into the ball pitched outside the off-stump and breaking.'

The body-line controversy was now at its height. The M.C.C. had come back from their 1932–3 tour of Australia amidst a storm of acrimonious comment on both sides. Jardine's support of Larwood's bowling had almost broken off cricketing relations between England and Australia. Only three weeks after Constantine had been accused of body-line bowling against the M.C.C. a cable went from that self-same body to the Australian Board of Control rejecting the term 'body-line' and describing the short bumping ball delivered to a packed leg-side field as 'leg-theory' and legitimate. But whether such bowling was called body-line or leg-theory, Constantine rejected implications that his own bowling was dangerous.

Nelson decided not to release him for the first Test, despite negotiations continuing up to the last moment, and his compatriots lost by an innings and 27 runs in a day and a half. Constantine was available, somewhat unnecessarily, for a mid-week game against Sir Julien Cahn's XI at his private ground in Nottingham. Cahn was a great cricket philanthropist between the wars who entertained his teams and their opponents in lavish style. No doubt Constantine enjoyed the hospitality, but he might have preferred to have played in the next game against Lancashire at Liverpool. Instead, he was a few miles away at Nelson, but managed to watch something of the game after the weekend.

Against Yorkshire at Harrogate he took nine wickets for 94 in the match—not enough to prevent a West Indian defeat by 200 runs. On a soft wicket, Constantine was told by R. S. Grant, the captain, to bowl fast on the leg-side in the second innings. Conditions prevented the ball rising at all and Yorkshire, in no hurry for runs, made enough to ensure them a large lead. It was a slow bowler's wicket, and Hedley Verity took fourteen West Indies wickets for 83 runs.

Rain spoilt the appearance of Constantine at Manchester against Lancashire, but he appeared in a minor match against Staffordshire, meeting the great Barnes whom he usually encountered in League cricket. Eleven wickets against Staffordshire and a nine wickets' win prepared him for the second Test at Manchester.

On the train from Stoke-on-Trent to Manchester, the players discussed whether to bowl 'body-line' in the match and Constantine agreed to do so. 'It would be pleasant to give Jardine and his men a little taste of what they had been handing out in Australia', was Constantine's wry comment.

The West Indies made 375, their then highest score against England in England. Constantine contributed 31 out of 36 made while he was at the wicket. England at once faced Martindale and Constantine, who bowled over fifty overs between them, a large number of which were, as *Wisden* put it, 'fast leg-theory with a packed leg-field'. Constantine admitted that the technique was responsible for the wickets of C. F. Walters, Hammond, Wyatt and Ames. Jardine, on the other hand, stood up fearlessly and scored a century. It was the first time he had faced the type of bowling which he had advocated in Australia. While there was admiration for his courage, the easy-paced wicket prevented any real likelihood of serious injury. One consequence of the West Indies' tactics in the Test match at Manchester was to turn the English public firmly against such bowling. In a sense, the West Indians had brought the matter to a head. P. F. Warner, who had joint-managed the M.C.C. tour of Australia, and who had personally been against the bowling tactics employed by Jardine, wrote to the *Daily Telegraph* as one who thought of himself as West Indian: 'I had hoped that my countrymen would avoid a type of bowling which I believe to be against the best interests of cricket.' But he accepted the fact that Constantine was 'at least two yards slower than Larwood' and lacked his control of the ball. Reviewing the whole position at the end of the season, the Editor of *Wisden*, Sydney Southerton, wrote:

'We saw in that particular match at Old Trafford what I should conceive to be a somewhat pale—but no less disturbing—imitation of Larwood in Australia, when Martindale and Constantine on the one hand, and Clark on the other, were giving a demonstration of fast leg-theory bowling. Not one of the three had the pace, accuracy of pitch or deadliness of Larwood, but what they did was sufficient to convince many people with open minds on the subject that it was a noxious form of attack not to be encouraged in any way.'

Constantine's bowling in this match leads us to consider his general relationship with English cricketers in the 1920s and 1930s. There were those, such as Hendren, the Middlesex player, with whom he formed a warm friendship. Hendren loved going on tour to the West Indies, and Constantine and he met frequently. The West Indian's brand of humour appealed to the English Cockney, and Hendren cheerfully accepted Constantine's declared efforts to get him out from the moment he arrived at the wicket. With Hammond, Constantine found relations more difficult. He had, as he thought, made a friend of the Gloucestershire player in England in 1923. When Hammond arrived in the West Indies in 1925, Constantine believed he was being snubbed. He was sure the England player preferred the society of 'white' West Indians, and he decided he would settle that score on the cricket field. Not till the Old Trafford Test in 1933 did the two men shake hands and establish a friendship that survived their very different temperaments. In 1944 they were rival captains at Lord's when an England XI played a West Indian XI during the war. Of Constantine in that game, Hammond wrote 'the West Indians could not have had a better captain or a more inspiring player to lead them'.

Perhaps their earlier differences arose because the player of the inter-war years had fewer opportunities to get to know opponents than does his modern counterpart. Constantine continued to believe, as he had done on his first visit in 1923, that many of the English players were 'reserved'. On their part, his natural exuberance was thought to be extravagant. Players who had not hesitated to pitch everything at the Australians in 1932–3 were ready to consider Constantine 'too aggressive a player'. And if 'aggression' were not a crime in a cricketer, conceit was. Some thought he possessed that characteristic in too great a measure. Constantine, in his incursions into the first-class game, never succeeded in establishing the rapport with players that came so naturally to him in League cricket. Right up to the war, he found himself ill at ease with the amateur in English cricket—men with whom he would associate on socially equal terms in later years.

The match at Manchester had been left drawn. England were one run behind on the first innings. The West Indies batted through the last day for 225, Constantine making the top score of 64 in just under an hour. He was not released for the third Test at the Oval, which the West Indies lost by an innings and 17 runs. His first appearance for a month came when the West Indies were at Blackpool and he was free for the mid-week game against Sir Lindsay Parkinson's XI. He contributed little and the tourists lost by seven wickets. It proved to be his last game for the West Indies in the tour. In his five first-class matches he had made 181 runs and taken fourteen wickets. The team had not done as well as it should have done, and Constantine, writing some years later, was to be critical of the captaincy of Grant. Constantine had seen enough of the West Indians in Test cricket and as tourists to know how important was able, experienced leadership. The time had come to select West Indies captains on merit and not on colour. Not until well after the Second World War would a coloured player be officially appointed captain of a West Indies Test team.

Just over a year later, in the English autumn of 1934, Constantine was invited to go to India to coach and to take part in the Maharajah's Gold Cup Tournament. The Indian visit was a great experience. Constantine stayed in a Maharajah's palace:

'I was given a suite of rooms, and to describe the palace would be to recount the marvels of the Arabian Nights! Gold couches, gold chairs, gold implements of every sort; diamonds and turquoises and sapphires mounted in every sort of setting; ivories and silks beyond price.'

The authority of the oriental despot caught his imagination. The sight of the Taj Mahal in moonlight was breathtaking. He was given a glimpse of the British Raj when he saw the Viceregal Lodge. He was aware of a land of contrasts: within a stone's-throw of the palace in which he dwelt lay the teeming masses of India where men, women and children toiled, starved, begged, bartered and died; Trinidad matched India in neither wealth nor poverty. Constantine knew Indians as part of the population of Trinidad. They had come, as indentured servants, from 1845 to 1917 from India to Trinidad and to British Guiana. Few ever went back. This was the vast land from which they had come. India opened for Constantine new dimensions of thought. He had seen white poverty in Nelson in the years of the Depression; now he saw coloured wealth in the possession of Indian princes. Hitherto, he had interpreted colour divisions as a straight social and economic issue. Nelson and India together made him realize that this was to over-simplify the situation. In the future, he would be a fighter against social distinctions between white and coloured peoples. He was less sure of his ground when faced with economic distinctions.

So far as the cricket was concerned, Constantine appeared for the Maharajah Kumar Ali Rajpur's XI—known as 'The Freebooters'—defending the Moin-ud-Dowlah Gold Cup, at Secunderabad against 'The Retrievers'. He scored 12 and 1, and took six for 72 and two for 69. (These are figures which some statisticians regard as 'first-class'.) The cup was lost by three wickets, largely as a result of a fine century by L. Amarnath, who was later to tour England with India and to succeed Constantine as Nelson professional at the beginning of 1938. Later, playing in a friendly match for the Maharajah of Patiala's XI against the Viceroy's XI at New Delhi, Constantine, bowling in terrific heat, was invited by his captain to pitch a few short. One can only conjecture the reaction to this. At once wickets fell, and a match that looked like being lost was won by a handful of runs.

Constantine was back in England in time for Christmas, after a voyage through the Suez Canal and the Mediterranean. He just had time to enjoy a family reunion at Nelson when a cable came from Trinidad asking him to play for the West Indies in their 1934–5 series against the M.C.C. Already the English party were well on their way and celebrating Christmas in tropical waters two days off Barbados. The family had been separated for so many months that Learie decided to take Norma and Gloria with him to Trinidad. The Constantines caught a later vessel from Bristol and sailed for Trinidad. His own habit of wintering in the Caribbean was being sustained; for Norma and Gloria it was their first visit for some years and their last until 1954. By the time Constantine reached Trinidad, England had won an extraordinary Test at Barbados on a wicket badly affected by rain. The scores were: West Indies—102 and 51 for six wickets declared; England—81 for seven wickets declared and 75 for six wickets. The West Indies had declared leaving England 75 to get, with any amount of time, and a batting side including Wyatt, Maurice Leyland, Hammond, Hendren and Ames. Yet there was every chance that the home side might have won.

Constantine appeared for Trinidad in the two colony matches. He had last played for the island in the matches against the M.C.C. in 1930, being barred from inter-colonial cricket because he was a professional. He opened the bowling at Queen's Park Oval before his home crowd, playing for the first time on the new jute matting—a flatter surface than the coconut matting it replaced. The M.C.C. scored fast,

Hammond getting a hundred before lunch, and reached 348 by late afternoon. Constantine took four for 72 and a fine slip-catch. Trinidad's first innings lead was largely due to a double century by Maynard, the first ever scored in Trinidad by a West Indian. Despite this performance, for which he was mobbed by the crowd, Maynard achieved little in the future in first-class cricket. He was typical of many youngsters in the West Indies who did outstandingly well at the game for their club and had an occasional hour of glory at a higher level. Some—Constantine himself—were lucky enough to be noticed, to prosper, to tour overseas, and to make a new way of life because of their prowess at cricket.*

In an exciting finish, the match was left drawn, Trinidad needing 19 runs with two wickets in hand. Constantine's 25 runs came in ten minutes including a six out of the ground into Elizabeth Street. In the return match, Constantine played for the only time in a colony side with his brother, Elias. Learie was bowling faster than he had done in the first game, and the M.C.C. struggled all day for 226. Trinidad lost six wickets for 42 when the Constantine brothers came together. Their partnership of 93 was a spectacular effort, Learie hitting several sixes with effortless ease. The Trinidad 'tail' wagged and the colony for the second match running secured a first-innings lead. The M.C.C. lost nine wickets for 56 and seemed certain to lose until the last wicket added 47 runs besides subtracting time from Trinidad's batting. The colony had to get 100 in forty minutes. Constantine opened the batting, was dropped from a skier, and soon fell to another big hit. Everyone ran into bat. When the last over began 32 were needed. Trinidad secured 18 of them. Both colony matches had been exciting games of cricket, fit prelude to the second Test match.

At the end of the first day's play in the Test, the West Indies were 284 for nine. They owed most to Sealey and Constantine. Sealey held the innings together while Constantine flayed a tired attack at the end of the day, often pulling balls

---

* On the day these words were written, an unknown player for the Windward Islands made a century against the M.C.C. on their 1973-4 tour.

from outside the off-stump to the square-leg boundary. It was an innings of beautiful timing. His dismissal on the following morning for 90 ended what proved to be the highest Test score of his career. Constantine never made a Test century. His whole approach was to attack from the start and take his chance of success. On the two occasions when the target was in sight, he continued to play his natural game. A century won by caution at the end would have been foreign to his temperament.

When England were 23 for five the crowd of 11,000—the largest ever to attend a Test match in the West Indies—were wild with delight, but a final total of 258 left England very much in the game. At the end of the third day, the *Trinidad Guardian* commented:

'With a lead of 194 runs and seven wickets still in hand, the West Indies are in a strong position; and if a change occurs which would warrant a declaration at lunch on Monday, and the wicket should give bowlers any assistance, there might still be a chance of an exciting finish.'

By lunch the lead had been increased to 324, Constantine's contribution being a frustrating 31 with the bowlers bowling as wide as they could to stop him scoring. The declaration duly came, and England had 325 runs to get in 210 minutes. There was no attempt to get them. If the West Indies were to win, wickets had to fall. By tea, five had done so. Immediately afterwards, Constantine had Wyatt caught and then ran out Hendren. Leyland was dropped off him, and the minutes ticked away. And then the umpire warned Constantine for bowling body-line and his captain took him off. At once the crowd barracked loudly for his return and Constantine came back to have Leyland dropped yet again. L. G. Hylton, at the other end, bowled full-tosses. In the end, Ames, unable to resist the temptation, was caught. His pads were scarcely off when the crowd roared at Jack Iddon's dismissal. E. R. T. Holmes—85 not out in the first innings—came in last to join Leyland: no tail-enders there. Seven minutes remained as Constantine, off a short run, bowled a maiden over to Leyland. Holmes played out Hylton's over, An epic tale was being unfolded: the crowd fell silent and held their gaze intent. The evening sun cast long shadows. Constantine bowled the last over: a fast one just outside the off-stump; another coming for the leg-stump; Leyland did what he had to do—and no more. The fifth ball was snatched back almost as it left the bowler's hand—enough to make it slower; enough to make Leyland hesitate; enough to hit his pads; enough to win a Test match. Not even seconds remained as thousands swarmed over the pitch. The gods had given them victory.

West Indian crowds get few opportunities to see cricket at top level. The game they had just witnessed was only the second Test match ever played at Port of Spain. Not for fourteen years would there be another.

After the excitement at Port of Spain, the third Test at Georgetown was something of an anti-climax. The wicket was lifeless and the game soon headed for a draw. Constantine's main contribution was three second-innings wickets in a spell of sixteen overs during which he conceded only nine runs.

A month later all assembled at Kingston, Jamaica. Constantine had spent his time in Trinidad, renewing old friendships, playing some games himself, noticing hints of political and economic change. Then came the voyage along the Spanish Main to Jamaica with days at sea in the clear blue waters of the Caribbean. At the end of the journey came the clear air of Jamaica, a different world from the humidity of Guiana and its waters yellow from the Orinoco.

The West Indies batted until tea on the second day in the fourth Test. Headley was dropped off an easy chance to square-leg by Kenneth Farnes when 70. He added 200 more while the rest of the side weighed in with some 300 more runs. Constantine made 34, upon which the Jamaican *Daily Gleaner* commented:

'Sealey was followed by Constantine, the greatest and most attractive personality in cricket the West Indies ever had. His spectacular batting arouses joy and excitement in all crowds. His bowling is always productive of some rare feat which makes spectators want to sit up and laugh themselves crying. His fielding with its unbounded energy, long striding catlike leaps and marvellous accuracy in effecting the most inconceivable catches and gathering of balls, just fascinates. Some of his work is essentially of Constantine's exclusive manufacture, there being no necessity for taking copyright or forbidding imitations. Will we ever again have a player like this?'

In the closing overs of the second day, England lost four wickets for 27 while Wyatt retired from the match with his jaw broken by a fast ball from Martindale—'a perfectly fair ball', as the M.C.C. vice-captain, Holmes, publicly announced. Before a Saturday crowd, the England innings staged some sort of a recovery. Ames made a century and received an ovation from the spectators. By five o'clock England were following on, 264 runs behind. On the Monday, Constantine and Martindale got a wicket apiece before two overs had been completed. Hendren was caught by Constantine, fielding five feet from the bat and flinging himself on to the bat's very edge. Just before lunch, Grant went off injured. Before he left the field he called the team together, and said: 'My ankle has been injured. I must go off. Learie, please take over the captaincy.' Constantine celebrated the event by collecting Ames's wicket. By mid-afternoon the match was over. The West Indies had won by an innings and 161 runs, and in doing so had won a Test series for the first time.

The match meant much to Constantine. He had captained his team to victory; he had taken six wickets; the local Press had eulogised him. That evening he attended a reception given by the Governor at King's House. His own notes on the day end in Pepysian fashion: 'and then to bed, to live it all over and over again in dreams, never to escape from the shattering roar of the crowd, continuous and splendid'. Never again, indeed, to play cricket in Jamaica; never again to play a Test match in his own islands; only once more to play a game of first-class cricket in the West Indies. All this lay hidden from Learie Constantine as he re-lived that match, and made his way to the north of Jamaica in the morning, to Port Antonio to board the S.S. *Camito*, a banana ship bound for Bristol.

Constantine continued to go to Trinidad when he could after the English cricket season was over. His last visit before the war led to his final appearance in first-class cricket in the West Indies when he was invited to be a guest player by Barbados in a 'friendly' match against British Guiana after the inter-colonial tournament for 1938–9 had been decided. The game took place at Bridgetown in January 1939. Constantine took four for 41 in British Guiana's score of 217, and contributed a single to Barbados's 248. Eventually, Barbados were set 166 to win. Runs had to be scored quickly, and Constantine's share was 11 in the Barbados total of 135 for seven wickets. The match was left drawn.

While Constantine was in the West Indies, he was approached about the possibility of his playing a full part in the 1939 tour to England. He was anxious to do so for several reasons: he had rejoiced in the West Indies victory in the 1934–5 series and wanted to see it repeated away from home; he knew it would be his last Test series (he was now in his late thirties); he wanted the West Indies to have the strongest possible side; he had not been too happy in 1938 playing in the Central Lancashire League. Two complicating factors arose. He needed to be assured that the best possible West Indies party would be selected—and he hoped his brother, Elias, would be favourably considered. He himself expected the pay and status of senior professional. If he were going to jeopardise his League cricket for the future, he wanted to feel it had been worthwhile. In the end, protracted negotiations led to his sailing to Barbados to see the Secretary of the West Indies Board of Control. Constantine was not entirely pleased with the final arrangements. He was paid £600 for the tour—less than he would have received as a League professional and no more than two other professionals on the tour who earned less than he did in League cricket.

Nor did he regard the party chosen as the strongest possible—for one thing, his brother Elias, was not selected. Elias had gone to Trinidad at his own expense, but had not been picked for the trial matches. But the time for recrimination was over. Constantine sailed for England and reported to the West Indies nets at Lord's where some of the party met snow for the first time.

For the first time since 1934–5 he was embarking upon a full season of first-class cricket. Taking the season as a whole, he would rarely fail. His fielding would be spectacular and he would usually make runs or take wickets. The official tour opened, as usual, at Worcester. Conditions were appalling. The ground was recovering from floodwater and the weather was bleak. In the circumstances the West Indies did well to hold their catches and dismiss Worcestershire for 83. The good start could not be sustained and the match was lost by 85 runs despite Constantine's top score of 47. Against Lancashire, the captain, R. S. Grant, had to go off injured, and Constantine took over the side. He took the decision not to chase 247 runs in three hours in cold conditions and bad light. To have lost the first two matches would have been disastrous for the financial prospects of the tour—always the spectre at the feast. But he was reprimanded for not 'having a go' and resented it.

Rain ruined two days of the match against the M.C.C. Against Cambridge University, in a drawn match, Constantine took seven for 94, and against Surrey, in a match lost by seven wickets, he made a half-century in an hour. The defeat of Oxford University by an innings and five runs went some way towards restoring morale, but Glamorgan beat the tourists despite 63 from Constantine (batting number nine), which included 16 in one over, and six wickets for 123.

Before the match with Essex, a team conference took place. Results were bad, and so were receipts. Headley and Constantine brought the much-needed first victory against a county. Headley made 164 runs without losing his wicket while Constantine took thirteen wickets for 91 in one of the best performances of his first-class career. The West Indies

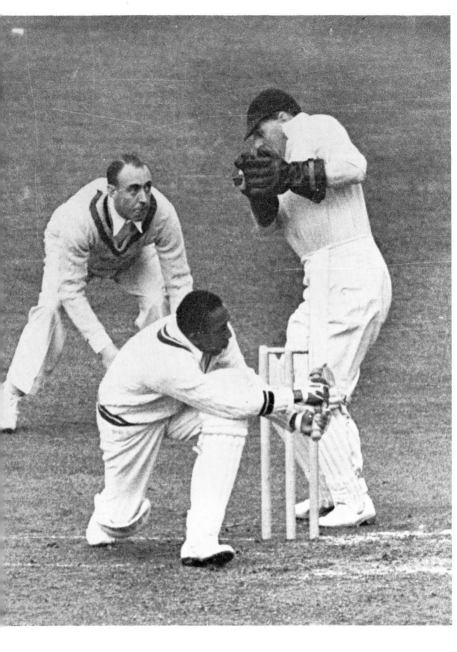

8. Constantine in the course of making a half-century for the West Indians against Surrey at the Oval in 1939. E. W. J. Brooks is the wicket-keeper, and H. M. Garland-Wells is at slip.

9. Constantine in 195 during his ministerial care in Trinidad. *Left to right a* Kamaluddin Mohamme Gerard Montano, Eric W liams (the Prime Ministe Constantine, Winston M habir, Wilfred Alexand and Ellis Clarke (la Governor-General of Tri dad).

10. Sir Learie and Lady Co stantine in London in 19 at the time he took up off as High Commissioner.

were never in a safe position and in the end scrambled home for a narrow two wickets' win. As Constantine himself noted: 'It was not enough, but still it was a victory.'

The victory of substance which the tourists needed came against Middlesex at Lord's—scene of Constantine's triumphs eleven years earlier. The West Indies amassed 665 (Headley 227, Sealey 181, J. B. Stollmeyer 117) and defeated Middlesex by an innings and 228 runs. Constantine took six for 107 in the match. 'There is no man now who can so completely bamboozle a batsman as Constantine can', wrote *The Times* correspondent.

C. B. Clarke, who played in all three Test matches on the tour, recalled Constantine's style of bowling: 'He was not the fast bowler of earlier years. He became a graceful medium-pace bowler who secured his wickets by subtle change of pace and by a beautifully concealed slower googly'. His action itself, Clarke thought, was calculated to mystify a batsman. 'He retained the ball in his left hand unduly long, transferring it to his raised right arm at the last moment—and looking up as he did so. The flinging of arms and the unorthodox direction of his head was calculated to deceive a batsman, and did so.'

From success at Lord's the tourists went on to beat Northamptonshire by nine wickets while the matches with Derbyshire and Leicestershire were drawn. The West Indies came to the first Test at Lord's having had no more defeats.

England had had a phenomenal scoring record in the past ten months. Since making 903 for seven wickets against the Australians at the Oval in August 1938, they had toured South Africa with Test match totals of 422, 291 for four wickets, 559 for nine wickets, 469 for four wickets, 215, 203 for four wickets, 316 and 654 for five wickets. It represented an average total of 640 in a completed innings. The principal scorers had been L. Hutton, E. Paynter, Hammond, and, after many failures, W. J. Edrich. Their opponents—the two greatest cricketing countries of the day—had averaged 351 runs for a full innings.

This was the measure of England's strength in 1939. It

was to the credit of the West Indies that they lost only one Test out of three, and suffered no discredit in drawing the other two. The comparison of figures may be taken further. England's wicket average for the series was 45.8 while that of the West Indies was 26.7. Statistically, the West Indies performed marginally better than had England's other opponents in the preceding ten months before the first Test at Lord's in June 1939.

Headley's century was the main feature of the West Indies innings of 277, to which Constantine contributed 14. Hutton got 196 of England's total of 404 for five wickets declared. In the end, after a second century from Headley, the West Indies left England 100 to win in 110 minutes which they accomplished with eight wickets and thirty-five minutes to spare. Thunderclouds of various kinds hung over the match. The conventional type threatened to end play, while appeals over the loud-speaker system were made by Hammond, the England captain, for men to volunteer for military service in preparation for the imminent war with Germany. The *Daily Mail* cartoonist, Tom Webster, depicted the match as 'Winter Sports', so cold and dark were conditions on the second day of play. Some people felt that Sport itself could soon be at a premium.

For Constantine no wickets came his way in the match. Eleven years later, one survivor of each side played at Lord's when West Indian calypsos celebrated the first victory of their country against England in England, a match which established Constantine as a broadcaster on cricket.

Between the two Tests, Nottinghamshire were convincingly beaten by an innings and 94 runs, Constantine taking six for 50 and three for 67. Rain spoilt the Yorkshire match when the game was reasonably balanced. Constantine took five for 28, including three in one over. The game against Lancashire was drawn. Thunder assailed the tourists at Durham and snow at Nottingham, against Sir Julien Cahn's XI. And so the West Indies came to Old Trafford for the second Test dismayed by the weather and distressed by adverse comments in the Press. They won the toss and put England in.

The match was largely spoilt by rain. England declared twice in an effort to force a result, leaving the West Indies 160 runs to get in seventy minutes of bad light. Understandably, no attempt was made to get the runs. Constantine, who took four for 42 in the England second innings, described it as 'essentially a game to be forgotten'. Once again, appeals were made for volunteers to join the Forces. As Constantine remarked, Hammond 'was addressing the right stuff, for only the lion-hearted remained' in the appalling conditions. After the Old Trafford Test, the tourists defeated Surrey by seven wickets and Hampshire by ten wickets. Somerset—much weaker than either—beat the tourists. Constantine figured only briefly in the score-book. Against Glamorgan at Swansea he took advantage of the heavy atmosphere to make the ball swing. Glamorgan went from 61 for no wicket to 127 all out, Constantine finishing with three for 44. By late afternoon, the West Indies had also batted, and Constantine took a further three before stumps were drawn. Twenty-five wickets had fallen in a day. After tea on the second afternoon, he scored 19 not out to help in a West Indies win by two wickets.

The rain, which had never really left the West Indies alone, even in the games they managed to bring to a conclusion, followed them to Edgbaston, but not to Cheltenham where they lost to Gloucestershire. So to the Oval, and the third Test, and what proved to be the last game of the tour. Constantine has described the scene he saw that mid-August weekend in 1939:

'Over the Oval ground hung silvery shapes of cruel omen— barrage balloons flying in case the German bombers should drone overhead during the match and make an unheralded murder attack on London at play. There was the drone of flying to be heard, unusual in London then; khaki and naval blue and a sprinkling of Air Force uniforms showed everywhere among the crowds; as we approached the Oval I saw gunners ostenstatiously moving an anti-aircraft gun by means of a tractor. Later we were told that this was strategy to deceive German spies into mistaking London's four guns for a large number. There was feverish hurry at the stations, and despite the glorious sunshine, one saw hard and frightened faces. August 1939, Test match cricket—and Death hovering in the air with a shadow everywhere.'

The first day's play was brisk. England scored 352 and the West Indies 27 for one. Constantine took five for 75, including the wickets of N. Oldfield, Hammond and J. Hardstaff. He also ran out M. S. Nichols, after bowling a slower ball to the facing batsman, following up the stroke to silly mid-off, and throwing the ball to the wicket-keeper's end before Nichols could complete a run. This sort of anticipation had given Constantine countless wickets or saved countless runs in his career. The West Indies batted throughout the second day's play to a total of 395 for six wickets—a lead of 43. Constantine was 1 not out overnight.

Tuesday 22 August 1939 was Constantine's last day as a Test cricketer. He was acutely conscious that it would be so, and he went out in fine style. His batting displayed all the exuberance which had made him the box-office attraction of the inter-war years. *Wisden*, soberest of reporters, described that final innings:

'It was a real joy to watch the carefree cricket of the West Indies on the last day. Constantine, in the mood suggesting his work in Saturday afternoon League cricket, brought a welcome air of gaiety to the Test arena. He revolutionised all the recognised features of cricket and, surpassing Bradman in his amazing stroke play, he was absolutely impudent in his aggressive treatment of bowling shared by Nichols and Perks. While the four remaining wickets fell those two bowlers delivered 92 balls from which Constantine made 78 runs out of 103. Seldom can there have been such a spreadeagled field with no slips, and Hammond did not dare risk further trouble by changing his attack. With an astonishing stroke off the back foot Constantine thumped Perks for 6 to the Vauxhall end—a very long carry—and helped himself to eleven 4's before he was last out to a very fine catch by Wood; running

towards the pavilion the wicket-keeper held the ball that had
gone high over his head.'

It had been Constantine's last chance to fulfil a promise
made to some friends earlier in the tour, that he would make
a century in his final Test series.

His innings took the West Indies to 498. There was little
chance of a result. Hutton and Hammond, the rising hope of
English cricket and the fading star, each scored a century.
English spectators were left with a memory to cherish
throughout the war. Constantine took his last Test wicket,
and his batting had provided, said one Press report, 'a glorious
hour of roman candles, rockets and giant crackers; it was
Constantine's Test match'.

Yet before the match began there had been an incident
with his captain, R. S. Grant. Constantine had disappeared
into the countryside, having got from the cook of the hotel 'a
packet of sandwiches and a bottle of pop'. He spent the day
walking and reading, delighted in the knowledge that no one
knew where he was. 'When I turned up in the evening I was
given a terrific trouncing by the skipper. I told him it was time
I took a little interest in my figures in a Test match. If I
failed in this one, I was prepared to take the criticism.'

Constantine had been worked too hard on the tour because
of the old West Indian reason—the need to get good 'gates'.
Suddenly, he had needed peace and quiet. He was the senior
professional in the party. No doubt he should have told his
captain in advance of his intentions.

As senior professional, he had been critical of the approach
to the game of some of the younger players—'they were piti-
fully anxious to play for safety'. In a broadcast in July 1939,
he spoke of his fears for the future of cricket. 'Scores and
aggregates count much more than they used to. The outcome
will be to standardise cricket and lead to competent medioc-
rity.' Yet there was the instance in the match against Essex
earlier in the season when he threatened to hit a young
member of the team over the head with a bat if he did not go
in and play a careful, restraining innings. Some of the team

could be forgiven for not knowing where they stood with their senior professional. One of them commented at the time, 'I don't listen to Learie when he is talking cricket, but when he talks money I pay attention.'

The West Indies had yet to beat England in a series in England. In the tour as a whole they had won eight games, lost six and drawn eleven. Since they had been handicapped by weather and disappointed by a bad start, they could, wrote Hubert Preston in *Wisden*, 'feel well satisfied'. Of Constantine, Preston said:

'He repeated all the amazing energy that made him one of the most dazzling cover points when he first came to England in 1923 and on his next two visits. No matter where placed, he performed wonders on getting to the ball. In bowling Constantine stood out by himself. By relying on varied spin and mixed pace, from quite slow to a very fast ball, sparsely used, Constantine altered his attack completely from the fast medium swingers which he employed formerly. He was the most unflagging member of this very alert side. His batting reached a climax of audacious adventure in the Oval Test but he often electrified onlookers with his almost impudent zest for runs.'

Statistically, Constantine's personal performance had been to take 103 wickets in the season for a cost of 17.77 and to make 614 runs for an average of 21.17. The figures were slightly less than his overall record in first class cricket, which (inclusive of one match to go in 1945) was as follows:

Innings	Times not-out	Runs	Highest score	Average
194	11	4,451	133	24.32

Balls bowled	Maiden overs	Runs	Wickets	Average
17,400	471	8,737	424	20.60

In 117 matches he took 133 catches, scored twenty-eight half-centuries and five centuries, took five wickets in an innings on twenty-four occasions, and ten wickets in a match on four occasions. None of these figures stood comparison with the spirit of adventure and the sheer pleasure of playing which encompassed all he did on the cricket field. When southerners saw his 79 in that final day at the Oval, they were treated to a spectacle which northerners had enjoyed Saturday by Saturday in the drab decade of the 1930s.

There was no more cricket. Kent cancelled the fixture due to follow the Test match. By Saturday, most of the West Indians were on board a ship from Greenock to Montreal. After three days at sea, it was ordered back to Scotland. Some hours later, the order was countermanded and the party was homeward bound to the West Indies via Canada. Meanwhile, Constantine had gone back to Meredith Street, Nelson. A man of moods, exhilarated by the cheers of a crowd and the bustle of people, he felt depressed. Cricket was over for the year; his law studies were a nagging reminder of other responsibilities. He wondered, as he filled sandbags at the Nelson Hospital, what the weeks and months would bring.

7

WAR WORK
1939-1945

War brought a new perspective to Constantine's life in Nelson. Within a couple of days he was filling sandbags with other men in order to barricade Reedyford Hospital. He got a job as a billeting officer, combining it with being an Air Raid Precautions (A.R.P.) equipment officer in the Town Hall. 'Visiting houses, grading them and organising the reception of children from Bradford and Manchester was no simple business', he commented. More significantly, it introduced him to the inside of the homes of the poor in Nelson. 'I never knew until then the extent of the slums and of poverty. It would do many of my own countrymen good to see and appreciate this for themselves', he was later to say in a broadcast. Just as India in 1934 had shown him the extreme wealth of some coloured men, so Nelson in 1939 showed him more starkly than hitherto the extreme poverty of some white men. He was aware that his own people back in the West Indies were ready to draw from their own experience of colonialism simple distinctions between white affluence and coloured depression. If, in years to come, Constantine seemed to be an insufficient advocate of the cause of coloured peoples, here lies something of the explanation. He recognised the economic circumstances governing the lives of many white people for whom neither today's nor tomorrow's world was Arcadian.

There was no question of the Constantine family leaving Nelson. 'I would feel like a rat deserting a sinking ship', he said. He, Norma and Gloria, all moved into one bedroom; 'if a bomb fell on the room, we all went; if the bomb hit the other room, we were lucky'. Nothing ever came nearer than half a mile away—some stray bombs intended for Liverpool.

With the outbreak of war, Constantine's income dropped considerably. There had been the offer of a contract with Windhill Cricket Club in the Bradford League for 1940, but clauses in it reduced its value in the event of war. But he took up the offer, and played for Windhill on Saturdays in 1940 and 1941.

Early in 1942 he applied to the Ministry of Labour in Manchester for a job while awaiting his call-up papers. Then came attendance for a medical examination at Blackburn and a telegram saying 'Do not take medical: report at Blackburn Employment Exchange.' There he was told that the Ministry of Labour and National Service, in conjunction with the Colonial Office, wanted him to become a temporary (war-time) civil servant in the welfare department of the north-west division of the Ministry with responsibility for West Indian technicians and trainees on Merseyside who had come to work in factories to relieve Englishmen for war service. He also held a watching brief on the needs of West African seamen in the port of Liverpool. 'I'd rather do it than "foot-slogging"', he commented, and took the job. His office was first in the Royal Liver Building and later on the fourth floor of 87 Lord Street, Liverpool. His assistant was Sam Morris (later Deputy Chief Officer of the Community Relations Commission), and he had a secretary and a small clerical staff. The office atmosphere was a happy one', Morris recalled. 'We all worked hard, and got on well together.' Constantine had met office work before, but this was the first time he had been in charge. Then, as years later in Trinidad and in London, he handled staff well and won their support.

Most of the West Indians who came to Merseyside were young men leaving their homes for the first time. The job of Constantine's office involved housing them temporarily in a hostel called Colwell House, finding them permanent accommodation, settling them in employment, and easing problems between them and English people. Put like this, it sounded straightforward. Constantine saw it rather more starkly:

'Anyone who believes he has difficulties working with people could never imagine the difficulties I had working for my own people. The men went to work and returned grumbling. They had difficulties about 'digs'. We had to do almost everything for them as you would for children—remittances to families at home; questions of clothing. . . .'

Those who were unskilled found especial problems in adapting and resented their low wages. Constantine's office had to explain that their wages could rise only when they acquired some skills and went on training schemes. 'Among such problems, I walked warily', he reflected. Indeed he might, for he rightly realised that white workers feared the possibility of a permanent Negro labour force. Constantine managed to allay these suspicions by securing from the unions temporary (war-time) membership cards.

Men who were more skilled caused other problems. Some were proprietors in their own country, owning garages and small businesses. They were sensitive to racial discrimination and subordination. Constantine was conscious of this. He would argue, to whoever would listen, that such men would take a poor opinion of Britain back to the West Indies with them. To firms reluctant to take on coloured labour at all, he found one solution: 'I used to get the Ministry to press those firms for most urgent delivery of orders, and they found they must take coloured workers. With urgent work to be done they were forced to give way.'*

In general, he found much co-operation from the unions as well as from management. Part of the job involved visiting factories to ensure that all was well or to settle disputes. Sometimes where an issue arose between employer and employee, Constantine's reputation and status might work to his disadvantage; he would be invited by the management to a meal or for a drink and, if he then decided that the employee was at fault, the assumption was drawn by the injured man

* A senior official of those days confirmed to the author the truth of this remark.

and his fellows that Constantine was not likely to be on the side of labour. When this happened, his colleague Sam Morris 'had to step in to try to restore confidence'.

These were not the only times in Constantine's life when the doors which opened for him so readily caused some ill-feeling among his fellow West Indians. It was the price of fame and of popularity. It made him, another of his colleagues of those days has recalled, 'a misunderstood and sometimes controversial figure', to which Sam Morris has added:

'But if Constantine was misunderstood by his own people, he could sometimes be an enigma to others. I accompanied him once to a factory where he was giving a pep talk and surprisingly, one of the white workers, despite all the publicity that Constantine was always getting both in the national and local press, including the printing of his photograph, was heard to remark, "Oh, is that Learie Constantine? I always thought he was a white man."'

The coloured men for whom he was responsible did not realise that he had his own racial difficulties. They saw a Negro who was always well dressed; whose laundry was immaculate; whose shoes were polished; who had acquired English customs and conventions. All this set him apart from poorer men, ill-clothed and casual in appearance. Constantine used his personal attributes for their benefit: he stayed himself in a factory hostel where there had been trouble because white and coloured lived in the same block. He hoped to demonstrate 'that I was an ordinary person like themselves'. In general, the plan worked, but Constantine had one unpleasant incident in the hostel dance-hall. An American Air Force officer, seeing him walked the length of the hall to shout: 'Get out—we don't allow nigs to mix with white people.' Constantine replied: 'Go away!' The American retorted: 'Get out, nigger, before I smash you.' Constantine has left his own description of the rest of the incident:

'He added a coarseness which really roused me, for I was

talking to a husband and wife and another girl who probably did not often hear such things. I said to the American: "Come outside with me" and I had every intention of thrashing him. I could have done it. I had marked the spot where I should hit him a formidable blow. But walking the length of that hall cooled me—I became aware of the newspaper headlines that would have resulted, and the general inflammation of the black and white problem that it would have caused, with England at that time filled with black and white American troops. So, rather sadly, I handed him over to the porter at the door, and he was promptly ordered outside. Later, the place was put out of bounds for all American troops.'

Could one have blamed Constantine had he struck the blow? He did not because he was a victim of his own reputation. Others might fight in anonymity. A blow from Constantine would probably have cost him his job. Far more important, it would have done immense damage to the West Indians whom he served.

His work brought him into contact with the District Manpower Office in Church Street, Liverpool, which had overall responsibility for recruiting labour for the war effort. A member of that office recalled the long hours they put in, for seven days a week—besides fire-watching. Constantine would 'cheer us up when he came in: always happy and jovial and smiling'. He also had connections with the National Assistance Board in the Liver Building, Liverpool. Another colleague of those days from that office remembered his association with Constantine:

'We ran a special scheme to prevent and relieve distress due to war circumstances affecting the West Indians. This was designed to meet the problems of their families back home during periods when they could not send remittances home due to illness. Here Constantine was a great help to us. He had a fund of first-hand information on the family customs and relationships of his compatriots, and on the "psyche" of West Indians—an important factor in maintaining harmony and in helping us to make decisions.'

The same correspondent stressed the important role Constantine played in 'ensuring equality of treatment and removal of prejudice. He was a man uniquely qualified for the task.'

The fundamentals of Constantine's work were associated with Colour. The war brought thousands of coloured workers and troops to Britain, from both the West Indies and the United States. This had an effect on the role of the League of Coloured Peoples with which, as we saw in chapter 5, Constantine had been associated. During the war the League's membership increased and so did its activities. Arthur Lewis, the St Lucian economist who had been a pre-war member, directed the League's attention to a growing anomaly in racial attitudes: 'Spokesmen of the British Government make speeches denouncing the vicious policies of Nazi Germany and affirming that the British Empire stands for racial equality', he said. 'It therefore seems to the League of Coloured Peoples that the time has come once more to direct the Government's attention to its own racial policy.' Harold Moody, the League's founder, made a similar comment. There was a risk, he said, of 'carrying on the Herrenvolk idea against which we are fighting'.

The League seized its opportunity. It took up matters such as commissions for coloured men in the Forces. It brought race relations home to the people of Britain by its practical concern for colonials living in the British Isles and by its pronouncements on the prospects of the Empire after the war. Constantine used the League as a means of making representations to the Colonial Office on matters related directly to his job in Liverpool. He believed the League had a part to play in ensuring that there *was* an Empire after the war. He was a patriot, wholly committed to the war effort, and he was deeply concerned about what might be the role of the Empire. He had blandly spoken of 'The Empire and cricket' in speeches in the 1930s. The phrase then had had a certain romanticism about it, and not much more. Constantine in the 1940s was far more politically-minded. The Empire, he believed, would have significance in a post-war world if it were ready to adapt itself to changed conditions.

He was instrumental in getting the League to hold its twelfth annual meeting outside London for the first time when it came to Liverpool in March 1943. The week was spent discussing the war-time problems of coloured people with special reference to Merseyside. Constantine, after only a few months in office, gave a picture of conditions which was cautiously optimistic. Others gave him the credit for the smoothness with which so many West Indians had been absorbed into the community.

The League of Coloured Peoples continued to be important while its founder, Moody, was still alive. He was a prolific writer, and his pamphlets *Freedom for all Men* and *The Colour Bar* had some influence on Constantine, who read them and drew on some of their ideas in his own book *Colour Bar* which was published in 1954. With Moody's death in 1947, the League lost some of its impetus. Constantine accepted the presidency for a spell, but by then the League's significance was historic rather than immediately relevant. In the 1930s and 1940s it had aroused interest and action in issues of race relations which were to lead ultimately to new political structures for Commonwealth nations in the 1950s and 1960s, and to fresh protective legislation for individuals. Constantine had been associated with an organisation whose ideals came to mean much to him.

The League was a national body. In Liverpool, a local body was set up during the war called the Liverpool Committee for the Welfare of Coloured Folk. It consisted of representatives of the Churches, the University and other official bodies. One member of the Committee felt that Constantine should join a body whose composition was entirely white people:

'On the spur of the moment I proposed he should be appointed. After a pause the idea was supported by a colleague and accepted. To my surprise, though he appreciated the thought behind the action, Constantine was unwilling to accept membership without an assurance that he would remain free and untramelled in his advocacy of the rights of his own people, as he was not prepared to become subordinate to the influential white people on the Committee.'

Constantine, after a dozen years in Lancashire, had not lost a certain distrust of white officialdom. He was then—and forever afterwards—suspicious of the Anglican clergy. His relations with the then Bishop of Liverpool were cool: 'he treated me courteously, but only apparently because he was obliged to do so as a matter of business'. At the meeting of the League of Coloured Peoples, when some discussions with local churchmen took place, he made a private observation that the Anglicans were inflexible with regard to colour segregation.

Constantine's work with West Africans widened his vision and took him beyond the parochialism of considering only West Indian affairs, which he was prone to do in the 1930s. Liverpool, as a shipping centre, had always had West African crews, but it had been a matter of pre-war policy to restrict their opportunities for shore-leave in Liverpool. The circumstances of war changed this, for shipping movements were uncertain and highly dangerous. West Africans found themselves often in port not only without a ship but also short of money. Constantine was called in when a group went on strike under their leader, Ekarte. An onlooker recalled their meeting, 'Ekarte kissing Constantine on both cheeks, weeping for the injustice his people suffered, and seeking Constantine's comfort'. It was a new role for Constantine. However he reacted to being kissed, he nevertheless did all he could to bring an improvement in the conditions and pay of West African seamen.

It was during the war that Constantine first began to broadcast with any regularity. He had spoken briefly in a programme on cricket in 1939. Three years later he was talking to West Indians back in the Caribbean on the contribution of their fellow-countrymen to the war effort and to charity cricket. Gradually he became recognised as a very competent performer. In September 1943 a talk on the life he had lived in England in the past fourteen years attracted widespread attention in the Press—'one of the most impressive and effective ever from Broadcasting House', said a review in *The Scotsman*: 'In a rich, musical voice, the speaker told, without a word of bitterness, of the treatment he and his family had received in different parts of England in a period of years on account of colour. It was calculated to evoke shame or sympathy in equal measure.' With reference to the work he was actually doing in Liverpool, Constantine had said: 'No one seems to want to know the colour of the man who fashioned a good piece of precision fitting.'

A few months later Constantine was invited to appear on a B.B.C. Brains Trust programme. One reviewer, in the *Daily Herald*, commented on his 'personality, commonsense and idealism' as 'an outstanding feature of an excellent discussion.' By the end of the war, it was clear that the B.B.C. had recruited a valuable freelance broadcaster. While the war years provided his first contributions, there were two more spells when he was much in demand—the early 1950s and the mid 1960s—besides an almost unbroken run of occasional broadcasting.

Constantine held his welfare post until early in 1946 when the Ministry of Labour division in which he served was disbanded. His final task was to deal with the repatriation of West Indians from England. As always, he was quick to act when injustice loomed. He has himself told of how forty West Indians, whose passages had been paid for by the British Government, were told to work their way as unpaid deckhands. Prompt action by Constantine rectified the situation, though Constantine later learnt that they were denied the sleeping bunks to which their tickets entitled them.

He had made an important contribution to Britain's needs in the Second World War by his share in ensuring skilled and unskilled labour both in munition factories and in essential public services. He worked long hours, travelling by car or train from Nelson to Liverpool two or three times a week, and constantly leaving his office to examine working conditions for himself. The war did not always put round pegs in round

11. Constantine was over sixty when he played his last games of cricket. Here he is going out to bat for the Authors against the National Book League in July 1964. He was to play three more times that summer.

12. Shortly before he died Lord Constantine sat for this bust in terra-cotta by Karen Jonzen.

holes. In his case, the peg fitted well. His organisational ability, personal prestige, experience of Lancashire and racial background made him the ideal person to deal with the absorption of West Indians into the Merseyside industrial and social scene; he could do no wrong in the eyes of Lancashire folk, recorded one of his staff of those days. In a word, the scheme had been a success, but Constantine acknowledged that its success owed much to others including Sir Godfrey Ince, Ernest Bevin and George Tomlinson. Ince was the Permanent Secretary at the Ministry of Labour—and a north-countryman interested in cricket! Bevin was the Minister himself and Tomlinson his parliamentary assistant. For his own efforts in the war, Constantine was awarded the M.B.E. in the 1946 New Year's Honours List.

Part of Constantine's spare time was devoted to lecturing to the forces on the West Indies. Some of these lectures were given under the auspices of the Liverpool University Extra-Mural department. Time was also found to visit wounded troops in Liverpool hospitals. On one occasion he went to a hospital where all the patients had lost one or two limbs. His ready humour was appreciated as he described how even his two arms were not enough to pick up all the dollar bills given to him when he played cricket in New York. 'I could have done with four arms, but made do with what I had', he added. Then came a different note which also won a response: 'I have had to go through the world with a drawback as great as losing an arm or a leg—the drawback of a black skin.'

Constantine played cricket with the Windhill club in the Bradford League until the end of the 1941 season. During the war a great many county cricketers joined the League so that they might play occasional games so far as war-time duties permitted. Constantine found himself in the company of men he had met in the English first-class season of 1939, such as Hutton, Paynter, Ames and Arthur Fagg, with Martindale from the West Indian party. His own performance for Windhill in the first year of the war brought him 366 runs for an average of 30.50, with one century, and seventy-six wickets at a cost of 11.80 runs. His hundred came against Brighouse in under an hour. He helped Windhill to win Division 'A' in the League. Constantine also appeared for an XI drawn from the League as a whole to play against Yorkshire at Bradford. The presence of Hutton, Herbert Sutcliffe and Leyland in the Yorkshire XI and Paynter, Constantine and Martindale in the League XI was enough to bring 7,000 spectators. Constantine's century came in an hour out of 141 runs while he was at the wicket—74 runs were in boundaries. The League declared at 259 for seven, Yorkshire replying with 209 for six. Sutcliffe, though past his best, scored 70 runs in boundaries in his 127. The match raised £380 for the Red Cross. It was the first large-scale charity match in which Constantine played during the war and it set a pattern for him. He realised that his own drawing-power could give pleasure in those times of stress besides raising money for war charities. Henceforth, his efforts on the cricket field were almost as important as his welfare work in making a contribution to the needs of the 'home' front. Sam Morris recalled one of those occasions:

'I went to see him play in a Saturday afternoon charity match. The grounds of the little Lancashire town were packed to capacity. Needless to say, the crowd came to see this fabulous West Indian cricketer. He prepared to receive the first ball. He did, and that was the only ball. Clean bowled one time. The look of incredulity on the face of the bowler was shattering. One could sense his sorrow at what he, or rather the ball, had done, and one felt that he wished the cricket laws could be bent to allow Constantine another go. There was a momentary hush among the crowd, but as Constantine continued to walk back to the pavilion less than two minutes after he had left it, the ovation he received was greater than the reception he had going in to bat. This spontaneous ovation was not for cricketing achievement on that day at least, but for the tremendous all-round reputation that he had already built up in this country.'

A year later, in August 1942, there was a return match

between Yorkshire and the Bradford League. This time Paynter got the runs and Constantine had to be content with 6. Yorkshire were left 46 runs behind the League's 192, with six wickets left, when stumps were drawn. Constantine had taken two for 13. The match came at the end of his last war-time season for Windhill, for whom he had made 322 runs for an average of 24.76 and taken sixty-eight wickets for an average of 11.96. It had been enough to assist Windhill to the top of Division 'A' of the League yet again. Constantine left the club to take up his Welfare Officer appointment. In doing so there was some sacrifice of income. Windhill had paid him for his war-time services £25 a match—an income of about £450 in each season of 1940 and 1941. Thereafter, all his war-time cricket was played as an amateur; he often refused even to accept expenses.

After leaving the Bradford League, Constantine played in the Liverpool and District League, in charity matches in Lancashire and Warwickshire, in a few matches at Lord's, in Scotland, and in occasional appearances for the British Empire XI. He admired the standards of cricket in the Liverpool and District League, and found 'many of the grounds really beautiful'. Those at Southport and Sefton he regarded as models of what a good county ground should look like. The competitive nature of the cricket made its appeal—'balls bowled years ago are still in red-hot dispute, more than I ever heard regarding county matches', he once wrote. He had one criticism: much natural talent, he felt, was being frittered away for lack of knowledge of cricket fundamentals. 'A little instruction on the basic things which cricketers must know if they are to employ their talents to proper advantage would repay players', he commented. Despite the freedom and enterprise of his own cricket, Constantine had a great regard for the importance of technique. Even on the aspect of batting he liked least—defence—he gave sound advice: 'If in your first few overs, you merely put your bat firmly in front of the wicket, and play the ball straight off the face of it (always remembering to keep the bat facing the bowler's arm) you will, in all probability, find yourself still batting after ten minutes, and the ball beginning to get big and easy in your sight.' He gave that advice in his book *Cricketers' Cricket* based on a lifetime of playing and watching good and not-so-good cricketers.

Many of the games in which he participated during the war, especially evening ones, did not give much time for defensive cricket. 'We found time,' Constantine said in the spirit of Sir Francis Drake, 'to play cricket and beat the Nazis too.' His patriotism evolved from his concept of what the British Empire ought to be. He firmly believed that the English way of life was not a process confined to the British Isles. He saw it reflected in the West Indies. Years later, in the House of Lords, he explained how a West Indian was far more in tune with English cultural patterns than was a citizen of any mainland European country. This conviction, which he held so firmly, led to his sadness at so much rejection of his own people. He was mindful of an incident which will be described later in this chapter, when he declared in his book *Colour Bar* that 'a German general—an enemy of Britain— would command more respect in a British hotel than a coloured citizen of the British Empire'.

Spectators as well as the cricketers found relief from the war in cricket. Games such as that between S. G. Shepherd's XI and L. N. Constantine's XI in aid of the Mayors of Bootle and Crosby War Fund, one evening in July 1943, provided three hours of entertainment for war-weary Liverpool folk before the evening's air raids. Shepherd's XI scored 149 —everyone making a few and no one very many. Constantine's side seemed to be sure of victory when they were within 11 runs of their target with five wickets left. Constantine had done his bit with 72 runs in fifty-two minutes, but it was not enough! Shepherd collected those last five wickets himself while 8 runs were scored. Last man out was Charles Leatherbarrow, whose own contribution to charity cricket in Liverpool as a player and organiser was immense.

On another occasion, 10,000 flocked to Fazakerley to contribute to the Lord Mayor of Liverpool's Charity Fund and to watch Constantine lead a West Indies XI of great names—

Martindale, E. St Hill, Clarke, E. Achong—against Lancashire in a drawn match. By 1942 no county was doing more
for charity through cricket than Lancashire. A colleague
of Constantine's in the welfare section of the Ministry of
Labour, Arthur Proctor, drew over 125,000 people to cricket
matches which he sponsored. Constantine found himself frequently recruited to play. When he appeared for an
Empire XI against North Wales at Colwyn Bay in a match
in aid of the Lord Mayor of Manchester's Distress Fund, over
£1,000 was raised. A year later this figure was far surpassed
when a single day's cricket at Colwyn Bay between the same
two sides raised £3,664 for the Red Cross Prisoner of War
Fund. Constantine's contribution to the entertainment was
57 runs and two for 50.

That summer of 1943 found him playing as far apart as
Didsbury, Longsight, Blackpool and Warrington. All this
meant travelling and more hours away from his home in
Nelson, but Constantine did not grudge it. He was no saint:
he enjoyed playing the game. But he also accepted the fact
that he was doing his bit towards winning the war, and once
he admitted that the hardships at home could not be compared with the strains and separations faced by men in the
battle-line.

It would be wrong to assume that Constantine had to be
playing if a charity match was to be a success. In the third of
the Colwyn Bay games, in 1944, he was not available, but
the cricket played by Sutcliffe, Cyril Washbrook and Martindale helped to bring in over £4,000 for the Red Cross Prisoner
of War Fund. Taking 1944 as a whole, Constantine was as
tireless as ever. At Didsbury he got 61 runs in twenty minutes,
and a standing ovation from a crowd of 5,000. At Old Trafford, restored after bomb damage, he took three for 63 and
made 25 in half an hour.

Whether in Lancashire or elsewhere, many of Constantine's appearances were for a West Indies XI. This was
raised from West Indians whom war work brought to Britain
or who were already in the country in 1939, as Constantine
himself had been. Quite apart from the cricket they played,

these West Indians brought their various homelands to the attention of British people. Lancashire people might have heard of the West Indians through Constantine's talks in the 1930s; intellectuals might have come across them as students in universities or thought about them by reading W. M. Macmillan's *Warning from the West Indies*, an important book published in 1936. But the great mass of the British public were singularly unaware of this area of the Empire. On many occasions, Constantine would give a short talk about 'The West Indies and the war' after the cricket match. The atmosphere would be relaxed as he drew the names of the winners of some cricket bat raffled for the charity of the day. Then, before people drifted away, there would be a few serious thoughts indicating what West Indians felt about the war in which everyone was involved—and, since Constantine could never be serious for long, a joke or two to send the crowd home happy. Constantine was an extrovert: he liked these moments when he held an audience in his hands. No other West Indian cricketer had the personality to do it.

The few appearances of West Indian XIs at Lord's were events. In 1940 a West Indian XI came to Lord's with three of the side who had last played there against Middlesex when the visitors had amassed 665 runs. No such luck attended them against Sir Pelham Warner's XI, for whom Hutton (44) and Denis Compton (73) laid the basis of a total of 263. The West Indies replied with 146 to which Constantine contributed 5.*

Constantine himself next appeared for the West Indies at Lord's three years later, in 1943, against an England XI. Twenty thousand spectators filled the ground and contributed over £300 to the Colonial Comforts Fund. The game itself was not a great success. A. V. Bedser, giving a hint of post-war successes, took six for 27 to dismiss the West Indies for 120. As one-day cricket of the 1960s and 1970s has shown, 120 by the side batting first is not enough to give promise of an exciting contest. Constantine sent back two Englishmen

---

* A curiosity of the *Wisden* 1940 report was the inclusion of one player's newly-won D.F.C. against his name in the score sheet.

cheaply but the game slipped away from them as Jack Robertson and Ames put on 134 runs to bat on after victory. In a final forty-five minutes to entertain the crowd on a glorious evening in early summer, Constantine hit 59, including two sixes off Douglas Wright—a bowler whose leg-breaks, wrote Constantine, 'did not seem to obey any laws', and for whom he had a great respect.

Later in 1943 Constantine was again at Lord's, though not for the West Indies. He, Martindale and Clarke joined cricketers from Australia, New Zealand and South Africa to compose a Dominions side to play England in a two-day game. England's 324 gave them a first-innings lead of almost 200 over the Dominions. The England side did not enforce a follow-on, partly to ensure that the game lasted its full time. A declaration after lunch on the second day left the Dominions 360 to get. C. S. Dempster made 113. Constantine, after making 21, was caught by Leslie Compton with his left hand at full stretch while leaning on the pavilion rails with his feet firmly on the ground. Constantine's comment in the pavilion was 'that is cricket' and he accepted equably a fair decision despite doubts raised in the Press. The Dominions failed by 8 runs and lost in the closing moments.

For Constantine the match was tinged with sadness. Fourteen thousand spectators and the newspaper critics were concerned to see that justice was done to him on the field of play. Constantine, the cricketer, he reflected ruefully, was a figure of status. But Constantine, the human being and fellow-citizen, could be denied bed and board in the great city where he had come to play cricket. Apparently someone had said: 'The hotel is coming to something if you are going to take niggers in.' Rather than be put out in the streets Constantine and his family went elsewhere. 'The time has come', Constantine said, 'to take things to the Courts.' In September questions were asked in the House of Commons over the incident in August in which Constantine had been persuaded to leave the Imperial Hotel, Russell Square, London, by an official of the Ministry of Labour. The Minister, Ernest Bevin, replied that Constantine had indeed been advised to leave by the official, but acting as a friend and not as a representative of the Ministry of Labour. The matter could not then be taken further since it was *sub judice* pending court proceedings. In June 1944, the case of *Constantine v. Imperial London Hotel Ltd* was heard before Mr Justice Birkett. Constantine had retained Sir Patrick Hastings, one of the most eminent advocates of the day, and Miss Rose Heilbron, a distinguished woman barrister.* The plaintiff asserted that the defendants had refused to receive and lodge him and his family in the Imperial Hotel, Russell Square. The defence stated that he left voluntarily and stayed in another of the firm's hotels, the Bedford.

It was argued that Constantine had booked rooms for himself, his wife and daughter, and had paid a deposit, and that the hotel knew the booking had been made by a coloured family. On arriving, Constantine was alleged to have been told that the hotel 'did not want niggers' and that he might stay one night only. It was then that his friend and colleague from the Ministry of Labour, Arnold Watson, persuaded him to leave. It was asserted by the defence that the hotel was acting in the interests of peace since the presence of large numbers of Americans in the hotel might lead to trouble. In his reserved judgement, Mr Justice Birkett accepted the evidence of the plaintiff. He considered that Constantine, in the witness box, had borne himself with modesty and dignity, and was not concerned to be vindictive or malicious but was obviously affected by the indignity and the humiliation. Judgement was found for the plaintiff and nominal damages of £5 were awarded. Such was the substance of a case which attracted considerable attention at the time and which has remained in the minds of many people when Constantine's name is mentioned.

The insult to his family he had felt deeply. For himself, he had learnt to live with slights and to regard them 'as an unpleasant part of living in Britain'. The occasion was para-

* The decision to retain Sir Patrick Hastings had been taken at the highest levels. The case was seen as one of great significance whose outcome might be related to the future attitude of coloured peoples in the Empire to the war cause.

doxical. Constantine had come to London as an honoured cricketer to play for the Dominions against England at Lord's. Years ago he had, in the words of C. L. R. James, 'revolted against the revolting contrast between his first-class status as a cricketer and his third-class status as a man'. Yet here the cruel distinction was again being made. He could entertain spectators in London: he might not be entertained in one of London's hotels. The affair confirmed Constantine in his belief that the best service he could render his own fellow West Indians—and coloured people everywhere—was to fight their battles for them. It was something he never forgot and explains why he continued to take up causes long after he himself was 'accepted and honoured in Britain'. His own comment was this:

'Had I been inclined to do so, I could probably have succeeded in a further action for defamation. But I was content to have drawn the particular nature of the affront before the wider judgement of the British public in the hope that its sense of fair play might help to protect people of my colour in England in future. From the tone of the hundreds of letters of congratulation I received from all over the country, I think my object was attained.'

Typical of his replies to his correspondents was a letter he wrote to a Kent lady:

'With respect to the incident at the hotel, I want to assure you that it has left no bitterness whatever and that I am not likely to judge the kind people I have met, and many others, by the attitude of such people. I apologise for being so tardy in replying but you will understand that the volume of correspondence has been tremendous.'

That generous reply remains in the possession of the person to whom it was written, treasured for many years. Typical of the reaction of British people to the original incident had been the offer to Constantine by complete strangers—a naval officer and his wife—to share their small flat in London.

At the time when the case was being heard in the courts,

Constantine was again at Lord's, this time captaining the West Indies against an England XI. His friend, Ernest Bevin, the Minister of Labour, came to watch, as did the Colonial Secretary. The best cricket of the day came from Hammond, his rival captain, whose century helped to ensure an England win by 166 runs. Batting in the last ten minutes of the game, Constantine scored 42 with a six to the members' stand and eight fours. He was immensely pleased with the standing ovation he received. 'It took me back', he said, 'to 1928.' In private he remarked that it had also made up for recent events.

Constantine was far too busy in Lancashire to come up to London more than two or three times a year. He did so for a Knights of the Round Table dinner at the Savoy in April 1945 as the representative of the West Indies. He came again for what had become the annual war-time fixture between England and the West Indies, which took place for the last time in 1945. Nine thousand spectators watched cricket on a cold, wet day. Once again, England won. Only Constantine's 32 made any sort of contribution to the West Indies total of 84.

The war was coming to an end. Germany had already surrendered. One almost takes for granted Constantine's achievements over the six years of charity cricket, but inevitably he was ageing. By 1945 he was forty-three—still fast in the field, still safe with his hands, but the ball in trajectory travelled less fiercely. He did a lot of bowling in relation to the wickets he took. Physically he had begun to put on weight. He often looked tired, and confessed the fact after a game. He had always known the strain of being expected to succeed, but it seemed even more important in these war-time games—not for himself but for those who had come to watch. Constantine had a certain Puritanism about him. If he was enjoying himself, he must justify the pleasure by pleasing others. 'Work I must, and work I want to', he once wrote. Cricket as much as welfare services in Merseyside was his war-time work.

Some of that cricket 'work' took him to Scotland. In

September 1944 he captained a team called the 'All-Blacks' at Edinburgh. His side included West Indians and players from Africa. The Negroes from the land of Constantine's ancestors came from Sierra Leone, the Gold Coast and Nigeria. The opposition, a strong Anglo-Scottish side, won a low-scoring game by 25 runs. Constantine spoke to an audience in Edinburgh on 'the West Indies and the War' on the following day before going to Kilmarnock to play for a combined West Indian and Australian Services XI against the same Anglo-Scottish opposition. This match, in which Constantine took two for 7, was won by the Combined XI before the largest crowd ever to watch cricket at Kilmarnock. Again, Constantine spoke to a meeting the next day. Immediately afterwards, he played for the same XI against substantially the same opposition at Troon, taking six wickets for 23. Again, he spoke. Whistle-stop matches and meetings were taking their toll. He was tired even of cricket, he admitted to a friend.

But after a winter's rest from cricket he went north again in June 1945, playing in more charity matches. On four consecutive days he appeared for a Colonial XI. Apart from 47 not out against a Scottish Select XI, neither runs nor wickets came easily. Then came a game at Alloa where his won XI beat a Services side, and he scored 64. At the end of the summer he was back again in Scotland playing at Kilmarnock.

At one point he had played cricket on ten successive days in Scotland because he had also committed himself to assisting Major H. B. Rowan's XI in his matches against schools. These games played an important part in Scottish schoolboy cricket in that the players gave instructional lectures and coaching to boys in the schools as well as participating in a match. Against Trinity College, Glenalmond, on one of the loveliest of school grounds in Scotland, Constantine scored 67 not out. To those schoolboys in the Highlands, one of them recalled, it was 'an innings of magic'.

An account of Constantine's war-time cricket career would not be complete without mentioning his few appearances for the war-time club called 'The British Empire XI'. This club had been formed soon after war began. It raised more than £20,000 for charity and played 238 matches in six seasons. It offered cricket, mainly in the south of England, to players on leave from the Services or from their various occupations. Constantine made eight appearances with 63 as his best score, and took fifteen wickets for 212.

Constantine's war-time cricket came to a triumphant climax in a three-day match at Lord's in August 1945, when England played the Dominions. As a game of cricket, it was described as one of the finest ever seen. Among its offerings were centuries by Martin Donnelly of New Zealand and Miller of Australia, and one in each innings by the England captain, Hammond. Wright took five wickets in each innings. Edrich, batting as low as number 8 in a powerful England order, scored 78 and 31. Fortunes swung either way and the issue was in doubt till the very end. Constantine crowned his first-class cricket career in this—his last first-class match— by captaining the Dominions. It meant a very great deal to be captain. 'I was "colony" while the rest of the team was "Dominion"', he remarked. What he meant was that he was black and the rest of the team white. It was the nearest he came to being a Test match captain. His own mark was stamped on the match on the third morning when he and Miller added 117 runs in forty-five minutes. For once, Constantine was the subdued partner. Miller's innings was faultless despite its pace, and his 185 runs came in two and a quarter hours. In the closing minutes of the game, when England needed 74 in forty-five minutes, a flash of the old Constantine brilliance ran out W. E. Phillipson.

'How I longed for that moment for youth again and the old lightning in my right hand. I should have loved to put myself on bowling, and try what one or two scorchers would do. But I had not got quite the pace for it, and so I had to think out something else very quickly.

'Davies was placing the ball nicely, wide of the fieldsmen at mid-on, and judging his timing of runs so exactly that we did not seem to have a chance to trap him. But at the end of an over I have a word with the bowler, and then manoeuvred myself to the mid-on position. In the ensuing over, two balls were sent down that could be placed fairly easily wide of deep mid-on. Runs were scored, and it looked as though there was nothing we could do. In the next over, I told the other bowler to feed one or two more of these bait balls, and I had to watch with anxiety as the score crept on and on towards victory. Just a little run of hitting, now, and we were finished; and Davies was getting very confident.

'Then came another over, and another bait ball. Once more, the flashing single, easily run, and the ball pantingly retrieved without any danger whatever to either wicket. A straight ball on the leg stump. Another straight one, carefully blocked. Then the other batsman made a single off what looked like rather a loose ball, and Davies was back facing the bowling, his eye, I saw, wandering round to that place wide of mid-on.

'The ball spinning through the air . . . the thump as it met the face of the bat . . . the ball so neatly directed to that wide-open space at the deep mid-on once more . . . the batsman, two striding white figures, on the move for a single . . . and I had picked up the ball thirty yards from the wicket, my hand shot out as in youthful days, and I saw Phillipson's wicket jump all ways into the air.'

With eight minutes left, the Dominions snatched victory by 45 runs. Constantine led off the Dominions XI and walked into the pavilion out of first-class cricket. One man's war was over.

8

SECOND INNINGS
1946-1956

Learie Constantine was less than his usual cheerful self as the 1946 cricket season approached. As a man of forty-four, he knew that his cricketing days were mainly behind him. He admitted that charity cricket had given him a new lease: 'I couldn't have kept going year after year in competitive League stuff,' he remarked, 'but the charity games gave me the cricket I wanted without the pressures.' Here he was less than honest with himself. The 'pressures' had always been there. If they had not been, he might have had a conscience about playing so much cricket in war-time. But he knew that by playing cricket he had helped charity and had entertained the public. It was part of his war work. As late as March 1946 he remained uncertain as to his future plans. In a B.B.C. programme that month he said:

'Now my job is coming to an end. My own future is obscure. At one time cricket was my life, my religion. It gave me the chance of a decent living. It brought me publicity and a wide range of travel. It gave me, as well, reasonable scope to educate my daughter. Now I am older and cannot maintain the old standard of bowling fast, catching almost everything that came my way and making runs at the rate of two per minute, a change is indicated. I must give up something. What is it to be? Strange as it may seem—it must be cricket. Cricket as a means of livelihood. But that is the way of life. It is Life itself. I want to complete my legal studies and if successful then take a decision. I would love to work for my people: work in the field of education and quicker progress to the goal of self-reliance and self government. This opens up a wide range of probabilities and for the moment confuses me.'

Constantine, in the parlance of our own day, had reached 'the mid-life crisis'. The first innings was over. How would he approach the second? He made an interim decision—to go on playing cricket—which had no substance as an answer for the future and contradicted his decision to give up cricket. But the game was 'life itself', and an invitation from Wind-hill Cricket Club to continue for a year or two more could not be resisted. Cricket was also a means of income. No other had suggested itself at the time, although early in 1947 an oil company in Trinidad asked him to consider a personnel post involving liaison between coloured workers and the company. Constantine went out to Trinidad for a month to study the implications of the job. He turned it down on several grounds. He sensed that he was expected to use his popularity as a cricketer 'to dissuade coloured rebellious-ness'; he was snubbed by being diverted, at the last moment, from having a meal in the staff club; and he knew it would be the end of his ultimate ambition to become a lawyer.

Meanwhile, in 1946, he had resumed his connection with Windhill. His three seasons of cricket for Windhill in the Bradford League were an enjoyable epilogue to his League cricket. He topped the bowling averages for the League in 1947 and 1948. His final appearance in League cricket brought him a wicket off his last ball and the chance to lead his side to victory:

'I went in for my farewell innings. I had to do something to mark the occasion, and despite fine and steady bowling, I managed to notch up 69 not out, winning the match with a final four that went humming to the boundary as clean as any ball I have ever hit.'

With the Windhill testimonial as a tangible reminder of his final League matches, Constantine forsook the scene which he had so much enjoyed.

Besides playing for Windhill, Constantine was professionally employed in 1946 as a cricketer in Ireland and
Scotland. During the summer of 1946 he flew on Mondays
from Manchester to Dublin to coach at Trinity College,
Dublin, Leinster Cricket Club and St Mary's College. There
was still rationing in Britain and he remarked that it was the
food in Dublin which attracted him. When he got there, he
found that the enthusiasm for cricket was another attraction.
He was immensely impressed with the fielding standard at
Trinity College.

He coached the boys of St Mary's in the lunch-hour.
Father Francis Berry, master in charge of cricket, recalled the
visits:

'He was really a fantastic coach; every moment of the hour
was used at the nets and no boy was idle; there was perfect
discipline and the boys picked up his tuition rapidly. It bore
fruit in the immediate subsequent years in our winning all
the inter-school competitions and in giving a great boost to
the game in the school which we still in some way feel thirty
years later.'

Of one of these boys, sixteen-year-old Gerald Duffy, Constantine wrote most enthusiastically prophesying for him a
future place in the England XI should he choose to cross the
Irish Sea. As an instance of Constantine's judgement of a
player's potential, Duffy's future cricket career may be mentioned. He went on to play for Leinster, had been capped
fifty-five times for Ireland up to the end of the 1973 season
and had won every individual cricket trophy offered by the
Irish and Leinster Cricket Unions. Had he crossed the Irish
Sea—who knows? Duffy's own recollection was that Constantine's success as a coach lay in his readiness to encourage
his charges and to give them confidence in what they did.

While in Southern Ireland Constantine met the President
of Eire, Mr Eamonn de Valera, a man who 'expressed strong
views about equality for coloured people'. Constantine was
photographed beside the President, but all attempts—including a solicitor's letter—failed to get him a copy of the

photograph for which he had paid. He later learnt from a friend that 'someone' had ordered the picture not to be circulated, but he never learnt who it was. It is difficult to give credence to an incident like this, and Constantine himself was not really prepared to—'but I never got the photograph I paid for'.

He also resumed his cricket in Scotland where he played both for the Colonial Cricket Club of Edinburgh and for H. B. Rowan's XI in 1946. By so doing he continued on the one hand to give his support to many West Indian students in Edinburgh playing cricket and, on the other, to help Rowan's coaching policy for Scottish schools which had begun during the war. Constantine paid a warm tribute to the organising powers of Jock McCurdie, the secretary of Rowan's XI: 'Nothing is left to chance. His precision is outstanding. He even tells you what time you are to go to bed and what time to get up. No one, not even that lazy fellow, Constantine, is a minute late for anything.' Campbell Douglas, who helped Rowan with the running of his XI, recalled his own impressions of one of Constantine's visits:

'We threw a dinner on the Friday and Constantine sat between our president and myself. Being a world figure, when I was introduced to him I naturally called him Mr Constantine. 'Mr Douglas', he said, 'Learie, please.' On the Saturday we had a game with sides made up of locals and visitors and R.A.F. Prestwick. Before the game started a little Austin 7 drove into Kirkstiple. What a roar was raised from a good attendance when the magnificent figure of Martindale, the West Indies fast bowler, stepped out, and the noise doubled when the young Martindales fell out of the back of the little car! Finally, came Learie.'

A few years later, in 1953, Constantine was invited by the prime minister of Ceylon, Sir John Kotelawala, to coach for three months in Ceylon. Norma went with him on the trip. Inevitably he played some cricket and he returned to the India he had known twenty years earlier when he accompanied the Ceylonese Cricket Association XI on its annual tour to Madras. When there he played against his Sinhalese friends for a Madras XI, scoring 10 and 12 and taking two for 110 in eighteen overs in Ceylon's total of 403 for four declared. Madras scored 68 and 178. A few weeks later he played in the south of Ceylon for Galle against a Ceylon XI, taking one for 9. 'He fielded brilliantly and took two fine catches', a correspondent wrote.

It was in these years that he began to establish himself as a cricket reporter. He had broadcast reports on war-time matches to listeners in the West Indies, which had been crisp summaries of the day's play with special reference to the performances of West Indians in England, and often a mention of players such as Ames, whom he knew that West Indian crowds remembered well. Constantine first made his mark on fellow-reporters in the Press Box at the Lord's Test against India in June 1946. The correspondent of a leading English national paper remembered the occasion well:

'The usual chatter was going on interspersed by reminiscences when Constantine came into the Press Box, greeted one or two friends, sat down next to me, and reduced the Press Box to respectful silence in a few minutes by the acuteness and originality of his remarks about what was going on out in the middle. He was not only a man who played the game really well—he understood it really well too, and every department of it. I have never in my life listened to such an illuminating and impromptu running commentary.'

Another fellow-journalist remarked: 'He observed everything going on in the field. Technically he was the equal of anyone else in the Press Box in those years and superior to most.'

Both as a reporter and as a broadcaster, Constantine was able to retain his close association with cricket. Although he wrote fluently and under pressure as a columnist, his real success lay in the broadcasting studio. With the visit of the West Indies side in 1950—the first to come since 1939, and the first to win a series in England—Constantine came into his own as a commentator. During that summer he earned nearly £300 from broadcasting on Test matches. In a letter to the B.B.C. he paid tribute to what he had learnt in technique from Rex Alston: 'I cannot fully express how much I owe to his help generally.' A tribute to Constantine's own performance came from an old man in Southampton after the Lord's Test:

I feel compelled to write and tell you how much I enjoyed listening to your commentaries. Your voice is so quiet, so cultural, in fact attractive too. I am now too old to sit on a hazel bench or to stand, so I have to be content to listen.

In the next three or four years before Constantine returned to Trinidad, he was in demand for a wide range of programmes including Women's Hour, Schools Broadcasts, Children's Hour, Commonwealth Club, London Forum, Radio Roundabout, West Indian Diary, The World Goes By and music quizzes. An internal B.B.C. minute of the time noted his 'excellent voice, sincere and unaffected. He is very intelligent and co-operative.' If this sounded like a schoolmaster's report, he earned a schoolmasterly reprimand for nearly landing the B.B.C. in legal trouble by citing, in a prepared script, the wrong hotel in a reference to the action he took in the courts in 1944. Indeed, a major criticism of him as both writer and broadcaster was his disregard for factual accuracy. Dates and statistics meant little to him. Errors would occur frequently. His poor father, if the scripts were to be believed, was for ever bobbing backwards and forwards across the Atlantic to play cricket—indeed, as early as 1886 at the age of twelve!

In the great majority of broadcasts Constantine talked about his life as a boy in Trinidad and then of his time in Lancashire both in the 1930s and during the war. He was at his best as a narrator, but less effective when he was the persuader. His 'persuasive' passages invited his listeners to sympathise with him in a situation—usually a racial one. He was apt to be long-winded in his determination to establish his views.

Broadcasting appealed to Constantine. The technique of sound radio calls for the extrovert qualities which he possessed.

Although errors might abound, fluency prevailed. This was what the B.B.C. wanted frequently and were prepared to pay him for. Broadcasting was an important outlet for him at this time. It brought him into contact with people, and it compensated for the toil of studying law, for Constantine had stuck to his declared intention to work at his legal studies. It contributed to his income when he no longer played for Windhill.

When, in March 1954, he gave his farewell broadcast, 'Return to Trinidad', a B.B.C. internal minute spoke of it as 'outstanding to the point of being a landmark in Light [Programme] History'. Here are the concluding sentences:

'I owe my country an effort. I owe something to them, coming back there and trying to teach them what I have learned; and perhaps learning myself a little bit of the progress they have made at the time. But whatever else I do, I want to say just before I go home that I have had my difficulties in England, but on the whole, measuring these difficulties against the pleasures and the successful friendships that I have made, I am almost prepared to ignore the difficulties altogether as if they never existed and to go home and get ready to come back to England for a holiday at the first opportunity. So that is my little way of saying thanks to the Englishmen in this country and to all those who have helped to make my life and the life of my family so happy and contented during our twenty-five years in what was then a strange land.'

Two fellow-broadcasters, a West Indian and an Englishman, commented on Constantine's technique. Alva Clark declared that he could talk without preparing a script. He was 'a superb broadcaster; a producer's dream. If he were talking into a microphone for a programme to be transmitted later, what he said scarcely needed editing'. John Arlott analysed this success. 'His approach was simple and direct. He never embarked on involved constructions. He was an extremely good natural broadcaster who adequately expressed the shape of a cricket-match.' One of his producers of these years adds that 'he was totally relaxed as a broadcaster. He loved talking.' These tributes from men of broadcasting experience in production and presentation give the measure of Constantine's calibre as a broadcaster. One might add that his voice had the right timbre, and he was articulate. He was again in demand when he returned to England in the 1960s.

Once or twice, Constantine had to decline an invitation to broadcast because he was too busy with his legal studies. By 1950 he felt confident enough for both. 'I am studying very hard but I think I'll pull it off', he wrote to a B.B.C. producer who had asked him to take part in a programme. The year 1950 was a half-way point in an eight year struggle which began in earnest in 1946 and for which he had already taken the first steps in 1944 when he was admitted to the Honourable Society of the Middle Temple. Ahead, as the immediate target, lay papers in Roman Law. Norma made him study Latin. Evening after evening, as Constantine ruefully remarked to a friend, 'she made me learn declensions and conjugations and irregular principal parts'. No wonder war-time cricket and welfare work acquired a retrospective glamour! It was his wife who kept his nose to the grindstone. 'I locked him in his bedroom several hours a day', she declared in a television programme in 1963. 'I knew that he wasn't getting on with his studies as he should be, with so many callers. If I hadn't taken some sort of action we both knew that he would never have become a barrister.' Whether or not she was making a good story out of it, the fact remains that it was Norma Constantine who played a dominant part in bringing about her husband's ultimate success. Behind the scenes she had determined many years earlier that they would stay in Nelson and face the future. Her confidence and her strength on many occasions enabled her more impulsive husband to accomplish what he set out to do. His first success in the bar examinations came in the Trinity Term of 1947 when he passed in Roman Law.

Various factors now led the Constantines to leave Nelson. Cricket was finally over, in professional terms. Opportunities for broadcasting were greater in the south. Gloria was about to leave St Andrews University where she graduated Master of Arts and go to the Institute of Education at London University. Most important, tutorials for the bar examinations were best obtained in London. The tenancy of number 3 Meredith Street was given up, and the family moved in July 1949 to a flat at 101 Lexham Gardens, off Earls Court Road. Once the Constantines had announced in Nelson that they proposed to move to London, farewell functions began. Among them was a dinner given by the Methodist men of the town. Constantine used the opportunity to talk about racial matters as he saw them and indicated that he had not felt it appropriate when he lived in Nelson in the 1930s to speak on public platforms on a subject which had, in those days, little significance for that community.

Once in London, Constantine continued to work, with the aid of tutorials in the chambers of Gerald Hart and lectures given under the Council of Legal Education, for the remainder of his Part I examinations. In 1950 he satisfied the examiners in Constitutional Law and Legal History and Criminal Law. In the following year he was successful in Contract and Tort and in Land Law. Ultimate success came in the Part II examinations in Michaelmas 1954 when he passed in Criminal Procedure and a special subject in Common Law; Equity and a special subject; Company Law and Practical Conveyancing; Evidence and Civil Procedure; and a General Paper. So far as expense was concerned, he had had to pay admission and call fees to his Inn of Court and lecture fees.

A few sentences do not convey the length of the struggle or the endurance involved. Norma, determined even more than he on success, spurred him on when he was depressed with the effort and deflated by failure. Their friend, C. L. R. James, who had been a close observer of the earlier studies in the 1930s when he shared their home, watched the papers for the results and 'more than once' found nothing.

'After another disappointment I called him up and commiserated with him. I thought I detected weariness. "You are not going to give it up?" I asked. "Who? Me? Not on

your life!" "Same as on the cricket field", I said. "Absolutely
the same."'

Despite the demands of cricket, broadcasting and the law,
Constantine did not let the rest of the world go by. He served
on a Colonial Office Advisory Committee on racial matters,
and in 1950 he played a leading part in the events which
followed the marriage of Seretse Khama to a white English
girl, Ruth Williams. Seretse Khama was the chief-designate
of the Bamangwati people, a tribe in Bechuanaland. He had
been educated in England, met and married Ruth Williams,
and taken her back to Serowe, the capital of Bechuanaland.
The girl was completely acceptable to Seretse's tribe, and the
young couple lived a quiet, undisturbed existence. All this
changed when Seretse was summoned to England for con-
sultation. Pressure was then brought to bear on him by the
British Government not to return to rule his tribe despite the
comment of the British Press that it was not the Government's
place to over-rule the domestic affairs of the Bamangwato if
they themselves accepted a white consort. Constantine became closely involved. He had no doubts that it was opinion
in the Union of South Africa that lay behind the policy of the
British Labour Government in forbidding Seretse's return.
Bechuanaland, with its quarter of a million Bantu, lay close
to the Union. A Seretse Khama Fighting Committee was
formed in March 1950 at a meeting of delegates representing
every organisation of coloured peoples in Britain, and Constantine became chairman. Protest meetings took place;
Constantine declared that feeling ran high and that the
British public were in sympathy with Seretse and his wife.
Despite deputations to the Government and the lobbying of
individual Members of Parliament, nothing was achieved.
Constantine's involvement showed his constant concern for
issues of colour and race, and his readiness to act in instances
of human distress.

His thoughts on the colour issue as a whole were crystallised in his book *Colour Bar* published by Stanley Paul in 1954.
It was written, said one reviewer, by 'one who is suffering

from an open wound, inflicted upon an obviously likeable and sincere man by the petty insults and injuries which coloured flesh is heir to at the hands of thoughtless, prejudiced and ill-mannered white people'. The author wrote as someone who 'knew the coloured person's position in sophisticated society'. *Colour Bar*, as Constantine said in his introduction, was written at the request of his friends in journalism and elsewhere to give the Negro's view of the black and white problem. In cricketing metaphor, Constantine declared that he could not resist the invitation 'to knock a few over the pavilion'. Yet its publication surprised others who felt that Constantine had had an enjoyable and happy life in England; they wondered at the bitterness underlying his writing. But *Colour Bar* was justified on three grounds. Constantine himself had continued to meet with instances of embarrassment and hurtfulness. Among those who knew him by sight scarcely any slights took place. When he was away from Lancashire and cricket circles it was a different matter. Television was not a conventional household possession in the 1950s and Constantine up to then had rarely appeared on it, anyway. Millions of people had heard of him but did not know him by sight. He walked the streets of London, an anonymous Negro. Still less were his wife and daughter known. Insults to them hurt him deeply. There had been one such when Norma and Gloria had booked two bunks in a four-berth sleeping compartment on the train to Scotland for Gloria's graduation and their fellow-passengers refused to share with them.

A second reason for writing the book, to which Constantine himself attached far more importance, was his concern to help those less fortunate than he. There were thousands of ordinary Negroes, and other coloured people, in Britain who had to face discomfort. For them, he was the spokesman. Thirdly, his book examined the world-wide nature of the colour bar. Starting from the premise that the United Nations had proclaimed a 'Universal Declaration of Human Rights' in 1948 he examined the extent to which mankind did *not* recognise 'the inherent dignity and equal and inalienable rights of all members of the human family'. The book paid considerable attention to affairs in South Africa, to which Constantine inevitably had not been, and in the United States to which he had. He pointed out the appeal of Communism to depressed coloured peoples and related the decline of Christianity to the failure of the Churches to take an uncompromising attitude on racial discrimination. Constantine once said that he intended the book to be called *Black and White* rather than *Colour Bar*, a title that his publishers chose. Colour bar, he said in a broadcast in 1950, was an abstract concept, a term used to describe so-called racial discrimination:

'There is the unofficial kind, from the cold-shoulder technique of social ostracism to the practice of making restrictive covenants in property leases, and the official kind, from denying the franchise to coloured peoples to specifying which seats they may sit on in buses. There has arisen in the modern world a basic situation between black and white involving misunderstanding, mistrust and misuse.'

It was his attempt to resolve this which led to the writing of *Colour Bar*. In general, Constantine lived at two levels—as, indeed, does many a coloured person of ability. There was the successful cricketer whom the crowds applauded, but there was also the West Indian Negro mindful of thousands like himself whose social and economic horizons were limited by resources, opportunity and prejudice. Very little of the cricketer appears in *Colour Bar*. It is the cry of the Negro, the black man, who has been turned out of restaurants, kicked out of churches, refused accommodation and cursed. These things came Constantine's way. He learnt to cope. He wrote the book for others who could not.

Colour Bar was published in August 1954 and reprinted in October. A few weeks later Constantine became a barrister. Both these events made 1954 an important year for him. It was made more so by an invitation to return to Trinidad Leaseholds Ltd as assistant to the Legal Adviser. Financially, the offer of £700 a year gave him security and the chance of a second career for the rest of his working life—he was now fifty-two. Yet he hesitated: he had lived in England for twenty-five years and had absorbed the English way of life. Despite the revelations he had made in *Colour Bar*, he knew that he was accepted by English white society. How would it be with the whites in Trinidad? Eventually, he took the job, sent his wife on ahead to make arrangements for Gloria's impending wedding, and sailed in December 1954. Something of these anxieties were later expressed by him in a broadcast he made in December 1963, entitled 'No Stranger Here':

'I left England to return to Trinidad. My hopes should have been high—the coloured student returning to the island where he had been born and brought up. I remember that my heart was in my boots. I felt like someone emigrating rather than someone returning home. I was not looking forward to the restrictive atmosphere of Trinidad—a colony where the white man held most of the power, made most of the money and kept himself pretty well to himself.'

How far were these fears realised when he disembarked from the oil-tanker *Regent Hawk* in Trinidad on 15 December 1954? At first there was the delight of being back among friends and relations not seen for many years. There was, that same week, the marriage of his daughter Gloria to André Valère, a barrister. Like many weddings, plans for a quiet, modest ceremony soon evaporated as more and more people had to be asked. Constantine's arrival was popular in many circles. 'Seldom has public acclaim been given so ungrudgingly to a son of the soil', reported Trinidad Leaseholds' house magazine, *Regent News*. There were welcoming parties and a civic reception in Port of Spain Town Hall.

Constantine was now a member of the Senior Staff of Trinidad Leaseholds Ltd. He had been given an expatriate contract, since his agreement had been signed in London. It entitled him to overseas leave at the end of three years. As a senior staff member he moved in predominantly white circles, enjoyed the facilities of the social club and occupied a staff bungalow at number 3 Immortelle Avenue, Pointe-à-Pierre. He received a copy of the staff handbook which told him all that a newcomer should know, and informed him that members of the staff did not 'as a rule' travel on Trinidad government railways and government-owned buses. Here irony lurked in the shadows: government transport would soon become a major political responsibility of his. Among old friends on the senior staff was Reynold Dolly, a medical officer, later a director, and in those days one of the comparatively few Negroes besides Constantine himself to be of senior staff status.

This was the environment in which Constantine began work on 2 January 1955. He was responsible to the legal adviser for studying draft legislation and reporting on its likely effect on the petroleum industry in general and on the Company's operations in particular. He examined notes on title to lands and mineral rights owned or leased by the Company and advised on the validity or otherwise of such title. He helped in the preparation and revision of agreements for way-leaves, rights of way and contracts between the Company and other parties. Lastly, he advised on legal claims made against the Company.

His wider knowledge of Trinidad—despite years of absence—had its uses when legal matters arose beyond the confines of company business. On one occasion, a white senior member of staff, John Smith,* was made the subject of a leading article in one of the island papers. The facts were wrong and totally unsubstantiated. What was said could not be regarded as damaging in a legal sense, but was certainly a cause of embarrassment to Smith—especially when the Press continued to give the matter some attention. Since the articles concerned suggested, among other things, that Smith had accepted an appointment outside the firm, he was called to account by management for infringing company convention. Staff members might not apply for outside posts without the firm's knowledge. Despite Smith's denials of the Press reports, his employers took a 'no smoke without fire' view

* The name of the staff member has been changed in this passage.

and some adverse comments were made. Smith took the matter to Constantine who eventually established the real reasons behind the newspaper articles, assured himself that Smith had been made a scapegoat in what was fundamentally a racial issue, and won a complete printed apology and withdrawal from the Press.

Relations between the Constantines and the white senior staff members were courteous rather than close. After five months, a party given by Learie and Norma in their bungalow had only one white couple in the guest-list. There were probably faults on both sides. The Constantines, understandably, sought to make friends with Trinidadians in the island as a whole. European staff members were, one may surmise, shy rather than indifferent about inviting a distinguished Negro to their house.

Time might have brought a change, but time was given no chance, for Constantine was approached about the possibility of entering Trinidad politics. Again he hesitated about making a change—and not only because he had given his employers an assurance that he would not identify himself with Trinidad politics. The hesitation went deeper. He was not at all sure that he wanted to stay in Trinidad at all. 'I didn't see eye to eye with my countrymen on so many things. As far as they were concerned I had been abroad for twenty-five years living it up, while they had been suffering in conditions where the feeling of oppression was never far away. There was an atmosphere of depression and an understandable frustration about which so many grumbled but took no action.' He even considered going to Ghana and working as a barrister. His friend Joe Appiah, married to the daughter of the English politician, Sir Stafford Cripps, and himself a Negro barrister like Constantine, offered to help him get established. Constantine was in danger of becoming Nobody's citizen—a stateless person in psychological terms for whom Trinidad was an uncomfortable *alma mater* and England a place of refuge for an exile. Would the Africa of his ancestors be any different?

To the first approaches to enter Trinidad politics, he

turned an indifferent ear. Later, when more formal approaches were made—involving chairmanship of a new party and the prospect of fighting for a seat in the Legislative Council—he discussed the matter with the General Manager of Trinidad Leaseholds Ltd, J. B. Christian. Christian was a Scotsman, 'one of the most decent people you could meet anywhere' Constantine once said. Their conversation, as reported by Constantine in a broadcast in later years, went like this:

'I said to Mr Christian that I was now being asked to be chairman of a party and Christian said, "well there's nothing wrong with it because people like you ought to make a contribution to progress in your own country and I wouldn't stand in your way. In fact, Learie, you can go along—you have my blessing." I took the chairmanship. Then I was asked to stand for a constituency. I went to him and he said, "Yes, Learie, go ahead, it's logical. If you win you resign, if you lose, you come back here." I went and I won my seat. Therefore I had to resign from the company. That's how I became a politician.'

He had discussed it with Norma, who said: 'Look, Learie. You know what will make you happy. I know what will make you happy. But I must leave it to you to decide whether you will join the party or not. And if it makes you happy, whatever your decision it will make me happy.' Constantine felt that that was the green light to join the party. His success in being elected as member for the constituency of Tunapuna brought his resignation from Trinidad Leaseholds Ltd* for the second time in his life.

Constantine's happiest hours at Pointe-à-Pierre were spent in helping with cricket. He was ready to coach at Guaracara Park where the Leaseholds Amateur Sports Club was open to staff and employees. There he found young Company employees such as he had been thirty years earlier. There was the same enthusiasm and the same high standard. Trinidad Leaseholds Ltd had given him his chance as a cricketer and

* In 1956 the firm became Trinidad Texaco Inc.

it was a policy which the Company had maintained. That great West Indies bowler of the 1950s, Sonny Ramadhin, had been a Company employee. Constantine also coached at Regent School where children of senior staff went. There were occasional games for Constantine himself, and the delight of getting, on Guaracara Park, his first wicket on Trinidad soil since before the war. He responded in these months at Pointe-à-Pierre in 1955 and 1956 to 'clamorous demands to assume the role of a cricket evangelist', reported *Regent News*; 'the whole of South Trinidad reaped big benefits from his return'. But cricket really belonged to the first innings of his life. Politics would now bring a new turn in the second innings on which he had embarked in 1946.

9

TRINIDADIAN POLITICIAN
1956–1961

Constantine's decision to enter politics brought him into direct touch with the affairs of the island which he had left in 1929 and known only as a visitor thereafter. Much had happened in the quarter-century he had been away.

In 1929 Trinidad's political status and economy were modest. There was only limited election to the Legislative Council, with seven members being returned by an electorate representing 6 per cent of the population. All other members of the Council were nominated by the Governor or were Colonial Office appointees. In this Trinidad was typical of some sixty other British Crown colonies in the period between the two world wars.

The affairs of the island were conducted on a budget which brought in £1,870,000 set against expenditure of £1,613,000. The pressures of a declining world economy were being felt, in particular in the sugar industry. Cocoa was also being affected by witchbroom disease for which abandoned cocoa properties were potential foci. Although oil production was nearly 9 million barrels (which placed Trinidad first in the British Empire), not enough benefit from oil royalties accrued to the island's overall economic and social needs.

Areas in which Constantine was closely involved thirty years later were the subject of attention in 1929. Schemes were afoot for completion of some major roads. The railways, traditionally running at a loss, showed some improvement in 1929. Plans were announced for the purchase of two steamers to replace the *Belize* on the Trinidad–Tobago run. Constantine was to find much of his time occupied with transport problems, especially shipping. By the time he came to office as a minister the two vessels which replaced the *Belize* were themselves to be outworn. What shipping should succeed them was to be a controversial subject in the Legislative Council of the 1950s and 1960s.

During the years 1929 to 1954 Trinidad's political and economic future was to be closely linked to the movement for federation within the West Indies, whose historic origins can be traced back to the seventeenth century. These issues were brought close together when the Moyne Commission was set up in 1938 to examine the need for economic development and a federation within the West Indies. Its adverse report doubted 'the readiness of West Indian opinion to accept federation in principle'. The main problem was posed by varying attitudes within the islands. While discussions and conferences took place in the post-war years,* differing views both among the various territories and within the territories themselves meant that federation in 1954—the year Constantine returned to Trinidad—still lay in the future.

Meanwhile, Trinidad's own political position had undergone some change. Gradually elective principles emerged. Once Trinidad had full adult suffrage, in 1945, the path was clear for the elected members to take the initiative in both the Legislative and Executive Councils. By then, new men were entering politics who played an important part in the growth of national consciousness in the island. Albert Gomes was typical of a new class of politicians of lower-middle-class origins who made a wide appeal as popular spokesmen and who identified themselves with the three interacting forces of federation, economic recovery and political aspirations.

Of all these events, Constantine had been a distant observer, not a participant. No Trinidadians could match his

* The Standing Closer Association Committee was set up in 1947 and was the subject of a London Conference in 1953.

knowledge of English affairs, but he was out of touch with the grass-roots of Trinidad politics. His return to Trinidad coincided with the birth of a new political grouping, the People's National Movement, with which he hesitantly became associated. To enter politics was to enter 'a world I was afraid of' he remarked, but the decision, with Norma's help, was made towards the end of 1955. By January 1956 he was the first chairman of the People's National Movement, a political party whose main figure for the next two decades was to be Dr Eric Williams, a formidable scholar and historian who by 1948 had become Deputy Chairman of the Caribbean Research Council of the Caribbean Commission for economic co-operation. Williams's active concern with the political and educational future of the West Indies had convinced him that the Commission, set up to examine social and economic co-operation, 'was determined to do nothing to promote the cause of West Indian nationalism and the education of the West Indian people', and he left it in 1955.

The People's National Movement aimed at independence for Trinidad within or without the structure of West Indian federalism. Williams himself has described in his book *Inward Hunger: the Education of a Prime Minister* his constitutional hopes for Trinidad in which his ultimate aim was a bicameral legislature and cabinet government, and his presentation of a People's Charter whose cause was not only Trinidadian nationhood but the social and economic policies by which the People's National Movement sought to transform standards of living, education, and agricultural and industrial development. The governing body of the People's National Movement was the General Council whose major office-bearers were elected at the Inaugural Conference in January 1956. The principal office was that of chairman, and to that post Constantine was elected.

Constantine's election was seen by himself as 'giving the party some standing in the world in which I was perhaps best known—though I had never thought that the ability to bowl, bat and field could make me a desirable political commodity. But I accepted the view of my colleagues and took on the job.' His personal standing was not the only factor in his selection. The People's National Movement needed to attract the support of moderate opinion in Trinidad if electoral victory were to be secured. Constantine was seen as a moderate who would conciliate certain elements in the community and broaden the basis of support.

His term of office was five years and his responsibilities were mainly administrative. The General Council, of which Constantine was also the new chairman, had overall responsibility for the efficient functioning of all aspects of the People's National Movement. The men with whom Constantine worked were well-known to him over many years. His deputy-chairman, Wilfred Alexander, together with Patrick Solomon and Andrew Rose, were all associates from his years of post-war study in England. 'We had all been students at one time or another and had probably met and measured out the future of our country many times.' Williams he had first known as a young Oxford undergraduate who had come to spend part of his vacations with the Constantines in Nelson. A light-hearted recollection of Constantine's was Williams's appreciation of beer. 'The kind he liked was German, and this could only be obtained at Clitheroe, twelve miles away. So after my cricket practice was over, we used to jump into the car so that he could get to Clitheroe for his beer.'

While Williams devoted the first nine months of 1956 to the political launching of the new party, Constantine and his colleagues ensured that the People's National Movement was ready, in administrative terms, to meet the electorate. 'He was often tired', recalled a close colleague. 'He would rise at 4 a.m., attend to paperwork for the P.N.M., do a day's work on the staff of Trinidad Leaseholds, and then attend the party meetings.'

By his choice of dedicated and able men Williams went a long way towards ensuring ultimate political success. Solomon, for example, was a doctor who had already played a major role in Trinidad politics but who had lost his seat in the 1950 election. Another colleague was Winston Mahabir, an East Indian doctor. Others were businessmen such as

Gerard Montano, teachers such as John Donaldson, and local officials such as Andrew Carr. If such men brought a combination of political experience and proven ability to Williams's new party, the acquisition of Constantine provided another source of strength because of the prestige role he occupied in Trinidadian minds. The long years away from Trinidad, for which he had his critics, could not detract from his reputation as the most famous cricketer Trinidad had produced. If the doctors* brought one sort of professionalism to the People's National Movement, Constantine brought another: that of a man who had been successful in sport. If these men were to succeed, their task was to persuade a working-class and peasant electorate that they had come to serve the people of Trinidad. Electoral victory in the end depended upon that fact: the means of achieving it lay, above all, in the mesmerism of the leader. Williams, as one of his middle-class supporters wrote in the *Trinidad Guardian* on 18 May 1955, was 'the apostle of revival . . . people of all classes, professions, colours, races, flock to hear him'. It was enough: in September 1956 Williams and the People's National Movement were carried by their supporters to an overwhelming electoral triumph.

In the election the People's National Movement won thirteen out of twenty-four seats, securing an overall majority in the Legislative Council and becoming the first example of party government in Trinidad. The People's Democratic Party—largely Hindu—won five seats, the Trinidad Labour Party two, and the Independents one. Seven parties contested the elections, the People's National Movement alone fighting all the seats and polling 38 per cent of the votes cast. It had been a victory won largely in Negro urban areas, especially in the towns of Port of Spain, San Fernando and Arima. Only in the oilfield area of St Patrick had the party not done well. The Jamaican *Daily Gleaner* called the electoral victory 'a triumph for a man with an ideal'. Some American papers felt that the victory would encourage foreign confidence and bring to Trinidad more investment.

* Williams himself had an Oxford doctorate in Philosophy.

Constantine himself had fought the constituency of Tunapuna, a town in the county of St George, not far from the villages of his childhood. He had owned property in the constituency where he had bought a house for his parents. His major opponent, S. Mathura, the Mayor of Port of Spain, represented the People's Democratic Party. Mathura was a popular figure expected to attract the Indian vote and that of the white middle classes. Constantine pinned his hopes on Negro support. Both men conducted lively campaigns, presenting the electorate for the first time with a sense of party political conflict. The results were:

L. N. Constantine (People's National Movement)	6,622
S. Mathura (People's Democratic Party)	6,443
R. K. Harrack Singh (Independent)	708
Mrs V. Thorpe (Party of Political Progress Groups)	412
M. A. Khan (Trinidad Labour Party)	287

Constantine's majority of 179 was not in itself a true reflection of the considerable victory which his party had won in the election as a whole. Slender or vast, that majority was enough to launch Constantine on yet another stage in his varied career. He formally resigned from Trinidad Leaseholds Ltd and moved to a house in Tunapuna.

The newly elected Legislative Council met on 26 October 1956, for the first time elected its own speaker, and heard the Governor, Sir Edward Beetham, declare the importance of the occasion in the political progress of Trinidad and Tobago.

Williams was elected as chief minister in the new administration and Constantine became minister of communications, works and public utilities. His ministry was answerable for the administration of the Meteorological Service, the Central Water Distribution Authority, Civil Aviation, the Licensing Authority, Port Services, the Post Office, Trinidad Government Railways and Works and Hydraulics. At a later stage he was himself to comment on how much government business lay in his care, and he was glad when some of the responsibility for these various public bodies and services was transferred to other departments. At one point his ministry was responsible for over half of all government expenditure.

The new government set about launching a five-year plan which was eventually to cost almost £248 million and whose implementation was to involve Constantine closely. It was a far cry from the economics of a colony whose annual income in 1929, when he had left it, was under £2 million. Among a host of policies, the government proposed to extend roads, expand electricity services and water supplies, establish an Industrial Development Corporation, subsidise small farmers, build schools and develop the island of Tobago and improve its links with the mainland. Williams also tackled the difficult field of industrial relations, setting up a joint Industrial Council and Boards of Inquiry into disputes.

In this atmosphere of political excitement and endeavour, Constantine, as a new minister, addressed the Legislative Council for the first time on 16 November 1956, when he gave an assurance that he would look into the question of additional street-lighting in some parts of the island. Street-lighting related to the question of road safety, and this was an area in which the new minister had to make his first major contribution in carrying out government policy. There was statistical evidence of increased traffic in the island and a corresponding increase in road accidents. The Government introduced a Motor Vehicles and Road Traffic Bill, the main provisions of which were to regulate parking and to declare one-way streets. There was a long debate on 7 December 1956 in which the Opposition suggested that the measure should be postponed to allow public discussion. Constantine argued that the Bill recognised the present state of public opinion. He discussed the vexed question of taxi-drivers and others who parked indiscriminately, not always using lights; 'the Bill should go through and we shall endeavour to get it through', he declared. 'We do need legislation to correct the reckless attitude of the people who use the highways. If drivers would only consider other users of the roads, the problems would become much easier.' The Bill which duly became law was the first controversial piece of legislation that Constantine had to negotiate through the House. He had taken the first steps towards establishing himself.

On 22 March 1957, Constantine won the approval of the House for the speedy way in which he acted over a water crisis in San Fernando, in the south of the island, which was due to a slipped joint on the trunk main caused by a landslide. The question was raised by a member at 10.15 a.m. and by 5.25 p.m. Constantine was able to present the House with a clear picture of what had happened, and of what had been done to restore the situation to normal.

Later that year Constantine dealt for the first time with an issue which was to recur throughout his period in office, eventually leading him in December 1958 to make an important speech upon the probity of Government and Civil Service. The subject of his concern was the sea communication between Trinidad and Tobago conducted by the two steamers, S.S. *Trinidad* and S.S. *Tobago*. These two vessels, which carried both passengers and cargo, needed to be replaced. Constantine had made efforts in the United States, Canada and other parts of the West Indies to find replacement vessels. A Norwegian ship would have proved suitable, but for technical difficulties in connection with navigation in the tropics. The *City of Port of Spain* was licensed temporarily and Constantine proposed that it should be used for three months while tenders for the construction of a new ship were invited. At the end of three months, Constantine told the House in November 1957 that the ship had been adequate, although there had been a disappointing decline in the number of passengers using the service. The ship's admirable 'drive-on and drive-off' system of cargo-handling had given the Government some guidance in deciding the design and general layout of the new ship. Meanwhile, the decision had been taken to go on chartering the *City of Port of Spain* after it had had an overhaul in a dry-dock in Martinique. For the moment, Constantine had handled with confidence a matter involving some technical complexity.

Early in the New Year of 1958, Constantine made an impassioned speech in the House on an opposition motion, introduced by B. S. Maraj, of 'No Confidence' in the Chief Minister's ability to deal with 'national and international interests'. The attack on Williams had a personal basis as well as a political one, and it led to Constantine declaring that 'the House had become a privileged forum for defamation of character'.

His speech not only showed his sense of loyalty to Williams and to the government of which they were both members. It also revealed increasing concern with the standards of debate in the Legislative Council. Party politics was being shown at its worst, and as an occasion for personal vendettas. He was to return to this theme later in the year when the Government was criticised not only over the affair of the inter-island ships but on broad issues of policy. The Government had sold the two ships S.S. *Trinidad* and S.S. *Tobago*. Although they had been condemned as unseaworthy, the suggestion was made that the *Tobago* had been subsequently made seaworthy. Constantine told the House, in December 1958, of the expert advice the Government had taken and denied accusations that the Government had been swindled. He dealt in detail with the negotiations for selling the ships, quoted the various offers the Government had had, and indicated that the Tenders Board had accepted one of £8,000 for both ships. 'I hope this is the last we shall hear about the S.S. *Trinidad* and the S.S. *Tobago* because all kinds of imputations and suggestions have been made about Government deals with the two ships.' He concluded:

'The suggestion has also been made that there is something dishonest about the *City of Port of Spain*, and I want to assure my colleagues that I have a reputation for probity abroad. I have travelled the five continents and I have been respected and looked upon as a man of integrity, a man that is honest, and I shall be loath to stand in this Council and have members make insinuations and charges against me without registering a solid word of protest. I hope I am not immodest when I say that many people never knew of the West Indies until they got to know of Constantine, and if this is the thanks

I am going to get from the country for the service I have rendered abroad, then I hope I will live long enough to regret the day that I entered into politics.'

The speech had been made in the Budget Debate, and Constantine went on to defend Civil Servants against accusations that there had been 'surcharges on public works and even heavy waste of materials on public projects, and that the cost of Government projects has been inflated by the necessity for contractors making substantial payments, presumably as bribes to public officers. . . . Civil Servants are the people on whom we depend.'

He ended with some remarks that were in line with his speech of ten months earlier:

'I want at this particular time to say that if ever there was a Government that made an effort to do a job properly, this Government is the one. I defy anybody, no matter where he comes from, to point his finger at any minister in this Government and prove by witness or by any other means he considers proper that the Government has been dishonest in any of its dealings. When people from abroad read *Hansard* and find this bankruptcy of thoughts in the Trinidad Legislature, and members doing nothing else but maligning Ministers, they will wonder what kind of people exist in the West Indies. I want to get the records straight. I resent for myself and for all my colleagues any imputations of fraud in any transactions we undertake. Many of us are the worse off for being in politics but it is because we love our country and our people. I hope Hon. Members opposite would be a little more careful about the way they hurl abuse at people.

I hope that a new relationship will be made in 1959 and that all of us will try to understand, and make a contribution, because this is equally as important for the Government as for the Opposition.'

It was the major speech of Constantine's brief political career and it had considerable repercussions for his future. While his colleagues appreciated his tribute to their collective endeavours and honesty, they resented his claim upon Trinidad's thanks 'for the service I have rendered abroad'. Some felt that the speech had reduced his asset to the People's National Movement. His reply to Opposition criticism was within the 'cut and thrust' of debate but did nothing to ease the bitterness of the political scene. Constantine himself began to date his own 'disenchantment with politicians' from this point.

Bitter relations between Government and Opposition had been a marked feature of the two years since the People's National Movement had come to power. There were four reasons for this. In the first place, P.N.P. economic policies were too extravagant for the Opposition. Secondly, the Opposition saw in Williams in particular a dictator with totalitarian ambitions. Thirdly, there was the constant harrying of the Government on grounds of both incompetence and corruption. Fourthly, the Opposition, hopelessly divided within itself and representing only the agglomeration of various defeated parties in the election, with little in common, found their sole identity in attacking the Government. These were the crosses Williams and the People's National Movement had to bear. Constantine was acutely conscious of this. The savagery of Opposition attacks and the depths to which their level of debate sank disturbed him. They explain the pleas he made in his speeches for an improvement in relations between Government and Opposition. He was to comment on this in a broadcast in England in December 1963:

'The worst thing about it was the bitter personal attacks. One might easily come in for an attack even though nothing to do with one's ministry was on that week's agenda. The statements made against me and my integrity so appalled me that I began to dread those Fridays. The things said could never be challenged in a court of law because they were protected by privileges. Politics is certainly a hard game.'

To an observer, there were too-frequent references by himself to his own reputation abroad, for Constantine was not modest in this matter. But his concern for Trinidad's reputation was genuine: if he himself, as a well-known Trinidadian, was held in high repute in the outside world, it saddened him to think that Trinidad's image to outsiders was something less. But he could not see Trinidad as anything other than a small world. 'I had grown up and developed in a large country. I had to restrict my experience in order to cope with my environment.' It was an attitude of mind hardly likely to win him friends in the Legislature. Constantine showed intense loyalty to Williams as party leader of the People's National Movement, because he believed that Williams had the best interests of Trinidad as his constant concern, and because he believed in Williams's ability.

1958 had seen more than merely internal disputes between Government and Opposition. It was the year in which—at last—the Federation had been inaugurated. Trinidad had been selected as the federal capital and Trinidadians shared in a gathering of West Indian public figures never before brought together. The Savannah, scene of Constantine's cricketing boyhood, was the setting in January 1958 for a spectacular firework display. Constantine, a close participant in the events as a minister in the colony's government, was not unaware of the difficulties they posed for Trinidad. The People's National Movement, it was true, was pledged to the support of the Federation with the ultimate goals of an independent West Indian foreign policy and independent West Indian representation in the United Nations, but there were immense problems needing a solution if the association was to prosper and endure. One difficulty upon which Constantine himself commented was the question of effective recruitment of civil servants to the federal structure. He believed that 'the best men should be in at the beginning so that they built a proper foundation', but he was concerned at the loss of talent in the administration of unit-structures.

Just as the Federation had brought change for the West Indies, so Trinidad was affected by constitutional changes which brought self-government nearer. July 1959 saw the introduction of a new constitution by which the chief minister was styled 'premier' and his administration possessed the powers of a responsible government in a way it had not done under the existing constitution. Constantine held a similar portfolio to his previous one.

During the months of September and October 1959, he visited England and Australia. While in England he did some broadcasts, and the internal minutes of the B.B.C. reveal some urgency in getting him to the microphone while he was in the country. His visit to Australia was as a member of the Commonwealth Parliamentary Association. He had not been there since 1931 and he took the opportunity, in a broadcast, to make a plea for the end of Australia's 'white' policy which he called 'outmoded and outdated'. He asked for quotas for African, Asian and West Indian immigrants.

Back again in Trinidad, the visit of the M.C.C. brought some diversion from the tasks of government, though not completely from political undertones. The M.C.C. came to Trinidad in January 1960 having drawn the first Test in Barbados. In Trinidad, the M.C.C. had won both colony matches, one at Port of Spain and the other at Guaracara Park, Pointe-à-Pierre. The second ground was that of Trinidad Leaseholds on whose new turf wicket Constantine had given advice. In the second Test at Port of Spain, by the afternoon of the third day the West Indies had lost eight wickets for 98 in reply to England's 382. Rohan Kanhai, Sobers and F. M. Worrell had made 14 between them. This was the state of play before a crowd of 30,000 when bottles started to be flung on the field. A riot developed and play was suspended for the day. The immediate cause of the incident was the umpiring decision which dismissed a local Trinidadian, Charran Singh, playing in his first Test. *Wisden* assessed the causes as 'probably due to a combination of circumstances; overcrowding on an extremely hot day, drinking and gambling, disappointment over the West Indies' batting collapse'. No doubt these reasons were true. Public figures in Trinidad deplored the outburst. Constantine himself caught a bottle which was coming straight for the head of the Governor of Trinidad—though not specifically directed at him.

Constantine believed he understood the underlying causes

of protest. They expressed the frustration of West Indian cricket linked to West Indian nationalist ambitions. Differences of colour and wealth had been divisive factors in West Indian cricket as in West Indian society as a whole. They had hindered the advancement of West Indies cricket, as Constantine had seen in the 1930s. Gradually such barriers had been broken down within the context of cricket. A West Indies side had won the series in England in 1950. Coloured cricketers from the ranks of the under-privileged were now more than mere performers in the game—as Constantine felt he had been in his career for the West Indies. Men like Worrell and Sobers were beginning to have influence. But there remained the last barrier—the question of captaincy. Constantine had long believed that West Indies cricket would be denied full expression so long as colour determined the captaincy. The crowd at Port of Spain that evening contained those who thought that Worrell must captain the West Indies, although not many bottle-throwers could have expressed the view so clearly. Some would have been ready to find a subconscious desire to beat the English in their own cultural game and to do it with a side of cricketers of colour. Later in the year Worrell had broken that final barrier, when he took the West Indies to Australia in the 1960–1 tour. Constantine in an obituary tribute to Worrell when he died in 1967 wrote that 'his greatest contribution was to destroy for ever the myth that a coloured cricketer was not fit to lead a team. Once appointed, he ended the cliques and rivalries between the players and islands to weld together a team which in the space of five years became the champions of the world.'

Back again in the Legislative Council, Constantine found that he had not heard the last of shipping. It arose again (in 1960) when the Government was subjected to bitter criticism for the low price for which it had sold the *Trinidad* and *Tobago*, and for its chartering rather than purchasing of the *City of Port of Spain*. By chartering the vessel, Constantine told the House, costs of repairs were avoided upon a ship which was not ideally suitable for the purpose and which, when it broke down (as it did) was repaired 'at the expense of the hirer and not at the expense of the Government'. The sea-worthiness of the ship was not in question, only its long-term suitability for the Trinidad–Tobago run. In a long debate, Constantine had defended government policy and during his tenure of the ministry it was not again debated. Before he left office he had the satisfaction of seeing the new vessels, built in fifteen months, in service. He was to say in April 1961: 'the steamers are running satisfactorily and there is nothing too much I can say in congratulating the people who handle the coastal steamers'.

Railways were to cause Constantine fewer political prob-lems than shipping. In an important debate on railways, on 11 November 1960, he outlined the Government's reasons for retaining the existing railway system for a further five years. Trinidad Government Railways, first opened in 1876, consisted in 1960 of some 120 miles of track, 30 locomotives and 42 coaches for passengers. The future of the railways was as much a matter of Government concern as it was in the United Kingdom at the same time, where the policy out-lined by Richard Beeching of axing unprofitable railways was gradually being implemented. Trinidad's problem was somewhat different. In the first place, as Constantine pointed out to the Legislative Council, no alternative transport was available capable of absorbing such large annual passenger traffic. Secondly, the roads could not cope with the bulk of freight. Indeed, some extra building of track had been necessary to ensure that heavy material could go straight from the docks in Port of Spain to a new industrial site near Arima.

While there was a strong case for retaining the railways, the condition of the rolling-stock could not be ignored. Con-stantine stated that of thirty locomotives, seven had already been condemned as useless while some had been in service eighty-four years—since the railway first began. The best coaches—steel-body ones—were over twenty years old; there was some doubt about the safety of twenty-five wood-bogie ones; four-wheel wooden coaches were down to a working four 'described as totally unsafe'. The Government therefore

recommended a policy of repair, where possible, and of pur-
chases. Constantine informed the House that £300,000
should be included in Estimates for 1961 and 1962 for the
purchase of new steel-body coaches, brake vans and diesel
rail car sets, and he proposed to set about purchase as soon as
possible.

Constantine's ministry had faced squarely a major problem, and arrived at decisions which were based on a thorough
enquiry. The future of Trinidad's railways in the mid 1960s
was to lie in other hands. He chose a debate in April 1961 to
give a general survey of what his ministry had accomplished
in the sector of public works:

'It may not be generally known that in the Works Department we do supervision of contracting jobs and we do direct
labour ourselves. We also have a maintenance and a Development Programme. In the Works Department we have had a
very busy time with a limited number of engineers. We have
supervised the building of schools whether they have been
built by contractors, or we have built them by direct labour.'

His Works Department had been a large employer of
labour, using 76,000 people during 1960 on these projects.
In road building alone twenty-eight miles of road had been
constructed since 1956, compared with just under eight miles
in the comparable preceding period of five years. In an
exchange with his predecessor, Ajodhasingh, Constantine
pointed out that not only had four times as much road-
building been undertaken, but it had been done at an
extremely modest cost. Added to this was a major programme
of bridge-building unmatched in previous years. On this
occasion, Constantine held the floor for most of the day's
debate, giving an impressive picture of government responsibility in the areas which were his particular concern.

Some months later, in September 1961, Constantine
turned from railways to buses when he moved a resolution
for the adoption of the Cabinet's proposals on bus transport.
He surveyed the position of public transport in the preceding
ten years which had been operated by various concession-

aires. He had considered the possibility of one single bus
company being formed as a single government concession,
but the various operators had failed to agree on this. He had
called in outside advice from the United States, and, as a
result, had decided that there would continue to be private-
enterprise bus transport with two concessions only. The two
concessions did not work out, and in the end—after Constantine's departure from office—a system of public owner-
ship of bus transport was established. The affair of the bus
concessions proved to be the last significant occasion on
which Constantine addressed the House.

Earlier in the year, Constantine was able to speak on a
non-controversial matter dear to his own heart. In February
1961 he announced the setting-up of a Committee 'to induce
West Indian cricketers to return to the native heath'. The
government hoped that the committee would consider ways
of attracting West Indians back to the country by making
proposals which would lead to the 'provision of suitable employment opportunities commensurate with the dignity of
their cricketing achievements, and the elevation of cricketing
standards in the West Indies'. Constantine was appointed
chairman and his colleagues included distinguished West
Indian cricket administrators and players in C. A. Merry,
V. H. Stollmeyer, L. Pierre and N. Asgarali. 'Human nature
is a copyist', Constantine told the House; 'seeing Sobers,
Kanhai and Hall will surely help to produce another Kanhai,
Sobers and Hall.' Despite the best of intentions, nothing came
of this plan. The only way professionalism could have been
maintained in the West Indies was by the appointment of
coaches, and there was a limit to the number of these who
could be sustained.

If Constantine was seeking a way of bringing cricketers
back to the West Indies, he himself was about to go on his
travels again. In 1960 further constitutional changes had
promised Trinidad full internal self-government in 1961. At
the close of that year, on 4 December 1961, a general election
took place to choose thirty members of the House of Representatives under the new constitution. The election, which

the People's National Movement won, was to some extent fought on the achievements of the government in domestic matters such as communications, much of which had been due to Constantine's work as a minister. Yet he himself was not a candidate. Several months earlier he had decided to leave politics and he had been contemplating legal work in Trinidad when he was asked to go to London as Trinidad's first High Commissioner.

Constantine's appointment as High Commissioner was in part a consequence of events affecting the Federation. Only three and a half years after its inauguration in Trinidad, the association was on the edge of dissolution. The appointment of a High Commissioner to London by the Trinidad Government was an assertion of independence by a unit member of the Federation, and a tacit admission of the fact that the Federation had no prospect of survival. By May 1962 it had formally ceased to exist. To examine the reasons for its collapse would be a lengthy task and beyond the boundaries of this book.* The overall reason was the separation of the islands themselves. In cricket alone had the West Indies presented a united front. Constantine himself knew how weak even that front could be when it came to the selection of Test-match teams in relation to island prejudices. Jamaica's secession from the Federation was followed by that of Trinidad, which became independent in August 1962. There we must leave events in Trinidad, launched in 1962 upon an independent nationhood of which Constantine was to be first an overseas representative and then an overseas observer. His intimate association with the island of his birth ceased.

What was the significance of Constantine's political activity in these years? He was undoubtedly handicapped by various factors. He did not really like being a politician; as he once remarked, 'political leaders squeeze the last bit of energy and effort out of you'. He admitted that the work was heavy; he was, indeed, several years older than any of his colleagues. Secondly, he would not allow himself to forget

* They are discussed in Eric Williams, *Reflections on the Caribbean Economic Community*, P.N.M. Publishing Company, Port of Spain, 1965.

his English experience. Political colleagues were aware of this and political opponents made capital out of it. As he himself said of one such opponent in a broadcast discussion in 1959: 'he lambasted me as an Englishman'. To the question, 'Were you regarded as a detribalised Trinidadian?' Constantine replied simply, 'Yes'. Thirdly, Constantine was disillusioned about politics. He had an intense concern with political honesty and disinterested action. He sought to 'make people alive to responsibility' and he believed that much had been accomplished, but he thought that the efforts required to create a thoroughly acceptable atmosphere of political responsibility and of society's recognition of that responsibility detracted too much from time which should have been devoted to the fundamentals of governing. Fourthly, he was not free from the jealousy of those who were ready to use his reputation but resented the credibility of his political achievements as a minister. Fifthly, he took no interest in political theories, and was content with the pragmatism of government. Finally, Constantine was not tough enough to be a politician. He was less able to take criticism than other ministers, and he allowed the rough and tumble of politics to disturb him.

Nevertheless his identification with the People's National Movement attracted wide support to the party in 1956. His well-proven ability to work with people had resulted in happy relations with his civil servants so that he had produced concrete results in his ministry and coped with problems, such as shipping, railways and buses, which had tested politicians wiser than he. By his concentration on domestic matters, he had freed other ministers to deal with the implications of Federation. If he was not an initiator, he had 'gone along', remarked a cabinet colleague, with the proposals of others and had not in that sense been an embarrassment to political colleagues. As a speaker his speeches had been lucid, sufficiently supported with facts, and relevant—qualities which others did not always demonstrate. He spoke effectively but was less successful when participating in debate. He had stood for purity in politics, and by his own example had done much to bring it about. To a political opponent, Albert Gomes, Minister of Industry and Commerce before the 1956 elections,

'he was of inestimable service to the People's National Movement at a crucial time in Trinidad's history when there was a popular movement for political change. His immense popularity as a West Indian figure certainly contributed enormously to the success of the People's National Movement and this, in turn, inaugurated quite clearly a new period in Trinidad's development.'

Yet, Constantine left politics with few regrets.

10

HIGH COMMISSIONER
1961-1964

At a luncheon on 14 June 1961 in the Guildhall in the City of London, the office of the High Commissioner for Trinidad and Tobago was formally inaugurated. In defining the nature of the office, the prime minister of Trinidad said that it was to promote investment in Trinidad, and to provide tourists with information. While the Federation survived and Trinidad did not yet have independence, the office was not seen as having any diplomatic importance. That evening at a reception at 10 Stratton Street, close to Piccadilly, Trinidad and Tobago's first High Commissioner, Learie Constantine, met his guests. He later returned to Trinidad, resigned his portfolio as a minister, and prepared to leave for England. In the New Year Honours of January 1962 the new High Commissioner was knighted.

The choice of Sir Learie Constantine as first High Commissioner was both predictable and popular. He was now a man of standing by virtue of his own personal qualities. He had wide contacts in Britain where he had lived for all but a few of the preceding thirty years. 'When I got to London I found that the doors which had been open to me as an individual years before were still open', he remarked. Although this recognition was basically an asset to him in representing the affairs of his country, there were pitfalls in having so vast a following. To the Press, Constantine was news-value. Other diplomats might go about their business in comparative obscurity: Constantine was inevitably in the limelight. This factor, in the end, contributed to the brevity of his term in office. By the nature of things, Constantine was not a career diplomat. He had to learn quickly the essentials of his new job and had no one to teach him. The presence of an experienced deputy would have been an undoubted advantage.

The post of High Commissioner requires its holder to maintain good relations with the government to which he is accredited, to have direct contact with members of that government and to know whom he ought to meet on various matters. He should be in close touch with other members of the Diplomatic Corps. In relation to his own country, a High Commissioner must see himself as the representative in London of every government department of his own country, and be concerned with the welfare and interests of the nationals of that country. Constantine's own view of the post was this:

'It is like being a Public Relations Officer of the highest possible status. One tries to sell one's country to the outside world. Part of this Public Relations function consists in going to diplomatic parties. . . . The real burden of the High Commissioner's job is fending for the interests of one's own countrymen in Britain. With so many more West Indians here now than there were ten years ago the problems have multiplied.'

Constantine found himself involved in both formal and informal events. He attended a Thanksgiving Service in Westminster Abbey in August 1962 in connection with the Independence celebrations of Trinidad and Tobago. In November 1962 he was received in audience by Her Majesty the Queen. He also took pleasure in being elected a vice-president of the West India Committee. This historic body provided in its offices a meeting-place where High Commissioners and others might discuss matters of social and economic importance common to the West Indies.

In January 1963, Constantine as High Commissioner took a close interest in events in connection with the arrest of two West Indians who were accused of stealing a car. The men concerned, a barrister and a schoolmaster, at once consulted Sir Learie, who instructed solicitors to act. At the proceedings in the London Sessions in March they were acquitted. Allegations were made that the case 'was a trumped-up charge against two coloured men occupying responsible positions'.

Constantine advised them to take out a civil writ against the two policemen who had arrested them, and they brought an action for compensation for false imprisonment and malicious prosecution. Notice of this intention was given during Constantine's High Commissionership. He sensed a potentially explosive situation between police and West Indians and, by his presence in court and his subsequent guidance to the men, indicated his concern.

The civil case was heard in February 1966 with Sir Peter Rawlinson appearing for the men and seeking a substantial sum. Damages were awarded totalling £8,000 in a case which attracted widespread attention in the Press. By then, of course, Constantine was no longer High Commissioner, but as a practising barrister he watched the outcome with a professional eye. His initial interest in the affair at the start probably isolated it from the risk of a hostile relationship emerging between West Indians in London and the police.

In April 1963, he was asked to go to the B.B.C. studios to see a film on Trinidad. No sooner had the performance begun than cinema gave way to theatre, and he was invited on to the stage as the star of the show 'This is your Life'. Gradually Eamonn Andrews unfolded the story of Learie Constantine's life through the dialogue, film and—most important—the introduction of those who had known him. Norma, his wife, talked about their first meeting and the time he spent on cricket rather than on her. Gloria, his daughter—flown from Trinidad—described her father's attempts to plait her hair when he was left in charge in Nelson days. He was the less strict parent! Elias, his brother, also flown from Trinidad, remembered the endless games of cricket with oranges or coconuts for a ball. Mrs Bessie Braddock, Member of Parliament for Liverpool Exchange arrived to say that in his wartime days as a welfare officer Constantine had shown 'all the tact in the world, and commonsense as well'. I. A. R. Peebles, the old England cricketer, called him 'the best entertainer of the lot'. From Manchester came John Kirk, who had been one of those who had urged the Nelson agreement in 1928—'Learie, you could have been Mayor of Nelson', he exclaimed. Betty Snowball, the England woman cricketer, praised his coaching of her, and Winifred Attwell, the Negro pianist, described how stage-struck she had been when she first met him. The prime minister of Trinidad, Eric Williams, paid tribute in a filmed contribution. All in all, it was an evening of 'extravagant nostalgia', as Constantine described it.

More nostalgia came a few days later when he received the freedom of Nelson. He and Lady Constantine returned to the town in Lancashire which they had left fourteen years earlier. They were extremely warmly received by the population although it was over a quarter of a century since many had seen Sir Learie play at Seedhill. The Mayor presented an illuminated scroll and a silver salver to the new Freeman. Among those who spoke was Councillor John Greenwood, a player from the cricketing days of the 1930s and later Chairman of Nelson Cricket Club. Old players such as Harold Hargreaves were among the guests who attended the ceremony in the Council Chambers and the dinner and social evening in the civic centre thereafter. During the ceremony Alderman John Shepherd said: 'If the title of a great man ought to be reserved for him who cannot be charged with indiscretion or a vice, who succeeded in all he undertook, and whose successes were never won at the expense of honour, justice, integrity, nor by the sacrifice of a single principle, then this title will not be denied to Sir Learie Constantine.' Constantine's reply was well judged. He brought laughter when he told them that they had done all this 'for the little dark fellow who came from a country they knew nothing about'.

Back in London in the following week, Constantine gave a lunch-time talk on cricket at the Royal Commonwealth Society. In introducing him, E. W. Swanton described him as one who 'excited and charmed and entranced and infuriated us all on the cricket field'. After talking on coaching, Constantine referred to South Africa's place in the cricket world:

'If I could go to South Africa and play as a coloured man and I could invite South Africa to my country to play, as a coloured country, then I would have been sorry that South Africa left the Commonwealth. But black men cannot go to South Africa to play.'

He then turned to the question of the captaincy of West Indies sides:

'This year Worrell has been appointed captain, the wisest of all West Indian thinkers, at the edge of his retirement. But other people less talented than himself, less knowledgeable have been selected as captain before because we had a South African attitude in the West Indies.'

Some of those present felt it was not the occasion to put the West Indian captaincy in the context of colour, but Constantine had always felt that West Indies cricket had suffered because of the policy up till 1960 of passing over coloured cricketers for the captaincy except for himself in the closing stages of a Test match in 1935 and Headley in one Test in 1948.

Worrell had just arrived that month as captain of the 1963 West Indies side. The tourists played their first match at Worcester. Their second was against Gloucestershire at Bristol, where Constantine's presence involved him in what proved to be a controversial aspect of his High Commissionership. To understand the events associated with his visit to Bristol, it is necessary to consider something of the background to West Indian immigration into Britain.

Constantine's period of office coincided with the increased immigration into Britain of Trinidadians and other West Indians. During the years he had been living in Trinidad he had seen the other side of the story: an outward flow of emigrants from the Caribbean, because of a shortage of opportunities for industrial and urban employment. Those who had come to Britain had gone to cities such as London, Birmingham, Nottingham and Bristol, where they had largely been employed in public transport services, hotels and hospitals. In August 1958 uneasy relations between West Indians and British in the overcrowded Notting Hill area of London flared up into riots which led to a visit to Britain by leading ministers of various West Indian territories. At the heart of the matter was the considerable increase in numbers which caused fears among the British of redundancy in employment and shortage of accommodation. By the end of 1958 there were 115,000 West Indians in Britain. All this had relevance for Constantine in his work as High Commissioner. Indeed, in the original manuscript of the passage quoted on page 180 he had written, 'The real burden of the High Commissioner's job—*and the part which I like*—is fending for the interests of one's own countrymen in Britain.' No doubt it was sensible while in office not to cite a preference for any one area of his duties as High Commissioner, but the phrase is revealing in the light of what followed.

Constantine's visit to Bristol to watch the touring West Indians play Gloucestershire came just after reports in the Press on 1 May 1963 that a West Indian had recently been refused employment in Bristol as a bus conductor. Constantine at once wrote to the Bristol Omnibus Company about the allegation and made plans to visit Bristol over the weekend when the West Indian cricket tourists were playing. It was announced from his office that he was going to Bristol 'for cricket only' but speculation at once arose as to the real nature of his visit. On Saturday, 4 May, West Indians made up a large part of the crowd of 7,000 who watched the cricket. Constantine stayed with friends in Clifton for the weekend and returned to the match on Monday 6 May. He made a statement to reporters deploring the decision of the Bristol Omnibus Company not to employ coloured bus crews. 'For it to be happening in Bristol of all places is even worse,' he said, 'when you remember that the West Indian sugar cane industry has helped, through the slaves sent from this country, to make Bristol great.' He went on to criticise the policy of the Bristol Company when he said: 'The evidence is quite clear that in the Bath branch of the Company coloured people are employed as bus crews, and it cannot be right on ethical grounds for there to be one policy for Bath and another for Bristol.'

Meanwhile other spokesmen were being heard. The chairman of the government-controlled Transport Holding Company which had managerial responsibility for the Bristol Omnibus Company announced that a colour bar was no part of his firm's policy and that Company employees were recruited on merit. The Bishop of Bristol, Dr Oliver Tomkins, preaching on Sunday, 5 May, at Christ Church, Swindon, declared: 'How racial integration can be realised is often a complicated business, calling for great patience and mutual understanding. Few moral conflicts are ever simple.' Unwittingly, the bishop echoed the war-time views of the League of Coloured Peoples when he continued: 'White workers have no right to denounce racial discrimination in South Africa or the Southern United States and then practise it in England.'

That same weekend, Paul Stephenson, leader of the West Indies Development Council, had organised a protest demonstration, which attracted singularly few supporters, and the Regional Secretary of the Transport and General Workers' Union had had talks with the chairman of the Bristol West Indies Association. Constantine was persuaded to speak on a B.B.C. programme when he admitted that the problem might be basically not one of colour but 'of a fear by bus employees that more workers would mean less opportunities for overtime'. He left Bristol after the match, having had the satisfaction of seeing the West Indians beat Gloucestershire by 65 runs.

Back in his office in London he issued a statement saying that he was happy at the developments that were taking place to resolve the matter. Later in the summer agreement was reached between the Bristol Omnibus Company and the Transport and General Workers' Union on the employment of coloured bus crews. Subsequently, Constantine contributed an article to a Bristol newspaper on the absorption of West Indians into Britain, in which he said:

'Do these persons who advocate reserving all their jobs for white people agree to the reasonable corollary that British people working in the coloured Commonwealth should receive the same treatment? More deplorable is the fact that this sanction is imposed because of colour only, since foreigners who cannot be readily identified by the colour of their skins are always welcome.'

Four questions may be asked about Constantine's part in the affair. Should he have gone to Bristol at all? Was he wise to comment once he was in the city? Should he have left matters alone thereafter? What else might he have done?

He should probably not have gone to Bristol. There were many other occasions later in the season on which he could have seen the West Indians—they were playing at Cambridge in the next match and at Lord's ten days later. His presence inevitably raised speculation. But once in Bristol, he could hardly avoid talking. He was hoist with the petard of his own fame. Reporters knew him as an impulsive spokesman. He was bound to find himself commenting on the affair. The writing of an article later in the Press—whatever were the rights and wrongs of his arguments—was not part of the role of a High Commissioner. To the fourth question—what else might he have done?—one may return the answer: acted differently. A career diplomat would have been no less concerned but he would have found other ways of acting. Constantine had been 'too sensitive and outspoken', commented a Trinidadian observer, 'to steer clear of the pitfalls of diplomacy'. He had been a victim of his own reputation. His actions were news.

His own view of the matter was expressed in a broadcast on 24 December 1963, in a talk 'No Stranger Here':

'It was while I was recovering from an attack of bronchitis and watching the West Indies play Gloucestershire at Bristol that I got dragged into the Bristol bus dispute. It had been openly stated that no coloured person would be employed either as a conductor or as a driver of a bus in the City of Bristol. I was asked to look into the trouble and quickly decided to raise the level of the negotiations because those immediately involved had adopted fixed positions and wouldn't budge. I went to the Mayor, and then I returned to London to see Frank Cousins whom I had known well—and indeed been friends with—since working in the Ministry of Labour. I knew that his Union was against a colour bar and I know that the Transport Board were against a colour bar, so it was clearly a matter of asking them to enforce their own convictions. This they did. We now have coloured conductors and motormen on the buses in Bristol.'

Constantine had meant well, though it is doubtful if he was 'dragged' into the dispute. A leading article in *The Times* put the Bristol affair into historical perspective. There was a need to consider the moral responsibility owed to new peoples if the Britain of the decade to come was to be a good place to live in. 'It was', concluded the writer, 'a sensitive and all too menacing field.' Sadly, Constantine was in the news for quite different reasons at the same time when thieves stole his Knight-Bachelor insignia from his home in Grove End Road. It was never recovered.

During that summer of West Indies cricket in England he was frequently in evidence on the cricket scene. In June he was present at the annual match between the National Book League and Authors. He spoke briefly at a lunch given in connection with the match, acknowledging his own debt to the literature of cricket and expressing a concern that cricket would not be played on 'assembly line' methods in the future. To Constantine, the flamboyant professional, the modern game was too precise in its demands on players. He was aware that as a spectator-sport the game was going through an adverse period. He was determined that West Indian cricket, at any rate, should do something to stem this tide and to bring back the crowds. Later, as a television commentator on Sunday matches, he made his own contribution to a revival of interest in the game. The chance to play himself came in August when he returned to the Seedhill Ground at Nelson to play in a match to raise funds for the club. The weather was appalling. No play was possible on the Saturday, and a game of sorts took place on a wet Sunday. Constantine, remarked a spectator, 'showed some of his old ability and timed the ball well.' After the match he wrote to the Secretary of Nelson:

'It was nice to play again at Seedhill after so many happy years. What memories were conjured up in such a short stay. To have been given the chance to help my old club when in need is a privilege and an honour. That the returns were not more substantial is my only regret. My thanks to all who helped to make our stay so enjoyable.'

The sum of £127 had been raised for club funds. There had been a day during the Depression when 8,000 people paid sixpence each to give Nelson a gate of £200. Constantine realised sadly that League cricket no longer drew the crowds it had done before the war.

Soon afterwards, he announced that he did not propose to continue in office as High Commissioner on the completion of his first-two year term. He denied that his resignation was due to reports that he had interfered in a matter of British domestic politics or that he had overstepped the bounds of normal diplomatic behaviour in his zeal to champion the cause of coloured Commonwealth immigrants in Britain. 'Whatever complaints were made', he said, 'were taken up between the Commonwealth Office and myself, and no third party was involved.' In October, he repeated in an address to a Rotary Club the denial that he had had any difference of opinion with the British Government. His resignation, he said, was for domestic reasons. Turning away from his own affairs, Constantine told that same gathering that he hoped British industry would invest in Trinidad since this would contribute to the island's economic growth and absorb more people in employment. He hoped Britain's links with the Commonwealth rather than with the new European Economic Community would be developed. He urged the large 'white' Commonwealth territories of Canada and Australia to absorb people from the over-populated countries—returning to a theme he had taken up when in Australia three years earlier.

By now the West Indian cricketers had departed. The summer was over and only a few months remained until the High Commissioner took his leave of Her Majesty the Queen on 6 February 1964.

The year 1963 had also brought the honour of being elected an Honorary Bencher of the Middle Temple, a distinction conferred on men of eminence 'whom the Benchers would like to dine with them from time to time'. 'It was unprecedented for a very junior barrister, who had been called to the bar only nine years earlier, to be so elected', commented a member of the Inn.

When Constantine took his own leave of the staff who had served him so well he made no reference to the reasons for his departure. It was a sad leave-taking. Those present had a feeling that things had not worked out as well for Trinidad's first High Commissioner as they might have done. 'We are good starters, but poor finishers' was the somewhat enigmatic remark he made in an aside to one of them. He had already made reference in the late summer to his resignation, and he had done so again in more detail in his broadcast talk, 'No Stranger Here'. On the successful outcome of the Bristol affair he said:

'That is a happy situation, but unfortunately, although my part in bringing it about was a minor one, I got into trouble with my own Government. You may have heard that I am leaving the High Commission very soon and now is hardly the time to explain why. Suffice it to say that amongst other things my Government felt that I had exceeded my duties during the Bristol affair and that I should have recognised it as an internal matter for Management and Unions and refused to intervene. That may be right, and I am sure that once I am rid of the protocol and conventions of the office of High Commissioner I shall be able to do a better job for my countrymen. My wife and I will certainly stay on in England.'

There Constantine was content to leave matters. Some years later he again referred to the affair in another Christmas Eve broadcast. This was in 1967 when interviewed by Rex Alston in the B.B.C. programme, 'Time of my Life'. The following dialogue took place:

Constantine: 'I thought I was doing a good job, but then other people have other views, and the arm of the politician is as long as that of the policeman, and when I thought it was going to reach me here, I thought, no. I got out of politics, I'm going to get out of diplomacy and I did.'

Alston: 'But you went back home first, didn't you?'

Constantine: 'Yes, I went back home. I had a disagreement with my Prime Minister and I went back home to get an assurance from him, and he wouldn't see me. I came back here and I resigned.'

Alston: 'You must have had plenty of opportunities of helping your fight for your people?'

Constantine: 'Oh yes, tremendous.'

Alston: 'Any particular one you'd like to mention?'

Constantine: 'I got in trouble for going to Bristol and interfering in a bus dispute. The dispute was that a Trade Union man there didn't want to employ coloured people as drivers or conductors, and somebody started a strike amongst the coloured people, or at least influenced the strike, and the white people decided to go on strike if coloured people were employed. I had a little experience during the war. I was in the welfare section of the Ministry of Labour and I used that knowledge to intervene and to save the situation, so the situation was saved, thanks to some help from Frank Cousins, and the Mayor of Bristol at the time. This matter was solved and then I found I was criticised by my Government because the people concerned were Jamaicans and I took the view that when a coloured man in London is getting his pants kicked, the people who kick his pants don't remember he is Jamaican or Trinidadian or St Lucian. It's a coloured man who's getting kicked and so for my Government to take the view that because he was a Jamaican I had no right to intervene, I could not accept.'

Four months after that broadcast, on 27 April 1968, he again alluded to his resignation in his Rectorial address to the University of St Andrews:

'I was certain that precedents could be established for a happier association of coloured citizens and the English. This brought me in conflict with my own Government who drew a distinction between a coloured Trinidadian and a coloured Jamaican and I resigned. I felt I was specially suited to do this job, for the English and myself enjoyed a degree of mutual trust and confidence.

Such were Constantine's views of the circumstances surrounding his departure from the High Commissionership. The significant point implied in one broadcast had been his reference to 'disagreement' with the prime minister of Trinidad. On this, one may suppose that Williams may have felt he had appointed something of a stormy petrel to office when a more anonymous figure might have been allowed to look after Trinidad's interests with less pressure from the Press and public opinion. Williams had sounded a note of caution in what he expected from the Office of the High Commissioner —admittedly before Independence—at its inauguration in June 1961. Constantine had exceeded that brief in 1963. Williams probably did little to stop Constantine from resigning and allegedly refused to see him in Trinidad.

The relationship between Williams and Constantine suffered an eclipse, the sadder because of their close association in the founding of the People's National Movement Party. Their paths were not to cross again in Constantine's lifetime. Williams later recognised what Trinidad owed to

Constantine when he recommended him posthumously for Trinidad's highest decoration, the Trinity Cross, in 1971.

How good a High Commissioner was Constantine? In his relations with his staff, he was successful. They appreciated the humanity of their first High Commissioner. A dozen of them set up the new office and organised the physical tasks of getting furniture moved into place, and files opened. They did this first in Stratton Street and then in South Audley Street. From the start, a 'family' atmosphere prevailed. Constantine was known as 'Sir Learie' rather than 'His Excellency' without any loss of dignity. The staff with their own personal problems of accommodation in London and adjustment to Britain found Constantine ready to listen and to help if he could. If charity begins at home, then Constantine practised this virtue. Once his staff were happy and settled, the office could devote itself to the needs of West Indian nationals as a whole. Constantine came to the office of High Commissioner with plenty of experience of managing staff. He had confidence in his subordinates from the start and did not interfere in the day-to-day business of the office. His concern for them was a factor in the decline in his relations with his government in Trinidad. He felt that the embassy in London ranked low in the list of priorities with which the new independent government in Trinidad was busily concerned. He was not happy at the salary-structure of his staff and wanted that to receive attention.

Possibly, he should have paid more attention to the work of the office. He was careless with time, and paperwork was sometimes set aside in the interests of people. His jealous concern with the ordinary West Indians in Britain meant that such individuals were apt to take up too much of his attention when they called at the office. Any 'lame duck' found him ready to listen. There were subordinates on his staff who could have dealt with such visitors and let the High Commissioner deal with the business of the moment.

He was highly respected by his colleagues in the diplomatic corps, one of whom thought his 'eminently fitted for the post'; he won the devotion of his staff and he continued to be acceptable to the British public. He was a suitable person to be High Commissioner when a West Indian cricket team was playing in England before so many of its own supporters. 'To have let him go was a mistake', commented another member of the diplomatic corps. Yet the evidence for arguing that he was a successful High Commissioner remains sketchy. In the one area in which he acted positively, he blundered—the Bristol affair. In the language of the game he loved, one might suggest that his timing was wrong though he was full of good intentions. To his office he brought certain known qualities which served him well but he added nothing to his stature or reputation during the term in which he held it.

II

THE LAST YEARS
1964-1971

Soon after he resigned from the High Commissionership, Constantine and his wife moved from Grove End Road to a flat in Kendal Court, Shoot-up Hill, London NW3. This was his home for the rest of his life. At the same time, he entered the Chambers of Sir Dingle Foot at 2 Paper Buildings, The Temple. It was a practice which gave some of its attention to appeals from colonies to the judicial committee of the Privy Council and undertook a certain amount of Commonwealth business as a whole. The work was largely criminal. Dingle Foot had first met Constantine when they shared a platform early in the 1950s at a meeting in protest against the handing over of Protectorate territories in Southern Africa to the(then) Union of South Africa. They kept in touch over the years, and when Constantine ceased to be High Commissioner he approached Foot about joining his Chambers. To enter upon a professional career at the age of sixty-two was extremely unusual, but Constantine managed, in Foot's judgement, 'to achieve a respectable junior practice'. At his age, one can hardly speak of a promising career opening up, but one may surmise that it would have become more extensive had not ill-health in the mid 1960s and onwards seriously curtailed his activities. Constantine's work at the Bar, limited as it was, meant the fulfilment of an ambition. Even if the solicitor's office in the 1920s was something of a drudgery, and the Bar examinations in the 1940s and 1950s a nightmare, he had always hoped he might one day become a lawyer.

During 1964 Constantine made his last few appearances as a cricketer. He was sixty-one years of age when he played for the Authors *v.* the National Book League (see p. 128) and shortly afterwards, on 26 July, for a Cricket Writers XI raised by E. W. Swanton. Others in the latter side were R. W. V. Robins, Richie Benaud and A. V. Bedser. The match, against Didsbury, was for the benefit of Tommy Greenhough. A Didsbury player remembered him 'despatching a half-volley over the boundary between deep mid-wicket and deep mid-on. The ball pitched at least twenty-five yards beyond the edge of the boundary—a tremendous shot for a young man, never mind a man of around sixty years of age.'

Two months later he played for The Bushmen, as Maurice Latey of the B.B.C. recalled:

'The Bushmen were a touring team based on the B.B.C. External Services at Bush House. We managed to prevail upon Learie to play for us on September 20 against the village of Great Missenden and bowl some of his leg breaks. When the Bushmen innings came I was soon out succumbing to a diabolical bowler of in-swing. Learie said :"I'll show you how to deal with that", and he did; putting his leg down the wicket and sweeping with a very short back-swing. He hit two colossal sixes and four fours in an innings of thirty-five in five or ten minutes. This was enough to persuade Constantine to make one more final appearance the following week against the village of Herongate in Essex on 27 September 1964. He made something like thirty in very quick time before being given out by a Bushmen umpire, much to the resentment of the local populace who had come to see him bat.'

So ended at the age of sixty-two—for his birthday had fallen between the Great Missenden and Herongate matches—the playing career of Constantine. Thereafter, his interest in cricket was maintained in many other ways. He had encouraged from the start the Wombwell Cricket Lovers

Society and was one of its early members and speakers. He and Sir John Barbirolli, the conductor of the Halle Orchestra, Manchester, were elected patrons of the Society. Sir John was a Lords Taverner, as was Constantine—members of a select band with an enthusiasm for the game elected for services to the arts or to cricket. When Sir Frank Worrell died in 1967, Constantine suggested the introduction of a Memorial Trophy to be given by the Society for the best player in Test matches between England and the West Indies, and the award has become a regular feature of these series. When Constantine himself died, the Society introduced the Learie Constantine Memorial Award for the best fielder in the Gillette Cup Final at Lord's. It was fitting that the first winner in 1972 should be Clive Lloyd, a fellow West Indian, whose reactions, powerful throwing and hard hitting were reminiscent of Constantine himself. Another society which elected him to membership was the Lancashire and Cheshire Cricket Society, whose members appreciated the long journey in wintry weather he had made to talk to them when he was High Commissioner.

It was announced on 4 February 1965 that a Sports Council had been set up to advise the British Government on the development of amateur sport and of physical recreation services. Denis Howell a junior minister in the Department of Education and Science and a former Football Association referee, was appointed chairman with Sir John Lang, a retired senior civil servant, as his deputy. Of the fifteen members appointed, Constantine was one. Howell had nominated Constantine because of his intimate knowledge of sport and because he knew that Constantine believed sport had an important part to play in creating an integrated community in Britain.

Much of the early work of the Council was directed towards the setting up of Regional Sports Councils bringing together Local Education Authorities and various sports bodies. This involved much travel within the British Isles and it proved an area where Constantine was of great service to the Sports Council. With the chairman, he would travel to conferences where his presence 'helped to secure us good-will from the start', as Howell recalled.

Constantine's services were also used on the Council's Coaching and Development Committee where his major contribution lay in helping to get the balance right between providing coaches and destroying natural ability. He would listen to proposals and his voice of experience would assess their practical value. Another of his concerns was the provision of playing space where children might be free to play games without having to spend money on travel or be hampered by undue restrictions on their activities. He remembered both the freedom of his own childhood in Maraval, and the limitations upon children's playgrounds in the industrial Lancashire he knew later.

Until the last year or so of his life, he was a regular attender at meetings of the Council and its sub-committees, and his contribution to this important development in the British Government's approach to sport was considerable. It was something which he had hoped to establish in a much more modest way in Trinidad in 1961 while a minister, but nothing had come of his proposals.

Constantine as a younger man had never been especially concerned with affairs in the continent of Africa. Only in the 1940s, through his closer association with the League of Coloured Peoples and through his work with West Africans in Liverpool, was his interest aroused. It was sustained in the 1950s, as his appearance on platforms in connection with Seretse Khama showed, and again in the mid-1960s when events in Nigeria led him to fly out to the land of his ancestors.

In 1966 tension between the tribal groups in Nigeria led to the kidnapping of the Federal prime minister, Sir Abubakar Tafawa Balewa, a member of the Hausa tribe, by Ibo army officers. The military coup seized power on 18 January, and this provided the prelude to bitter divisions, the secession of the Eastern Region, and civil war.

Amnesty International at once sent a cable to General J. T. U. Aguiyi-Ironsi who had retained control of the army:

DEEPLY DISTURBED PROSPECT OF FURTHER KILLINGS
OF POLITICAL LEADERS STOP ASK YOU TO TAKE STEPS
TO PROTECT LIVES OF ABUBAKAR BALEWA AND CHIEF
AWOLOWO AND THEIR COMPANIONS STOP HAVE
ARRANGED FOR SIR LEARIE CONSTANTINE TO BE AVAIL-
ABLE TO FLY TUESDAY TO LAGOS OR DOUALA FOR TALKS
ON MEASURES TO PRESERVE LIFE.

Constantine left London late on the night of Wednesday,
19 January. His instructions were to find out what had
happened to the kidnapped Federal premier, to act on
behalf of Amnesty International for all political prisoners,
and to seek the release of Chief Awolowo. He arrived at
Lagos at midnight on 20 January and was allowed, after
encountering one military barricade, to go to the Federal
Palace Hotel.

The next morning he told the Press that he hoped 'to be
of some use . . . I know most Nigerian leaders. I will go
anywhere and meet anyone if it will help.' Repeated in-
quiries about Balewa's fate produced no response, and by the
end of the week it was known that he had been assassinated
on the day of the coup. Constantine failed to see Ironsi
(subsequently also killed) but obtained an interview with the
Chief Justice, Sir Ade Ademola, whom he knew, and with the
Deputy Permanent Secretary for External Affairs, L. O.
Harriman. Constantine reported in a letter to Amnesty International, 'the chances of Awolowo's case being re-
examined are excellent and I hope to see him in prison at
Calabar'. The rest of his visit was devoted to assessing events
by seeing people at the University of Ibadan and delivering
a letter to Awolowo, though not seeing him. Constantine felt
able to assure the imprisoned Chief, after his talks with the
Chief Justice, that his case might come up for review in the
not too distant future and to tell him that old friends continued to take an interest in his condition. In the event,
Awolowo was released in August.

Constantine left Nigeria after a visit of six days. His
report to Amnesty International helped to bring to public

notice the tragedy of human events in Nigeria. Subsequently, practical help was organised in Britain for victims of the war. What might in different circumstances have been an occasion of public importance and some happiness for Constantine proved instead to be furtive and pathetic. He had chosen a time of tragedy for his only visit to the Niger from which his forebears had come.

Back in Britain, Constantine became closely involved with racial questions which by 1966 were assuming greater importance. The Labour Government, elected in 1964, had introduced the Race Relations Act in 1965 making it a criminal offence to stir up hatred on grounds of race or colour. It became the duty of the newly-created Race Relations Board to investigate alleged offences under the Act, and to achieve reconciliation between offending and offended parties. At first the Board was small in number and modestly housed in offices near Westminster Abbey. Constantine was appointed in July 1967 as one of its three members, under the chairmanship of Mark Bonham Carter. Their number was completed by B. S. Langton, a former Lord Mayor of Manchester. A staff of conciliation officers and clerks administered the Board's business, much of which related to instances of discrimination in public houses.

Immigration to Britain, particularly of Kenyan Asians, became an important issue in 1968 in which year two important legislative measures were passed—the second Race Relations Act (December 1968) and the Commonwealth Immigrants Act. On the subject of Immigration, Constantine spoke on 23 September 1968, on the B.B.C. programme 'The World This Weekend', on British political attitudes. 'Should not the coloured peoples of the Commonwealth be given preferential treatment to aliens?' he asked. He attacked Conservative Opposition plans for tighter control of immigration, and returned to the theme a few days later when he spoke of one aspect of immigration policy which was especially distressing—the question of financial loans to immigrants. He had made an attempt to have a separate building society set up for them which had proved unsuccessful, and he was aware of many cases of hardship where coloured immigrants were denied financial loans and benefits. The new Race Relations measure made such discrimination illegal. To deny anyone facilities for banking, insurance grants, loans, credit or finance was a civil wrong, and a subject for consideration by a regional committee or the Race Relations Board itself. If conciliation failed, court proceedings could follow. The Act also increased membership to the Board to twelve, and set up the Community Relations Commission.

Constantine's contribution to the Board was important in that he was a well-known figure and a representative of coloured peoples who knew the West Indies well. He was, commented Mark Bonham Carter, 'a regular attender at Board meetings so far as his health allowed. When the Board set up an employment committee in 1968 his contribution was particularly important'. To the end of his life he regarded his work on the Race Relations Board as one of the ways in which he could be of service to a new generation of West Indian immigrants.

Shortly after his appointment to the Race Relations Board, Constantine was invited by a section of the student-body at St Andrews University to stand for the Rectorship. The Rectorship of the four ancient Scottish Universities is an office of statutory authority under the Universities (Scotland) Act of 1889 to which the holder is elected by the matriculated student-body. Traditionally, the Scottish universities attracted to the office a distinguished list of noblemen, politicians, and leading figures in the arts. The Rector is President of the University Court. He is senior to the University Principal although the authority of the latter is preserved by his nomination, by the Chancellor of the University, to the superior post of Vice-Chancellor. The Rector is thus third in the University hierarchy. Constantine was successful in the election which took place on 12 November 1967. The results were:

> Sir Learie Constantine　　　691
> The Rt Hon. Joseph Grimond　498

Alexander Gibson   281
Sean Connery   178

The news cheered him in the Westminster Hospital where he was recovering from an operation. He had succeeded a man distinguished in very different fields: Sir John Rothenstein, an art critic and a former Director of the Tate Gallery.

Between Constantine's election as Rector of St Andrews University and his installation in office, there was some possibility of his becoming a candidate for the vacant parliamentary constituency of Nelson and Colne. Sydney Silverman, who had sat as Labour member for the seat since 1935, had died. Constantine had known him for some thirty years, and they had met frequently when Constantine had lived in Nelson. The leader of the Liberal Party, Jeremy Thorpe, saw Constantine as a possible candidate at a time when Liberals sought to lead the fight against legislation restricting Commonwealth immigrants and seeking to end the entry of Kenyan Asians into Britain. On 28 February 1968, Thorpe cabled Constantine from Barbados inviting him to consider candidature—though convention would, of course, demand acceptance by the local party committee. On the very same day, the Commonwealth Immigrants Bill was passed in the House of Lords. Constantine declined the invitation on the grounds of age and of his friendship with the former Labour member, Sydney Silverman, whose party might lose the seat by Constantine's invervention. He had retained many associations with Nelson. He chose not to set himself up as a Liberal candidate in a seat which he had always known as a Labour one. The Press suggested that the best place for Constantine's contribution to the political issues of the day was the House of Lords—and so it proved, in a few months' time.

Early in the New Year, the Rector-elect had made his first gesture in relation to the University when he cabled from the Bahamas—where he was recuperating—his opposition to a rugby match between the University and the touring side from the Orange Free State University in South Africa:

FIXTURE WITH SOUTH AFRICANS DEPLORABLE.
GOVERNMENT WHICH BY LEGISLATION REDUCES
HUMAN BEINGS TO LOWER ANIMALS UNWORTHY
TO ASSOCIATE WITH DECENT GOVERNMENTS AND
PEOPLES.

The fixture took place, but the incident anticipated the growing revulsion against participation in sport with the Republic of South Africa which was to lead to the abandonment or cancellation of cricket and rugby tours. South Africa's apartheid policy had intensified since the Bantu Self Government Act of 1960.

Constantine was installed as Rector of St Andrews University on 17 April 1968. The day began with a church service in Holy Trinity Church, St Andrews, followed by an informal lunch and a chance for Sir Learie and Lady Constantine to rest before the remainder of the programme. At 3 p.m. the ceremony of installation took place in the Younger Hall. First of all, the Rector-elect received the honorary degree of Doctor of Laws. His fellow-graduands were Sir Harold Mitchell, a Scotsman who was an expert in Latin–American studies and had business interests in the West Indies; Sir Philip Sherlock, the Vice-Chancellor of the University of the West Indies; and Sir Alec Douglas-Home, the former British prime minister and a past-president of the M.C.C. The University had happily ensured that Constantine's colleagues all had an interest in common with him—either the West Indies or cricket.

After his installation as Rector, Constantine gave the customary Rectorial address to about a thousand students—in their turn, a customarily good-humoured but noisy audience. His theme was 'Race in the World'. He took particular pleasure in the fact that the young had elected him to office 'at what I may call the climacteric of my life. Being not far from the allotted span, there are few marks of public approbation to which I shall look back with greater pride.' He told his listeners something of his life as a young man in Trinidad and of his work as a member of the Race Relations

Board. He concluded, 'You have by the election of a coloured man to be your Rector served notice on the world that you have broken down the barriers and removed the obstacles standing in his way of progress.'

There were those present who felt that much of the address was irrelevant and that an account of Constantine's rise from humble origins was inappropriate. But, one may ask, what is relevant or irrelevant on such an occasion? Clearly a university in Scotland would be unlikely to elect a white professional cricketer who had achieved success in other directions in English public life to office. Constantine was entitled to his assumption that he was elected Rector because he was black.

He was given an enthusiastic reception by the students, and the day concluded with a dinner in St Salvator's Hall. Constantine commented to a friend afterwards, 'It was like getting the Freedom of Nelson but with new faces around instead of old ones.'

The Rector of a Scottish University may appoint an Assessor to be his representative on the University Court. Rectors busy in public life or living some distance away have traditionally done this, and Constantine followed the custom. In consequence, there was some surprise when an unofficial meeting of students in October 1969 decided by 151 to 100 votes to ask him to resign because ill-health prevented his attending meetings. Although the decision was overruled by the official Students' Representative Council, there had been grounds for the original action by the unofficial meeting. Constantine's Rectorship had proved a disappointment in that he never came back to the University after giving his rectorial address. His supporters felt that, despite his ill-health, he could have found ways of showing some interest in the University's affairs. 'He let us down. We felt disappointed' commented one.

By the summer of 1968, the crisis in sporting relations with South Africa which had been becoming increasingly evident in recent months came to a head over the selection of the M.C.C. team to tour South Africa in 1968–9. The facts were these. Basil D'Oliveira, the coloured South African cricketer who had played in English first-class cricket and been 'capped' for England, had had a moderate season in 1968. At the last minute he secured a place, vacant through injury, in the fifth Test against Australia at the Oval. He scored 158. Immediately afterwards the team for South Africa was announced, and his own name was omitted. Loud protests followed from many quarters, and D'Oliveira himself was deeply upset. The Reverend David Sheppard, later Bishop of Liverpool, and a former England captain who had taken a strong line against competing with South Africa, felt it was a mistake, although he was not prepared to condemn the selectors on grounds other than of cricket misjudgement. Constantine spoke out from three points of view:

Speaking as a cricketer, the omission of D'Oliveira is to be regretted. Speaking as a West Indian, the circumstances of this omission are positively suspicious. Speaking as a member of the Race Relations Board, even if there were racial discrimination, it would not be unlawful under the 1965 Act, nor—so far as I can see—under the 1968 Bill.

Subsequently, D'Oliveira received a late invitation to join the side, again because of a player's injury. The South African government regarded it as a political manoeuvre and indicated that D'Oliveira would not be acceptable. In consequence, the M.C.C. tour was cancelled.

Constantine felt that not all his cricketing friends had taken the stand he might have expected of them. Instead of unity of opposition to the idea of playing South Africa, he found an equally strong lobby who felt that sport and politics could be disassociated by sportsmen ignoring political attitudes. The point was validly made that the Western world played with the Communist countries while not identifying themselves with support for domestic policies pursued in those countries. Understandably, it was not a point of view that Constantine could accept. It left him with the feeling that 'Britain has a long way to go along the road of racial tolerance'.

As earlier chapters have shown, Constantine had been a

frequent broadcaster. His performances over many years had been widely praised for their technical competence and ease of presentation. Through radio he had been able both to express his views on matters of concern to the West Indies and to discuss the game which had brought his rise to fame. When he decided that he would relinquish his High Commission-ship he made approaches in August 1963 to the B.B.C. to find out how much work he might anticipate in the future. The Corporation could make him no guarantee but he was assured that his reputation and experience in broadcasting made it likely that his services would often be required. Con-stantine was without any regular source of income from 1964. His livelihood was derived from legal briefs, book-royalties (very nominal by this time), and broadcasting. It seems clear that he hoped for more work than he actually got from the B.B.C. Between 1964 and 1968 he earned almost £1,300 from broadcasting. It could not be the basis of an income for him, but it must be said that the Corporation gave him many opportunities to broadcast. In 1965, for example, he was a contributor on the Home or Overseas services of the B.B.C. to programmes with the following wide range of titles:

Australian Cricket Tour of the West Indies
Race Relations in Britain
Caribbean Topic—Legislation against Racial Discrimina-
    tion in Britain
What makes a Cricketer?
A tribute to Sir Winston Churchill
Sports review: a tribute to Tich Freeman
Caribbean Magazine
Controversy in International Cricket
Commonwealth Immigrants
Sports Review
Voices
Listen to this Space
The Griffith Bowling Action Controversy
The Possibility of Neutral Umpires
The Duke of Edinburgh Award

The Informal Cricket Conference
Twenty Questions
The M.C.C. Team for Australia
Can the Commonwealth Survive?

At the beginning of this busy spell of broadcasting—indeed, just before he had ceased to be High Commissioner—Constantine had broadcast on Christmas Eve 1963 under the title 'No Stranger Here'. Extracts from that broadcast have been used in different parts of this book. Constantine was asked by the producer to say something which 'would send our listeners to bed on Christmas Eve happy and reassured but perhaps a tiny bit thoughtful of something beyond themselves'. He was given a list of suggested titles—'No Stranger Here', 'A Guest No Longer', 'My People and Yours', 'A Stranger No More'—from which he chose 'No Stranger Here'. Constantine looked back over the years he had spent in England and adjudged how far he had been accepted in the country to which he had come as a young professional cricketer in 1929. He also left his listeners to ponder upon the thought that long absence from his own native land had made it difficult for him to live in Trinidad.

Constantine also did a certain amount of work on television in connection with Sunday cricket. During the 1960s the English first-class game underwent considerable change. A side styled the International Cavaliers began to play Sunday matches, and shortly afterwards, in 1963, the Gillette Cricket Cup began a knock-out competition for the first-class counties (and some minor counties). None of these one-day games was technically first-class, but this was something for the administrators and statisticians to ponder upon rather than the spectators. One-day cricket, of which Constantine had long been an advocate, brought cricket of a first-class standard to a wider range of spectators. Games were begun and concluded before the same crowd. The finances of cricket were restored. Sponsorship took place. Constantine took part in some commentating but he found it more exhausting than other types of broadcasting. On many grounds, studio facilities did not exist and it was necessary for him to climb a ladder to a commentary box. The effort in doing so tired him and made breathing difficult. He was often uncomfortable during the time he was commentating. Then he had to get down the ladder. He gave up contributing to commentaries on televised matches just before the John Player Sunday League began in 1969. He had been less successful as a television commentator on other grounds as well. A good television commentator must be a judge of when to be silent and let the scene shown to the audience tell its own story. Constantine found difficulty in deciding when he should keep quiet.

In these years the B.B.C. took advantage of Constantine's experience by asking him, in 1964, to serve on its General Advisory Committee, 'where he talked sound sense especially on those issues upon which he was knowledgeable' and 'we knew him at his delightful best'. In July 1968 came an invitation to serve as a Governor of the Corporation for a five-year term. This meant that Constantine could draw no more emoluments for broadcasting, but would receive a fee of £1,000 annually for his governorship.

At the time there were twelve governors, whose appointment was in the gift of the prime minister. They may be described as the watchdogs of the public whose interests they safeguarded. They represented the final word in B.B.C. policy, met fortnightly and made decisions which were carried out by the Board of Management. It was an important time in the history of the B.B.C. The Chairman and Governors were to be associated with a forthcoming publication, *Broadcasting in the Seventies*, which came out in July 1969 and discussed issues such as local radio stations and financial policy. It was also a period when the B.B.C. was coming under considerable criticism in some quarters for the lack of moral standards in some of its programmes. Television programmes designed for viewing at 'family' times were accused of being morally offensive and distasteful. Yet the Corporation had to serve its customers in an age of permissiveness and changing social values and attitudes. It was a far cry from the stern Puritanism of Lord Reith who had stamped his image on the Corporation in an earlier generation. Constantine's contribution as a governor was brief but not without some importance. On one occasion, soothing words of his after a stormy meeting prevented the resignation of one governor whose financial expertise was important to the Corporation. Professor Glanmor Williams recalled vividly his association with Constantine as a governor:

'I had never met Learie until he became a governor of the B.B.C., but during the years that he served on the Board we became firm friends.

'I always thought that his appointment to the Board of Governors of the B.B.C. was one of the most imaginative ever made to that body. My only regret—and I think my fellow-governors shared it—was that the appointment had not been thought of some ten years earlier. By the time Learie joined the Board he was already in broken health and this prevented him from making as great a contribution as he might otherwise have done. Nevertheless I remember vividly the remarkable courage and sense of public duty that he showed in attending Board meetings when he was really not well enough to have done so. I have seen him there at times when his face was literally grey with strain and weakness, gasping desperately for breath and racked with bouts of the most painful coughing. Yet throughout it all he preserved the most resilient patience and good humour.

'As a governor he naturally felt very deeply on such issues as immigration, race relations and the needs of the developing countries of the world, and he expressed himself firmly and eloquently yet even-temperedly on such subjects. What always struck me about him was that he never became obsessional about these issues and could always be counted upon to see them in perspective. He once said to me, with that characteristic twinkle in his eye, 'Even the Alf Garnetts of this world are human beings and have to be thought of as such.' He also had a particular interest in industrial relations and here again his attitudes were those of a wise, tolerant and percipient observer.

'When it came to the sporting scene his knowledge of cricket and cricketers was unrivalled, but he also seemed to know and understand a great deal about other sports also.'

Lord Hill, Chairman of the B.B.C. at the time, commented:

'Alas, the sad truth is that Learie came to us too late to play a really effective part. Already his chest had begun to give him trouble, with the result that his attendance was uneven and his contribution was inevitably marred by illness. His few contributions had the qualities of clarity and directness— sometimes lawyer-like—coming from a man, not from a representative of a particular group, minority or otherwise. But almost from the beginning, it was so evident that we had lost a first-class governor because he came to us ten years too late.'

Constantine's final broadcast was in 1970 on the subject of cricket. He had first performed in 1939 on the same subject. In the intervening thirty-one years he had earned nearly £2,500 from broadcasting. He had been used regularly, especially in talks to the West Indies, during the Second World War. His best year as a cricket broadcaster had been 1950 during the triumphant West Indies tour of England. He had, in the evening of his life, been in demand in the middle 1960s. As a broadcaster he had achieved much because he combined technical competence with a relaxed manner and a warmth and directness in presentation.

The year 1968, in which Constantine became a governor of the B.B.C., had been his busiest year since he ceased to be High Commissioner. Despite ill-health, he had been active in his work for the Sports Council, the Race Relations Board and as a broadcaster. He had considered entering British politics. He had become Rector of a University. It was not altogether a surprise when the New Year Honours on 1 January 1969 brought the announcement of his peerage. It was unquestionably the honour given special attention by the Press, radio and television, although fellow-peers included Professor Patrick Blackett, the President of the Royal Society, Sir Joseph Garner, former Head of the Diplomatic Service, and Sir Donald Stokes, Chairman of British Leyland

Motor Corporation. Congratulations poured in by letter and telegram from many parts of the world. The new Lord Constantine commented that he felt his peerage 'must have been for what I have endeavoured to do to make it possible for people of different colour to know each other better and live well together'. And, 'it was recognition for all West Indians', he remarked to a fellow governor of the B.B.C.

Yet the peerage might have come earlier. Allegedly, the Trinidad Government was not prepared to approve the honour, and ultimately only the influence of certain people in Britain was instrumental through the office of the then High Commissioner in obtaining approval of the creation. No clear reason for Trinidadian opposition emerges, although it may be said that the decision not to use the British Honours List for Trinidadians after Independence was a factor. Sadly, Constantine was an ill man, and the appearances he made that evening on television were an effort. One B.B.C. colleague described his appearance before the arc lights as a 'feat of endurance'.

It was announced on 25 March that the new life baron would take the title of Baron Constantine of Maraval in Trinidad and of Nelson in the County Palatine of Lancaster. He thus honoured Maraval, the place of his origin, and Nelson, the town which had given him a home for so long and conferred its freedom upon him. Baron Constantine was not the first coloured peer. That distinction went to Sir Satyendra Prasanna Sinha, a member of the Viceroy's Council in India, who was given a baronage in 1919, and whose grandson was the third baron but had never taken his seat. The new peer was the first Negro to be so honoured, and his introduction to the House of Lords on 26 March 1969 was made a great occasion.* The Earl Marshal of England, the Duke of Norfolk, and the Lord Great Chamberlain, the Marquis of Cholmondeley, both took part although they did not normally attend such introductions. The House itself was full as a procession formed to lead in the new peer. First came Gentleman Usher of the Black Rod, then Garter Principal King of

* In 1975 a peerage was conferred on Dr. David Pitt.

Arms carrying the peer's Letters-Patent to the title, and resplendent in a heraldic uniform showing the four royal emblems of the United Kingdom. The Earl Marshal with his baton came next followed by the Lord Great Chamberlain with his White Staff. Then came Baron Constantine, bearing his Writ of Summons, with his supporters, two peers of his own rank. These were Baron Beswick, a junior minister in the Commonwealth Office, and Baron Brockway. Lord Brockway had had a long and distinguished career as a politician and writer with an especial interest in the Labour Movement, colonial freedom and the cause of Peace. The procession moved up the Chamber; the new peer took the oath; and there followed the ritual of bowing and doffing the black cocked hat to the Lord Chancellor seated on the Woolsack. As customary, the Lord Chancellor remained seated while Baron Constantine and his supporters sat down after each gesture and then stood up again. After these courtesies, the procession again paced slowly down the Chamber with bowing to the Table and to the Law Lords, and this time Lord Constantine bowed to the Lord Chancellor and shook his hand. Blessed by antiquity and redeemed by solemnity, the quaint ceremony finds justification in a twentieth-century world. 'The new peer and his sponsors went through their motions with beautifully drilled precision', wrote Philip Howard, *The Times* correspondent. Baron Constantine had played 'a marathon, heraldic innings'. Among those watching in the gallery had been his wife, Norma. Baroness Constantine was proud of the distinction Learie had won, thankful his health had spared him for the occasion.

Norma Constantine had been a devoted partner through the years. She had encouraged her husband in adversity and rejoiced in his success. She had lost the shyness of earlier years, and had been a gracious hostess both during the High Commissioner years and, more modestly, at their flat in Kendal Court. She remained, in her sixties, strikingly attractive. Close friends alone noticed towards the end of the 1960s an increasing tiredness and some signs of ill-health.

Soon came the summer and the prospect of cricket and

the West Indian and New Zealand tourists. But Constantine dared not make his hay fever worse by getting too near the grass of an English cricket field, and by June he was really ill. The source of his ill-health was bronchial. An announcement in the Press in 1968 had described him as suffering from a chest complaint, bronchial catarrh and hay fever. Three months in Trinidad in the late months of 1968 had been a pleasant meeting with relations and friends but had done nothing to improve his health. The remaining two years of his life were a constant struggle against ill-health.

In May 1970, Lord and Lady Constantine were invited to go to Brazil as the personal guests of the Brazilian cultural attaché at the consulate-general in Manchester, Mr Ernest G. Dashwood-Evans, a friend of many years standing, but the last moment the trip was cancelled on health grounds.

While Constantine had been dogged by ill-health in the 1960s, to some extent his personal finances were also a source of worry. After he resigned from the High Commissionership in February 1964 he had no regular source of income. Broadcasting (until he became a governor), journalism, the Bar and diminishing royalties from cricket books brought in only a little. His work at the Race Relations Board gave him £1,000 a year from 1968 onwards, as did his governorship of the B.B.C. from the same year bring another £1,000. From 1967 onwards he drew an old age pension and from 1969 an attendance allowance (rarely claimed) at the House of Lords. The Constantines' close friends understood the position. Social invitations were given and accepted so far as health allowed. Only simple hospitality was expected in return. The wider field of their acquaintances were not sure of the position. When a testimonial fund was mooted in 1970, there were doubts as to whether it was necessary. In the end, a decision was put off.

Constantine had gone to the Lords—as to the B.B.C.—too late. He was able to do little in 1970 and it was not until nearly two years after his introduction to the House of Lords that he made his maiden—and only—speech. He chose the debate on Britain's entry into the European Community, a subject on which he had spoken publicly during his High Commissionership. In a speech on 10 March 1971, he urged that Britain should enter the Community only if the other member nations agreed to accept the Commonwealth Sugar Agreement. Sugar had been a major issue in discussions between Britain and the Community, and between Britain and the Commonwealth countries involved. The European territories of the European Economic Community had a surplus of sugar produced domestically from beet, while Britain was committed to imports under succeeding Commonwealth Sugar Agreements. Lord Constantine pointed out the economic hazards for certain Commonwealth countries if sugar and other cash-crops such as citrus fruits and bananas were affected by European Economic Community policy:

'A great deal of production by many Commonwealth countries has developed and has been extended in response to demand in the United Kingdom. The great danger of Britain's entry into the European Economic Community is the loss of this outlet without the prospect of any alternative, unless the conditions of entry enable the Commonwealth countries to export to the enlarged Community. Uncertainty about the future places estate-owners in difficulties. No bank wishes to lend money in this precarious situation, with the result that sugar cane production may be reduced, and the allocation of sugar hampered. I hope Britain will say today that this sugar agreement will be accepted by the Six before Britain enters the Common Market.'

Constantine linked his argument to the more emotive one of Britain's relationship to her West Indies subjects. The West Indians, despite the remnants of African culture to which they clung, had developed over three centuries cultural links with the English. Constantine had brought off, said the Press, a notable triumph. He had taken a subject of topical importance—Britain and the Community—and had linked it to his own personal stand-point and ancestry, the economic and social hopes and fears of the West Indies. It had been a speech which he had been urged to make.

Influential figures in Caribbean sugar had felt that an important statement in the House of Lords might make a significant contribution to the campaign to safeguard the sugar economy of the West Indies. Lord Constantine was the obvious man to make it.

Six weeks later, in May 1971, the Community agreed to a 'specific and moral commitment' to safeguard sugar interests, and in June 1971 a meeting of Commonwealth countries and United Kingdom representatives met in London to 'declare their satisfaction at the Community's readiness to recognise the United Kingdom's contractual commitment to all the Commonwealth Sugar Agreement member countries'. It would be fanciful to give Constantine credit for a decision which had been worked towards for many months, and had involved much discussion on Britain's part by Geoffrey Rippon. Nevertheless, in so far as the issue of sugar was important to the West Indies, their spokesman in the House of Lords had—in his solitary performance—commanded attention for their needs. In the past, Parliament had its members who spoke for the West Indian sugar interest in the days of slavery. It was an interest that had no humane feeling for the ancestors of Learie Constantine, bound as it was to the concept of slave-produced sugar. Now the wheel had come full circle: a West Indian politician spoke for the 'sugar interest' in terms of his own people, and his voice was heard.

Meanwhile, there had been a final cricket occasion when he attended, on 2 April, a luncheon at Lord's to celebrate Norman Preston's twenty-one years as editor of *Wisden*. Two months later, he announced that ill-health made it necessary for him to end his days in the warmer climate of Trinidad. What was probably his last letter was written at the end of June to an old cricketing friend in Manchester: 'Yes, I must go home. My health has broken down. I can stay in one place but I cannot move around without a lot of discomfort. A warm climate should help me, at least I hope so. So I am going to it. Give my best wishes to all my friends.' Two days later, on 1 July 1971, Learie Constantine died at his home in London. He was sixty-eight.

12

ONE MAN IN HIS TIME

Lord Constantine's body was flown to Piarco airport, Trinidad, where its arrival was heralded by a guard of honour and a 19-gun salute. From the airport it was borne to Port of Spain where a lying-in-state took place in the Roman Catholic Cathedral. On Thursday, 8 July 1971, Lord Constantine was buried with the ceremonial of a State Funeral. The service in the Cathedral was conducted by the Archbishop of Port of Spain and attended by the Governor-General, Sir Solomon Hochoy, the prime minister of Trinidad, Eric Williams, diplomats from many countries and representatives of various aspects of Trinidadian public life. A gun-carriage carried the coffin through streets lined twelve deep, accompanied by the Regimental Band and the Corps of Drums of the Trinidad and Tobago Regiment. At the committal, at Arouca cemetery, Lady Constantine was supported by her daughter, her son-in-law and Dr Reymond Dolly, a lifelong friend of the family. Trinidad had honoured one of her greatest sons, a man, said the prime minister, in the *Trinidad Guardian* who had earned a place in his country's history.

Among the thousands who stood motionless in a day of rain and sun, were vast numbers of young people, despite the fact that Constantine must have been unknown to them, except as a legendary figure of West Indian cricket.

Later, on 23 July 1971, a Memorial Service was held in London, in Westminster Abbey. Her Majesty the Queen was represented by Lord Nugent, a permanent lord-in-waiting and a past president of the M.C.C. The prime minister,

Edward Heath, was represented by Lord Jellicoe, Lord Privy Seal and Leader of the House of Lords. The Dean of Westminster officiated and representatives attended from many areas of public life—politics, the Bar, the Commonwealth, the B.B.C. and, of course, cricket. Sir Dingle Foot gave the address.

On 14 August, it was announced that Constantine had left in his will £3,555 net. He left his property to his wife. Sadly, she did not survive him long. Her own death took place on 4 September in Trinidad where she had gone to live with her daughter. Norma Constantine's devotion to her husband contributed to her own death so shortly after his, since her concern for his health made her ignore her own. When at last, back in Trinidad, relations and friends realised how ill she was, there was little that could be done.

Norma Constantine had filled an important role in her husband's life. She had provided the security and encouragement he needed. She had led him to make decisions, and to regard them as his own. She had been 'a charming hostess' and 'a gracious lady'. Underneath her quiet, shy exterior lay a fierce determination to watch over her husband, either to prosper his fortunes or to guard his health.

Learie Constantine was one of those men of whom the statement 'he was a legend in his own lifetime' was no more than the truth. Sir Dingle Foot wrote in a tribute in *The Times*: 'I have never met anyone who inspired more widespread affection among all sorts and conditions of people.' There are many examples one might give of this. Sir Dingle himself has told of Constantine's first professional appearance in a criminal court. He was sent for after the proceedings by the Judge, and he wondered what procedural misdemeanour he had committed. He was greeted by a beaming figure: 'My dear Sir Learie, what an honour to have you in my court. I have never forgotten your innings at the Oval in 1939. You must stay and have a drink with me.' When Constantine left the court some time later he was stopped by the police on duty and asked to join them in their canteen for another one.

Constantine took trouble to remember people. Towards

the end of his life he was getting his hair cut one day in Holborn when another customer recognised him in the mirror. On introducing himself, that customer was at once remembered: 'We played against each other in the Glamorgan match in 1928', exclaimed Constantine. Even when he failed to remember someone, he had the celebrity's trick of giving the impression he did. He once told the story of how he accompanied Frank Swift, the England goalkeeper of the 1930s, down a Manchester Street when a man accosted Swift: 'Do you remember when the ball passed over the goal line in the match against Scotland? I was the one who threw it back to you.' Swift shook him by the hand and said how glad he was to meet him again. Constantine noted the incident and treated his own admirers with similar courtesy. 'All sorts and conditions of people' wrote to the author of this book bearing witness to the appeal that Constantine had. To the booking-clerk who often sold him his rail ticket in Southport, 'he was a fine gentleman'; to a B.B.C. producer, 'a man of charm and without malice'; to a British Labour politician, 'a man of great integrity'; to a Conservative politician, 'a delightful person to talk to'; to a West Indian living in Notting Hill, 'a friend who helped coloured people'; to a housewife in Nelson, someone who had influenced her life; to a cricketing opponent, 'a great man who earned the respect of all classes'. These stand as tributes to Constantine's essential friendliness, a quality shown as well in his relationship with children.

The Nelson children had enjoyed rides in his Austin Seven. As the years went by in Nelson he continued to give this simple pleasure to successive groups of children. In the early 1950s he had taken out an English family for the day, and received a charming 'thank you' letter in return from the parents of Martin who 'arrived home and immediately put your picture in a frame in his bedroom and went to sleep'. Back in Trinidad a year or two later, children—boys and girls alike—crowded round him when he coached at Regent School, Pointe-à-Pierre. At an informal drinks party in someone's house in Hampstead in the late 1960s, neighbours' children rushed in and begged him for autographs. Constantine's delight in the company of children may be related to his own natural innocence. There were qualities of honesty and simplicity in him which belonged to the nature of a child, and which never deserted him. He was a man of sobriety and chasteness. He hated being away from his wife on long cricket tours, and he took her with him whenever he could on short expeditions. It was understood, his fellow cricket commentators agreed, that Learie would usually bring Norma to a match which he was reporting. He was a 'man's man' at lunchtime rather than after the day's work was done. There were many lunches with colleagues in broadcasting, journalism and cricket in the 1960s, but Constantine would seldom be found at the bar after stumps were drawn. He would have gone home.

Throughout his life Constantine retained a sense of humour even when one imagines that the jokes against him might have been offensive. There had been the occasion far back in Nelson days when Harold Hargreaves accused him of being late because his wife was blackleading him. In 1965, fellow-contributors in a B.B.C. broadcast sent him a copy of *Little Black Sambo* autographed by them all. It is to the credit of the jokers that they could judge their man aright; to the credit of Constantine that he accepted such humour in the spirit in which it was intended.

Constantine, as E. W. Swanton observed in a tribute in the *Daily Telegraph*, was 'one of the personalities of his time'. How far did he remain a modest man before so much adulation? So far as cricket was concerned there was no false modesty about him. He had assessed his cricketing abilities at a very early stage and he soon learnt their currency value. He knew he could make money from his cricket and he did not hesitate to secure the best terms he could. One must accept that his vanity in cricketing terms sometimes jarred. In later years cricketing colleagues could be bored with reminiscences in which Constantine himself was always the centrepiece. Yet this vanity was seldom carried into other areas of his life. His war-time colleagues in Liverpool had difficulty in getting him to talk of his cricketing exploits. When he was decorated in 1946 and knighted in 1962 he was glad of the honours for 'the sake of the West Indies'. He disliked being addressed as 'Sir Learie' or as 'Lord Constantine' by those who knew him well—'look man, my name is Learie'. Only very rarely did he sign letters with the customary 'Constantine' as used by a peer of the realm. He used 'Learie Constantine', although headed notepaper indicated his style. As a cricket spectator he did not necessarily look for special treatment. On one of his last visits to the North of England to a ground he knew well, he paid at the gate and sat down on a bench beside the sight screen so that he could watch the bowler's line. He seemed 'genuinely pleased and surprised when we recognised him and asked him to umpire for a few minutes', remembered the secretary at Didsbury. Modesty on another occasion made him at first decline an invitation to appear on a B.B.C. Brains Trust, although he could have done with the money. In the end, second thoughts prevailed.

On the other hand, those who knew Constantine in politics thought him opinionated. It was his frequent references to his own achievements which disconcerted fellow members of the Trinidad Legislative Council, and it created a certain hostility towards him which reduced his 'personality-value' for the People's National Movement Party. He found political criticism difficult to take and his defence against it was to create an armoury of personal successes with which to confront his opponents.

Throughout his life, Constantine had a determined approach to money. He made a swift adjustment from the £50 a year he earned as a solicitor's clerk in 1921 to the £500 he commanded as a Nelson cricketer in 1929. He accepted a situation that gave him not only ten times as much as he had earned in Trinidad but ten times as much as his fellow-cricketers in Nelson. Gradually, his broadcasting fees increased as he became more in demand. On one occasion he wrote to the B.B.C. requesting a higher fee for a broadcast for which he had already been paid, and his request was met. Later he employed an agent to negotiate his contracts. Over his working life Constantine probably earned about £36,000. There were two periods—1946–54, and 1964 onwards—when he was less fortunate and could rely on no steady income. In prosperity he was quietly generous. West Indians in financial distress in the 1930s were given help, nor was he one to stand by and watch others pay the bill, but generosity could be expressed in ways other than financial. 'In the living room of many a Nelson cottage,' wrote John Kay, 'there were stories told of a helping hand.' The poor were visited in their homes, and the sick at home or in hospital. In adversity, the Constantines kept up appearances. In their declining years they made sure their friends were not embarrassed by their circumstances. Because of this, help—which many would have given generously—was not contemplated until it was too late.

In the year before his death, Constantine was invited by the sculptor Karen Jonzen to sit for her. At first he declined because of the physical effort involved in going to her studio and posing. When she explained that she hoped to place the finished model in an exhibition of people who had made a contribution to human rights, Constantine agreed to her proposal. The result was a sculptured head in terracotta stained in a bronze colour. It represents him as an old man whose eyes have a far-away look as if in reflection of past deeds. Humour lingers at the corners of the mouth. It is a face in repose; an open face revealing none of the subtleties of the politician. Only the short hair and the thick lips suggest his Negro origins. There is something European in the sculptor's interpretation as if trying to convey the two worlds which were his. No hint of the athlete is betrayed. The sculptor had not known him as such. While he sat, a picture of Sir Alan Herbert caught his eye and he fell to telling the sculptor of their acquaintanceship. The time came to go. Karen Jonzen never saw him again but she understood why her subject had been such a widely respected person. 'He had a warmth in his manner to which one instantly responded.'

To that sculptor Constantine's life as a cricketer meant nothing. One is led to ask: what did Constantine accomplish in his life apart from cricket? At school he achieved little. Even though the opportunities for success in terms of scholarships were very strictly limited, he made little effort to seek them. During the years as a clerk in Trinidad there is no evidence of any real determination to work hard—except in mastering the skill of typing quickly. Once Constantine had married, the impetus to work came from Norma Constantine. She urged him to read in the Nelson public library, to study for the Cambridge 'Locals', to spend some time in a Nelson solicitor's office, and to settle down after the war to qualify as a barrister. As late as 1967 when Constantine was asked why he was so determined to become a lawyer, he replied: 'It was important that in the life of a little black boy that he had an independent profession.' Constantine was well past boyhood before he recognised that importance.

Constantine's few years as a politician must be seen as the least satisfactory side of his life—at least from his own point of view. He had embarked upon a political career with high hopes for himself and for Trinidad. 'It was to be the turning-point of my life', he said. He had worked hard. He had, in the view of a close ministerial colleague, 'handled well the complex issue of the ships, S.S. *Trinidad* and S.S. *Tobago*'. The 1959 election had largely been fought on the achievements of his department. His relations with his civil servants were effective and acceptable. He had the ability to put ideas into practice. Yet the years in office ended in some sadness. There had been fundamental differences in attitude and temperament between Constantine and those politicians whose centre of interest was Trinidad and who had travelled little. Neither side showed enough give and take. Constantine was apt to cite with frequency English parliamentary practice as the paragon of good government, and his critics resented his emphatically English standpoint. Constantine himself offered the shortest answer and probably the best when asked why his career as a minister did not last long: 'because I am not a politician'. Critics of Constantine would agree that this was true.

Constantine's reluctance to enter the mêlée of politics also explains his lack of a total dedication to the cause of coloured people for, fundamentally, he was not a militant for coloured men's causes. He had seen too much of the world—whether wealth among Indian princes, or poverty among Nelson cotton-workers—not to realise that economic divisions in relation to race could be over-simplified. Where he was concerned, it was social injustice on the grounds of colour that mattered. Then he would speak on platforms from time to time—and the issues might not be purely West Indian matters, as for example in the Seretse Khama affair—but his instinct was to act behind the scenes. One Trinidadian critic felt 'it was hard going to convince a majority of West Indians' that Constantine had their interests at heart. Those who came to the offices of the High Commissioner between 1962 and 1964, who heard his views in the late 1960s at a time of controversy on immigrant problems, or who read reports of his speech on West Indian sugar in the House of Lords in 1971 must surely have realised his sincerity. But to others he remained 'a black white man'; the Negro who had 'sold out'; 'Uncle Tom'.

Of these allegations Constantine was well aware. In 1963 he said in his Christmas Eve broadcast:

'I'm one of the West Indians. And although I have been very lucky in the way that I have been accepted here, I always try to remember that we have hosts. There are so many antagonisms in the world today and indeed Britain has plenty of its own. We don't want to add to them. We should like to think that the West Indians give variety, and warmth, and humour to your society and that most of them do a jolly good job of work as well. We want integration established without squabble, rancour or sacrifice of lives. This can be done and life will be richer when it is eventually achieved.'

Yet this was said by the author of *Colour Bar*—a book which some white people felt was ungenerous from a man who had lived in Britain so long. Constantine was once asked what was his aim in writing the book and he replied: 'I like people. I like to see happiness, I wanted to see my people make any advances in any particular field for which they were suited.'

There is a clue to his whole approach. He was a man concerned with human relationships rather than politics. It mattered more that coloured men and women found social happiness than political fulfilment. In the last year or two of his life, when the British politician, Enoch Powell, adopted an extreme view on the presence of coloured people in Britain, Constantine did not counter him with extremism. In the late 1960s, neither health nor inclination encouraged him to be a powerful advocate for the coloured races. What was required in Britain, he said in an interview with Fenton Bresler of the London *Evening Standard* in March 1969, was

'understanding: a platform for tolerance and an appreciation of each other's point of view. With no Wolverhampton speeches! . . . Coloured people have been derogated all the way down the line. You cannot suddenly jump up and say they are equal. I realise that. The people who come to England should be prepared to accept the laws and customs of this country. Once people are here, they should behave like good guests—and Britain should help.'

Yet none of this is to deny Constantine's genuine distress for those whom he called 'hurt and bewildered immigrants'. Had there not been this genuineness, there would have been no visit to Bristol in 1963 when he was High Commissioner. The consequences of that well-meant gesture contributed to the end of his career in public service. They give the lie to those who say that Constantine was a man ready to 'be still in the face of oppression or unfairness'.

But suspicions of Constantine's real allegiance remained to the end. His last public statement, made at a Press Association lunch on 9 June 1971—three weeks before he died—followed the announcement that for health reasons he proposed to return to Trinidad: 'My roots are all here, I have enjoyed a status that I would never had had at home.' In social and economic terms this was indeed true. Constantine enjoyed membership of various British clubs. To have been elected to the Marylebone Cricket Club, the Royal Automobile Club and the Forty Club brought him into institutions largely identified with the English middle classes and with professional and business men of standing. He was a welcome guest in several London clubs. His peerage gave him the entrée to another institution that had some of the characteristics of a London club. His governorship of the B.B.C. had something of the same guise.

But Constantine was equally 'the people's man'. Nelson had given him as much as London—indeed, far more. He was delighted with the banner headline in the *Nelson Leader* which declared, in 1963, 'Local boy makes good'. That same paper had said of him when he left Nelson in 1949:

'Yet for every memory of this town and its cricket this great player takes with him he will leave a dozen behind. His name will be revered not only as one of the greatest all-rounders of all time; not only as a good sportsman; it will be remembered in writing as what is probably the most glorious chapter in League cricket history.'

John Kay in his *Cricket in the Leagues* wrote of 'Learie Constantine of Nelson, and the West Indies. I do not think he will mind me placing Nelson first in order of importance.' Such was Constantine's social position in England. One might add that he took an even kindlier view of the Scots, whose country he loved to visit and of which land he wrote in 1943: 'my experience has been that there is no colour-bar'. In economic terms, he had earned a livelihood in the British Isles which would not have been possible in Trinidad.

What would have been Constantine's social position if he had lived in Trinidad in his last years? In the view of one friend, a Trinidadian Negro who had spent almost as many years in Britain as Constantine did himself, Constantine's social background—that of a Negro from a cocoa estate— would have made it difficult for him to be accepted by the middle classes—white or coloured—in Trinidad.

Constantine had felt something of this before he returned to Trinidad in 1954. 'The Englishman we know in the colonies is not the Englishman I know in England.' As well as expatriate English in Trinidad there were the white

Trinidadians. Constantine was ill at ease in relation to that group. Significantly, he had not been elected to the Queen's Park Cricket Club in Trinidad as he had been to the M.C.C. at Lord's, though it is only fair to say that his absence from Trinidad militated against election to the Queen's Park Club, and there lingered a mutual mistrust from the 1920s. Constantine's relations with middle-class Negroes and Indians in Trinidad had been tested during his six years in politics. While personally friendly with many of them, he had felt detached. He regarded their political attitudes as insular and he was always conscious of the gulf created by his own years of absence from the island. A distinguished Trinidadian contemporary, 'privileged to call Constantine a friend', had no doubts about the division which existed between Constantine and his fellow West Indians:

'He was a name, perhaps to some a legend, but there had been no personal contact, close association, or sense of oneness and belonging. He was widely recognised for his great gifts but all had been accomplished in England, not Trinidad.'

Where the Constantine 'mystique' remained was among the Trinidadian masses. They would have supplied, had he ended his days in Trinidad, the crowd-worship for which part of his nature craved, but there could have been no cultural *rapport* between him and them. The honours accorded to Constantine by his own country came late and were posthumous—Trinidad's highest decoration, the Trinity Cross, and a State Funeral. His 'search for recognition', said the *Trinidad Guardian* when he died, 'could only be won in the metropolitan area'.

Constantine's pursuit of political moderation led him to value the role of the British Empire and Commonwealth in world events. As a young cricketer making one of his first public speeches, he had spoken at Inverness in 1929 of the links between the Empire and cricket. He had been distressed when imperial relations were damaged by the body-line controversy in 1932–3—although this did not stop him adopting the same tactic himself in the summer of 1933. He had become far more involved in the work of the League of Coloured Peoples during the war once it had drawn attention to the irony of fighting German racialism and not stamping out racialism within the Empire. His hopes for the post-war concept of Commonwealth were expressed on several occasions. In July 1953, he said in a B.B.C. Commonwealth Forum programme: 'If by education and helping people on you create a condition by which partnership could be fostered, then you also create a condition by which the process of the Commonwealth of Nations could be fostered.' He went on to stress the need for 'peoples in subject countries' to see their responsibilities as well as their rights. The Commonwealth offered prospects of unity of colour, creed and concept and would 'survive the process of time'. To the end of his life he was a believer in this, without sentimentality or illusion. His interpretation of the role of Commonwealth made him something of a lonely figure, in political terms, in the 1960s. On the one hand, many British politicians were looking to a future alignment with Europe. On the other, many Commonwealth politicians were questioning the value of sustaining the partnership and of retaining Westminster modes of government. His benevolent view of Commonwealth was fast becoming an anachronism at the time of his death. Yet is was something to which he clung. Towards the end he wrote, 'the friendships I have made have been a constant source of happiness and satisfaction and exemplify the phrase that nothing has solidified the Commonwealth for good more than cricket has done'.

For Constantine, cricket made all things possible. He was the first West Indian to catch the eye of English critics. His career spanned the inter-war years. In the chronology of his cricket he was lucky. He was ready to enter the first-class game soon after 1919. Save for one match, he left it in 1939. R. C. Robertson-Glasgow wrote of him in that year as 'one of the few unquestioned geniuses of cricket'. *Wisden*, featuring him as one of the 'Five Cricketers of the Year' in its 1940 edition, described his 'passionate love for the game, lissomness of limb, rapidity of vision and elasticity of muscle'. To that great observer of the cricket scene, Sir Neville Cardus:

'His cricket was a prophecy which has gloriously come to pass; for it forecast, by its mingled skill, daring, absolutely un-English trust to instinct, and by its dazzling flashes of physical energy, the coming one day of Weekes, of Worrell, of Headley, of Walcott, of Kanhai, of Sobers. All of these cricketers remain, for all their acquired culture and ordered technique, descendants of Learie, cricketers in Learie's lineage.'

To the Australian, A. G. Moyes, he was a 'showman'. He 'gave you pleasure because his own joy was so evident, because he sought the unattainable and was full of adventure. If he failed, he failed gloriously.' G. O. Allen, who played against him many times in the 1920s and 1930s, remembered him as 'one of the most colourful cricketers who ever played; a beautiful mover who always attempted the impossible. He was one of the greatest entertainers in the game.' When Constantine died, Sir Leonard Hutton in *The Observer* described him as the most natural cricketer he had ever seen; 'a law unto himself, enjoying every minute of his game and spreading joy among cricket followers wherever he played. He ran as though his feet did not touch the ground.' To his fellow fast bowler, E. A. Martindale, 'he was a great crowd-pleaser and a potential match-winner'. E. W. Swanton of the *Daily Telegraph* wrote: 'There have been all-rounders with better records with both bat and ball: but it is hard to think of one who made a more sensational impact, in either department, and above all, to imagine his superior as a fielder anywhere.' Eustace Ward in the *Trinidad Guardian*'s tribute said that 'he identified the West Indies cricketer in a manner which led to the emancipation of West Indies cricket'.

In one area of the game Constantine had comparatively little experience except during the war. This was captaincy. Had he lived in a later generation he might well have led the West Indies. He once said, with something of that cricket 'conceit' of his, 'some captains leaned so heavily on my advice that it might have been imagined it was I who was making the decisions'. Nelson elected him captain when they went on tour in 1929. He often led his own side in charity matches and he was elected captain of the Dominions in that exciting match at the end of the war, at Lord's. Those who knew him as a captain regarded him as tactically very sound, erring only in under-bowling himself. But it is difficult to make a judgement—so many of the games in which he led a side were designed purely to provide entertainment and to last a guaranteed length of time. He was an infrequent captain in serious contests.

There is a danger is assuming that Constantine hit every ball he got for four or six, that he was a 'slogger', pure and simple, whose talents were successful in League cricket but insufficient at a higher level. To say this is to do injustice both to the standards of the League game in his day and to his own view of batting. In one of his books on technique, he defined 'hitting':

'Hitting does not mean swiping. Beginners must realise that. It does not mean hitting sixes either. It means getting at the bowler, going for him, refusing to be tied up in defensive postures and allowing him to do what he likes. It means stroke play and aggression'.

Stroke play and aggression for Constantine might represent cutting a ball off the middle stump and striking it with more force than any other contemporary could.

At the highest levels of the game, Constantine was a greater bowler than he was a batsman. To a purist, his technique could be faulted in that he looked up at the ball, rather than at the wicket of the batsman, as he delivered. In practical terms, this made no difference. The long arm, coming down from the highest possible height projected a ball of very great speed (in his prime). And when guile (and advancing age) dictated that a different delivery should be sent down—the slower ball concealing a googly—no hint was given to the batsman.

At once the bowler became the fielder. As soon as he had

finished his task of presenting the ball to the batsman so that play might proceed, he darted into some forward fielding position ready to make a catch or effect a run-out. To the bowler, his own advice in one of his books was this: 'Every ball, with rare exceptions, should be a direct attack on the wicket; study batsmen's peculiarities; bowl to the field; never neglect the non-bowling arm—fling it up to balance and down to add momentum; find out the minimum run you require.' All this—and much more in several chapters of advice—he taught, wrote and practised.

The game was never dull for Constantine. If he failed with bat or ball, there was always fielding. In that department of the game, the critics have allowed his reputation to stand unchallenged. As a cover-point in his earlier days he had few equals. In the slips or gully, in the view of those who saw him in the 1930s, he had none.

Constantine's life-pattern stemmed from that Middlesex match in 1928. From his batting and bowling on that Tuesday afternoon everything else followed—Nelson, broadcasting, politics, public service. Yet to one acute observer of that day's cricket, the runs and wickets against Middlesex destroyed his cricket career, for Constantine wanted to play cricket in that cavalier fashion all the time. Had he done less well against Middlesex—the argument ran—he would have had a more consistent first-class career. Within the narrow context of first-class cricket, it is an opinion that might be sustained. He might, for example, have accomplished more for the West Indies in the five Test series which remained to him after 1928. But there would have been a price to pay. Better statistics in the cricket of one hundred days spread over eleven years would have given Constantine some entitlement to be placed in the classical tradition of great cricketers, among whom he would have felt entombed.

For Learie Constantine must be set amongst the romantics. His suppleness and flexibility of muscle, his gaiety and sense of fun, his impulsiveness, all evoke the response of romanticism. Constantine expressed himself as Nature intended he should. His was the cricket of lyric and freedom.

STATISTICAL APPENDIX

Only the major figures of Constantine's career, and those less easily available to the researcher or statistician, are included.

All first-class cricket

Season	Matches	Innings	Batting Times not out	Runs	Highest score	Average	Bowling Wickets	Runs	Average	Catches
1921–2	1	2	—	24	24	12.00	2	44	22.00	1
1922–3	2	4	—	58	17	14.50	4	109	27.25	1
1923	20	31	4	425	77	15.74	37	809	21.86	15
1923–4	2	4	—	38	25	9.50	12	109	9.08	—
1924–5	2	4	—	37	36	9.25	—	48	—	4
1925–6	5	8	1	99	29	14.14	12	284	23.66	2
1926–7	1	2	—	24	13	12.00	3	211	70.33	2
1927–8	3	4	—	135	63	33.75	11	202	18.36	1
1928	26	43	3	1,381	130	34.50	107	2,456	22.95	33
1928–9	3	5	—	224	133	44.80	21	309	14.71	10
1929–30	5	10	—	150	58	15.00	21	572	27.23	16
1930–1	13	23	—	708	100	30.78	47	950	20.21	21
1933	5	9	—	181	64	20.11	14	310	22.14	5
1934–5	5	9	—	296	90	32.88	25	344	13.76	5
1938–9	1	2	—	12	11	6.00	4	69	17.25	—
1939	22	32	3	614	79	21.17	103	1,831	17.77	17
1945	1	2	—	45	40	22.50	1	80	80.00	—
All	117	194	11	4,451	133	24.32	424	8,737	20.61	133

Number of centuries: 5 5 wickets in an innings: 24 times 10 wickets in a match: 4 times

For Trinidad
(Inter-colonial and versus M.C.C.)

Season	Matches	Innings	Batting Times not out	Runs	Highest score	Average	Bowling Wickets	Runs	Average	Catches
1921–2	1	2	0	24	24	12.00	2	44	22.00	1
1922–3	2	4	0	58	17	14.50	4	109	27.25	1
1923–4	2	4	0	38	25	9.50	12	109	9.08	0
1924–5	2	4	0	37	36	9.25	0	48	—	4
1925–6	3	5	1	61	29	15.25	5	155	31.40	1
1926–7	1	2	0	24	13	12.00	3	211	70.33	2
1927–8	2	4	0	135	63	33.75	11	202	18.35	1
1928–9	3	5	0	224	133	44.80	21	309	14.71	10
1929–30	2	4	0	44	15	11.00	3	75	25.00	9
1934–5	2	4	0	127	68	31.75	10	147	14.70	2
All	20	38	1	772	133	20.86	71	1,409	19.85	31

For Nelson

Season	Runs	Batting		Bowling	
---	---	Average	Wickets	Average
1929	820	34.16	88	9.12
1930	621	38.00	73	10.40
1931	801	50.00	91	9.00
1932	476	22.66	91	8.15
1933	1,000	52.63	96	8.50
1934	657	36.50	90	8.28
1935	493	30.81	79	10.50
1936	632	33.26	86	11.22
1937	863	43.15	82	11.11
All	6,363	37.65	776	9.52

Test matches

Season	Matches	Innings	Times not out	Runs	Highest score	Average
Batting:						
1928	3	6	0	89	37	14.83
1929–30	3	6	0	106	58	20.75
1930–1	5	10	0	72	14	7.20
1933	1	2	0	95	64	47.50
1934–5	3	5	0	169	90	33.80
1939	3	4	0	110	79	27.50
All	18	33	0	641	90	19.42

Season	Overs*	Maidens	Runs	Wickets	Average	Catches
Bowling:						
1928	71.4	19	262	5	52.40	6
1929–30	163.4	42	497	18	27.61	7
1930–1	127.3	15	407	8	50.88	9
1933	25.0	5	55	1	55.00	2
1934–5	109.1	36	197	15	13.13	3
1939	71.3	8	328	11	29.82	1
All	(balls bowled) 3,553	125	1,746	58	30.10	28

* Some eight-ball overs.

A NOTE ON SOURCES

NEWSPAPERS

During his career in first-class cricket, Lord Constantine's name might be found occurring regularly in most newspapers in the British Empire and Commonwealth. Reports of inter-colony cricket matches in the 1920s appeared only in West Indian newspapers. Details of his cricket career with Nelson may be found in the *Nelson Leader* and in other newspapers with a circulation primarily in Lancashire.

Constantine's political career as a minister received little attention outside the West Indian Press, but his period as High Commissioner in London attracted wider coverage. *The Times* index has many references to him in both sporting and public life between 1923 and 1971. The following newspapers were consulted in writing his biography:

The *Barbados Advocate*
The *Bristol Evening Post*
The *Daily Argosy* (British Guiana)
The *Daily Gleaner* (Jamaica)
The *Daily Herald*
The *Daily Mail*
The *Daily Telegraph*
The *Evening Standard*
The Glasgow Herald
The *Manchester Guardian*

The *Manchester Evening News*
The Nation (Trinidad)
The *Nelson Leader*
The *Regent News* (house
   magazine of Trinidad
   Leaseholds Ltd)
The Scotsman
The *Sun* (Sydney)
The Times
The *Trinidad Guardian*
The Western Morning News

BOOKS AND JOURNALS: CRICKET

Apart from newspapers, the main sources for Constantine's cricket career are *Wisden Cricketers' Almanack* and *The Cricketer*.

He is the subject of more than passing interest in the following books on cricket:

Arlott, John (ed.), *Cricket: the Great All-Rounders*, Pelham Books, London, 1969

Barker, Ralph, *Ten Great Innings*, Chatto & Windus, London, 1964
Batchelor, Denzil, *Game of a Lifetime*, Werner Laurie, London, 1953
Cardus, Sir Neville, *The Playfair Cardus*, Dickens Press, London, 1963
Constantine, L. N., *Cricket and I*, Philip Allan, London, 1933
Constantine, L. N., *Cricket Crackers*, Stanley Paul, London, 1949
Constantine, L. N., *Cricketers' Carnival*, Stanley Paul, London, 1950
Constantine, L. N., *Cricketers' Cricket*, Eyre & Spottiswoode, London, 1949. (Later titled—(1) *How to Play Cricket* (2) *The Young Cricketers' Companion*)
Constantine, L. N., *Cricket in the Sun*, Stanley Paul, London, 1946
Constantine, L. N., and Batchelor, Denzil, *The Changing Face of Cricket*, Eyre & Spottiswoode, London, 1966
James, C. L. R., *Beyond a Boundary*, Hutchinson, London, 1963
Kay, John, *Cricket in the Leagues*, Eyre & Spottiswoode, London, 1970
Nicole, Christopher, *West Indian Cricket*, Phoenix Books, London, 1957
Thomson, A. A., *Cricketers of My Times*, Stanley Paul, London, 1967

BOOKS AND JOURNALS: POLITICS

The main source for Constantine's work in the Legislative Council of Trinidad and Tobago is the *Official Report of Debates*, vol 7–11, Government Printing Office, Port of Spain, 1956–61. With this Report should be consulted the *Trinidad Guardian* and *The Nation*. Some background to the history of Trinidad, to the political events associated with Trinidad's attainment of independence ad to the West Indian Federation will be found in the following books:

Burns, A. C., *History of the British West Indies*, George Allen & Unwin, London, 1954
James, C. L. R., *A Convention Appraisal*, P.N.M. Publishing Company, Port of Spain, 1965
Macmillan, W. M., *Warning from the West Indies*, Faber & Faber, London, 1936
Mordecai, John, *The West Indies: The Federal Negotiations*, George Allen & Unwin, London, 1968

Oxall, Ivar, *Black Intellectuals come to Power*, Schenkman Inc., Cambridge, Mass., 1968

Sherlock, P. M., *West Indian Story*, Longmans, London, 1960

Springer, Hugh W., *Reflections on the Failure of the First West Indian Federation*, Harvard University Press, Cambridge, Mass., 1962

Williams, Eric, *From Columbus to Castro: The History of the Caribbean 1492–1969*, André Deutsch, London, 1970

Williams, Eric, *From Slavery to Chaguaramas*, P.N.M. Publishing Company, Port of Spain, 1959

Williams, Eric, *History of the People of Trinidad and Tobago*, André Deutsch, London, 1964

Williams, Eric, *Inward Hunger: The Education of a Prime Minister*, André Deutsch, London, 1969

Williams, Eric, *Reflections on the Caribbean Economic Community*, P.N.M. Publishing Company, Port of Spain, 1965

BROADCASTS

Constantine's broadcasts provide the main source (and in many cases the only one) for his own views on events belonging to his years as a politician and diplomat. They also throw some light on his childhood, his work in Liverpool during the war, the years in Nelson and his thoughts on the Empire and Commonwealth. They are mostly on microfilm in the B.B.C. Reference and Registry Services at Broadcasting House, London.

OTHER RELEVANT BOOKS AND ARTICLES INCLUDE:

Constantine, L. N., *Colour Bar*, Stanley Paul, London, 1954

Constantine, L. N., *Race in the World* (Rectorial Address at St Andrews University), St Andrews, 1968

Edwards, David T., 'The Economy of Trinidad', in *West Indian Economist*, March 1950

Morris, Sam, 'Learie Constantine', in *New Community*, January 1971

Patterson, Orlando, 'The Cricket Ritual in the West Indies', in *New Society*, 28 June 1969

Patterson, Sheila, 'Cricket and Other Odes', in *New Community*, April 1973

Wooding, H. O. B., 'The Constitutional History of Trinidad and Tobago', in *Caribbean Quarterly*, May 1960

INDEX